ALSO BY ROB MUNDLE

Bligh: Master Mariner

Bob Oatley: A Life Story

Bond: Alan Bond

Cook: From Sailor to Legend – the story of Captain James Cook

Fatal Storm: The 54th Sydney to Hobart Yacht Race

Hell on High Seas: Amazing Stories of Survival Against the Odds

Learning to Sail

Life at the Extreme: The Volvo Ocean Race Round the World 2005–2006

*Ocean Warriors: The Thrilling Story of the 2001–2002 Volvo Ocean Race
    Round the World*

Sir James Hardy: An Adventurous Life

Sydney to Hobart: The 1995 Golden Anniversary

The First Fleet

FLINDERS

THE MAN WHO MAPPED AUSTRALIA

Rob Mundle

Author of the bestseller *Bligh: Master Mariner*

People of Aboriginal and Torres Strait Islander heritage are advised that this book contains images of people who are deceased.

hachette
AUSTRALIA

First published in Australia and New Zealand in 2012
by Hachette Australia
(an imprint of Hachette Australia Pty Limited)
Level 17, 207 Kent Street, Sydney NSW 2000
www.hachette.com.au

Trade paperback edition published in 2013
This edition published in 2016

10 9 8 7 6 5 4 3 2 1

National Library of Australia
Cataloguing-in-Publication data:

Mundle, Rob.
Flinders: the man who mapped Australia / Rob Mundle.

978 0 7336 3738 4 (pbk.)

Flinders, Matthew, 1774–1814.
Explorers – Australia – Biography.
Coastal mapping – Australia – History.
Australia – Discovery and exploration – British.

910.92

Cover design by Design by Committee
Cover image courtesy of Ian Hansen
Maps by Ian Faulkner
Picture section by Agave Creative
Typeset in Bembo by Kirby Jones

Printed in Australia by Griffin Press, Adelaide, an Accredited ISO AS/NZS 4001:2004 Environmental Management Systems printer The paper this book is printed on is certified against the Forest Stewardship Council® Standards. Griffin Press holds FSC chain of custody certification SGS-COC-005088. FSC promotes environmentally responsible, socially beneficial and economically viable management of the world's forests.

This book is dedicated to the likes of Matthew Flinders — the heroes of maritime history. These exceptionally brave explorers sailed into the unknown where, through daring, determination and great skill, they completed the map of the world.

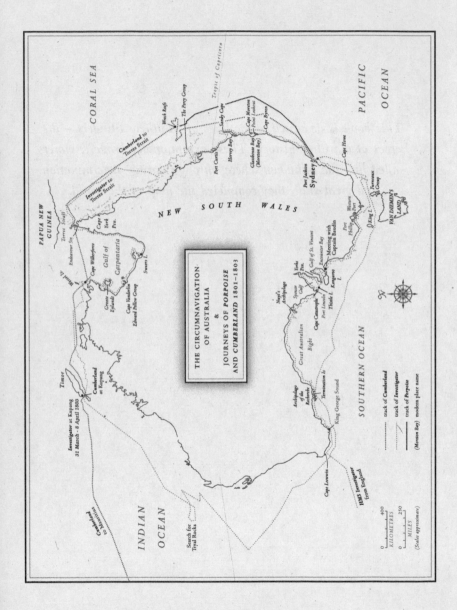

THE CIRCUMNAVIGATION
OF AUSTRALIA
&
JOURNEYS OF *PORPOISE*
AND *CUMBERLAND* 1801–1803

CORAL SEA

PACIFIC OCEAN

INDIAN OCEAN

SOUTHERN OCEAN

PAPUA NEW GUINEA

NEW SOUTH WALES

VAN DIEMEN'S LAND

Tropic of Capricorn

Wreck Reefs
The Percy Group
Sandy Cape
Cape Moreton
Point Lookout
Cape Byron
Cumberland to Torres Strait
Investigator to Torres Strait
Port Curtis
Hervey Bay
Glasshouse Bay (Moreton Bay)
Port Jackson
Sydney
Cape Howe
Furneaux Group
Cape York Pen.
Gulf of Carpentaria
Cape Wilberforce
Wessel Is.
Groote Eylandt
Cape Vanderlin
Edward Pellew Group
Sweers I.
Endeavour Str.
Torres Strait
Meeting with Captain Baudin
Western Port
Port Phillip
Q. King I.
Encounter Bay
Gulf of St. Vincent
York Pen.
Spencer Gulf
Kangaroo I.
Thistle I.
Port Lincoln
Cape Catastrophe
Nuyt's Archipelago
Great Australian Bight
Timor
Cumberland at Kupang
Investigator at Kupang 31 March – 8 April 1803
Archipelago of the Recherche
Termination Is.
King George Sound
Cape Leeuwin
HMS Investigator from England
Cumberland to Mauritius
Search for Tryal Rocks

track of *Cumberland*
track of *Investigator*
track of *Porpoise*
(Moreton Bay) modern place name

0   400
KILOMETRES
0   250
MILES
(Scale approximate)

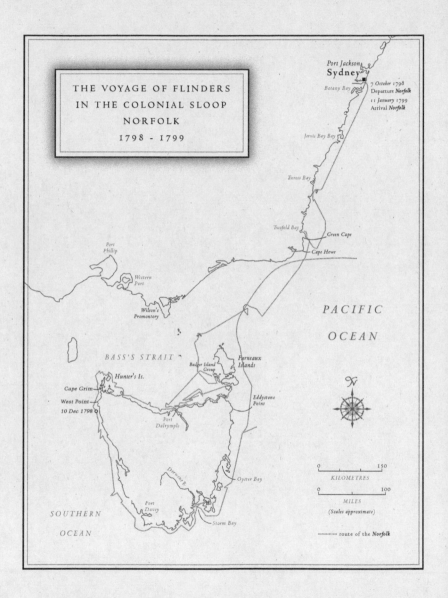

THE VOYAGE OF FLINDERS
IN THE COLONIAL SLOOP
NORFOLK
1798 - 1799

Port Jackson
Sydney
Botany Bay

7 October 1798
Departure *Norfolk*
11 January 1799
Arrival *Norfolk*

Jervis Bay Bay

Turots Bay

Twofold Bay
Green Cape
Cape Howe

PACIFIC

OCEAN

Port
Phillip

Western
Port

Wilson's
Promontory

BASS'S STRAIT

Hunter's Is.

Badger Island
Group

Furneaux
Islands

Cape Grim
West Point
10 Dec 1798

Eddystone
Point

Port
Dalrymple

Derwent R.

Oyster Bay

SOUTHERN

OCEAN

Port
Davey

Storm Bay

0   150
KILOMETRES
0   100
MILES
(Scales approximate)

route of the *Norfolk*

Contents

Author's Note

Today we are in awe of the idea that astronauts will, in the near future, take to the heavens and spend years exploring the moon or Mars. How will they cope with being away from the sanctuary of Earth for so long? And what of the dangers they will face? So much could go wrong.

Now, step back more than 200 years, into the eighteenth and early nineteenth centuries, and consider a somewhat similar scenario. This time, though, the mode of transport is a stout-looking, wooden sailing ship just 100 feet long and carrying 80 or more seafarers, which is launched on a voyage of exploration into what is truly the unknown. Unlike today's astronauts, these remarkably brave Argonauts held only a vague notion of where they were headed and what they might find. They sailed on the whim of the wind, and from the moment their ship went beyond the horizon they were gone, possibly forever.

These explorers took with them little support material in the form of charts and maps, and only the most basic of navigation equipment. Except for a small cutter or gig lashed to the deck, they had no safety equipment as we know it, and there were no instant communications with home should anything go wrong in a world where an uncharted reef was the nautical equivalent of a rogue asteroid in outer space. Should fair winds and favour be with these adventurers, they would reappear on the horizon after some years, often with exciting news of a new frontier. Alternatively, should the ship be overwhelmed by the boiling fury of a storm-lashed sea or smashed to splinters on a reef or rock, taking all hands with it, the world would have one more maritime mystery to ponder.

Needless to say, the masters of these expeditions were a special breed – great seafarers and leaders of men who were relentless in their resolve to succeed. One such man was Matthew Flinders, the brilliant explorer who put the rudimentary outline of Terra Australis on the world map and strongly advocated for the continent to be named Australia. The challenges he faced demanded almost every skill imaginable – seafaring, navigation, dedication, cartography, leadership, compassion, fortitude and planning – and there are few, if any, other names that can stand alongside Flinders as Australia's greatest explorer.

Matthew Flinders was a large cog in the mechanism that established early Australia. However, all too often, his substantial contribution via exploration, together with the circumstances of his lengthy incarceration by the French on Île-de-France, are not generally recognised. It is also disappointing to note that this great English navigator and explorer has received virtually no public recognition in his home country: no statue, plaque or other form of acknowledgement honouring his life exists in London. Sadder still, within 40 years of his death, his grave in St James's Garden could no longer be found. His remains are now thought to lie under London's Euston railway station, originally built in 1837.

Like so many great men of his era, Flinders was a modest man who never ventured into the area of self-promotion: while he named hundreds of headlands, bays, harbours and points of interest around the coast – including the Barrier Reef, which came through casual reference more than intent – he did not ascribe one placename to himself. The intention of this book is to pay high tribute to a stoic, determined and illustrious explorer. It is the story of an indomitable individual who, through unfortunate circumstance, was prevented from fulfilling his life's mission of completing a more highly detailed map of the entire coastline of Australia.

I have written this factual story of an extraordinary man not as an historian, but as a storyteller with a passion for sailing and the sea – a writer whose maritime heritage dates back to the era of square-rigged ships. The story of Matthew Flinders leaves me convinced that he can rightfully be recognised as the third member of a remarkable triumvirate of seafarers and explorers – Cook, Bligh and Flinders.

CHAPTER ONE

Wreck Reefs

The large, tattered British blue ensign, flapping wildly in the strong breeze, was flying upside down for good reason. It was the internationally recognised signal for distress.

The scene around the salvaged topsail yard that carried the flag said it all. Eighty unkempt, sunburned and bearded men were scattered around the small, low-lying and treeless sand cay where the flag flew. Some were taking shelter from the strong south-easterly trade wind and the blistering tropical sun under makeshift tents formed by sails, while others were labouring on the construction of two somewhat crude-looking boats. There was another surprising oddity in the setting, too: a curious and intrepid black cat.

The reason for this desperate scene was apparent just a few hundred yards away: the skeletal remains of a ten-gun, 308-ton and 93-foot brig, HMS *Porpoise*. What was left of her was lying on a jagged coral reef amid turbulent white water. However, all evidence of the larger, full-rigged and armed cargo ship, *Cato*, which had been wrecked at the same time, was gone. Her timbers had proved no match for the pounding ocean swells, and within hours of her grounding there was little of her to be seen.

Porpoise and *Cato* were part of a three-ship convoy when they smashed onto the uncharted reef in the depths of darkness on Wednesday, 17 August 1803. At the time, their respective captains believed the vessels were on a safe course well wide of the dangers posed by the coral reef that stretched for hundreds of nautical miles along the adjacent coastline to the west, but a coral outcrop had ambushed them. It was part of a 13-nautical-mile-long mid-ocean blotch of reefs, islets and cays that had been lying in wait for unwary sailors at the surface of the Coral Sea for millions of years.

That afternoon, there had been an alert that there were uncharted reefs in the area. At around two o'clock, *Cato* was sailing some distance to leeward and astern of *Porpoise* when her captain signalled that land had been sighted. *Porpoise*, which was the faster ship, changed course to investigate, while signalling to *Cato* to hold her course and continue on. The sighting was confirmed by *Porpoise*'s crew – it was a dry sandbank. Its position was noted on a chart and given the name Cato's Bank. That done, all possible sail was set on *Porpoise* so she could catch the other ships and again take up her station ahead of them.

By the time it did, the vessels were 35 nautical miles north of their discovery, and in that distance no other sightings of land had been made. Instead of heaving to for the night, it was decided to proceed with caution through the hours of darkness under reduced sail. There was a fresh south-easterly breeze blowing, so the call from *Porpoise*'s master was to double-reef the billowing topsails, in order to slow the ship while it held a course of north-by-west.

That evening, at eight o'clock, the lead line was again cast over the side, and it confirmed that *Porpoise* was in very deep water – more than 85 fathoms. But less than one hour later, the serenity suddenly became mayhem.

'Breakers ahead!' was the panicked call from *Porpoise*'s lookout, a seasoned old salt who had been peering into the darkness from a position on top of the forecastle. An even greater sense of urgency came when the same call was made by the master of the watch, who was standing on the quarterdeck: they were on the brink of disaster.

The helmsman, who until then had been enjoying his evening trick at the wheel, responded in an instant, putting the helm hard down, his intention being to dramatically change course and tack the ship so that disaster could be avoided. But with so little sail set, *Porpoise* was slow to respond: she went into irons, near head-to-wind with her sails either aback or flapping, and virtually stopped.

On hearing the commotion, the captain, Lieutenant Robert Fowler, rushed onto the deck. His immediate thought was that a tiller rope had carried away and caused *Porpoise* to go out of control, a failure that was not uncommon on a ship. But the panicked look on the helmsman's face and a concerned comment from the master confirmed that things were far worse. Terror-laden eyes peered into the darkness to leeward and saw ghostly white breakers a mere quarter of a cable length away – only 50 yards! That was the distance between shipwreck and salvation, and the ship was making more leeway than headway. There was no question: *Porpoise* was doomed.

A noted landscape artist of the era, William Westall, was aboard *Porpoise*. He later wrote:

> We were all assembled in the cabin, when I suddenly heard the crew in great confusion, and hurrying on deck, behold breakers on our larboard bow. The coral reef showed itself in a long line of foam, seen indistinctly through the approaching gloom of the night. When the ship struck, one general groan resounded throughout, for not a possibility appeared that anyone could be saved.

Less than a minute after the warning call came, a mighty swell picked up the ship and smashed her onto the reef with brutal force. From that moment the fight was over: *Porpoise* was mortally wounded, her hull planks already being gouged to pulp by the coral. The next wave rolled her onto her port side, then two more mighty jolts brought the thundering sound of splintering timber as the foremast went crashing over the side and the hull was breached.

Regardless of the immediate danger the ship's men faced, it was imperative to fire a cannon and warn the following ships of the danger. But the shuddering violence that came with each subsequent wave, combined with the amount of surf that was crashing over the vessel, made this impossible.

Clinging to whatever they could reach, those aboard *Porpoise* watched in horror as, minutes later and only two cable-lengths away, *Cato* met a fate even worse than theirs. Dark as it was, they could see her silhouette as she was driven onto the reef with horrendous force; she immediately capsized. Her masts disappeared in seconds.

Fortunately, *Porpoise* had capsized with her deck downwind and away from the hammering waves, but *Cato* had fallen the other way and was far more vulnerable to punishment from the seas. In no time, every structure on deck was being torn asunder by the booming waves. For those aboard *Porpoise*, it appeared that death and destruction had come to *Cato* in one mighty blow. Only daylight would confirm it.

But what of *Bridgewater*, the third ship in the convoy? She was a 750-ton cargo vessel sailing under the flag of the East India Company, en route to Batavia then India. A crewman aboard *Porpoise* pointed into the darkness and shouted that he could see the shimmering light of *Bridgewater*'s masthead lantern in the distance. Yes, *Bridgewater* had avoided disaster. That could only mean she would sail back to the reef at first light and take aboard all the survivors.

At least, that is what those aboard *Porpoise* believed would happen.

The reef that had claimed the two ships was extremely remote – it was in the Coral Sea, 140 nautical miles east of the southern end of the Barrier Reef, and 250 nautical miles off the northern coast of the landmass known as 'New Holland' or 'Terra Australis'. In very recent times, however, it was occasionally being referred to as 'Australia'.

The man proposing most strongly that it should be named Australia had, only weeks earlier, been lauded in Sydney Town for his remarkable achievement in becoming the first explorer and navigator to circumnavigate the great landmass – and he was aboard *Porpoise*. Commander Matthew Flinders, then aged 29, was sailing home from Port Jackson to England as a passenger, having captained the 100-foot sloop-of-war, HMS *Investigator*, on the voyage of exploration and in doing so proven New Holland was a continent. Less than halfway through that voyage *Investigator* had become a leaky tub so Flinders had no option but to expedite his return to Sydney Town, in Port Jackson, where the vessel was subsequently deemed unseaworthy. Now, he was sailing home aboard *Porpoise* with other members of his crew, including his brother, Lieutenant Samuel Flinders. Also making the journey was Flinders' feline friend, Trim, a black cat with a daub of white on his chest and four white paws.

The trip had promised to be even more pleasurable for Flinders because Lieutenant Fowler had sailed with him aboard *Investigator*, serving as his first lieutenant during Flinders' epic voyage around Australia. Fowler had subsequently been appointed to command *Porpoise* by the infant colony's third governor, Philip Gidley King, a man who, not surprisingly, was extremely impressed by Flinders' pioneering exploration of the continent's coastline.

Now, with *Porpoise* and *Cato* wrecked and Flinders being the most senior naval officer among all aboard the two ships, it was his duty to stand alongside Lieutenant Fowler and take command of the situation.

Flinders had been away from England for more than two years and was returning home to present the Admiralty with an impressive collection of charts, logs and books, which described in great detail the outstanding discoveries he had made during his voyage around Australia, and during other exploratory excursions out of Sydney Town. His Majesty's Royal Botanic Gardens in Kew would also be a beneficiary on his return: it would be the recipient of hundreds of plants gathered during the voyage of *Investigator*. They had been potted and stored in a purpose-built greenhouse on *Porpoise*'s quarterdeck.

These achievements promised to be very satisfying for a young man who was already enjoying an outstanding naval career, but there was one other, far more exciting reason for his return: he would be reunited with his loving wife, Ann. They had been married more than two years earlier but had spent little more than three months together before Flinders was directed by the Admiralty to sail for Sydney and explore new regions.

For Flinders, that directive to survey the waters around the continent was even applicable to his voyage home aboard *Porpoise*, as he explained in his later book, *A Voyage to Terra Australis*:

> The examination of Torres Strait was one of the most
> important articles of my instructions which had been
> executed only in part; and although I could not pretend to
> make any regular survey in the *Porpoise*, it was yet desirable
> to pass again through the strait, and lay down as many more
> of its dangers as circumstances would admit.

Torres Strait crowns Cape York, the large peninsula forming the north-east corner of Australia; the cape had been named by Captain

Cook in 1770 in honour of the deceased brother of King George III, Prince Edward, Duke of York and Albany. Flinders was all too aware of the dangers the strait's reef-strewn waters presented to navigators. He had already experienced two passages through it, one aboard *Investigator* and the other in 1792, when he was a lieutenant aboard HMS *Providence*, under the command of Captain William Bligh. Flinders also knew that, should he be able to chart an easily navigable passage, significant benefits would be enjoyed by all vessels. A safe course through Torres Strait would save around six weeks on a voyage from Port Jackson to India, when compared with the alternative – sailing around the northern coast of New Guinea.

Accordingly, prior to *Porpoise*'s departure from Port Jackson in company with *Bridgewater* and *Cato*, Governor King delivered a memorandum to Lieutenant Fowler. It read in part:

> The objects which captain Flinders will have to finish in his
> route through Torres Strait, requires that he should be
> assisted with boats, people, and have the entire direction of
> the ship as to the courses she is to steer ... You are therefore
> further required to comply with every direction he may give
> you, to enable him to execute the orders of my Lords
> Commissioners of the Admiralty.

That directive was now irrelevant. With *Porpoise* beyond salvage, Torres Strait – 1000 nautical miles to the north – was the most distant thing from Flinders' mind. His priority was to save lives aboard his ship and *Cato* – if there were any survivors.

Being heeled towards the reef meant *Porpoise*'s hull created a lee where the impact of wind and waves was minimised, even though the waves were bursting over it, so Flinders – in consultation with Fowler – ordered that the ship's boats, which were lashed on deck, be launched as lifeboats. A small four-oared gig was successfully launched, but the larger cutter was stove in and flooded when sudden wave action washed her into debris from the damaged ship, so the procedure was stopped. They could not afford to lose any support boats.

Flinders and Fowler also had to consider how long it might be before the lightly constructed ship began breaking up as a result of the constant pounding from the waves. They decided that the best way to prolong the life of *Porpoise* was to lighten her, and that this should happen post haste, even though it was still dark. Their hope was that the hull would be pushed further onto the reef and become more stable. Fowler called for the rigging to be let go so that the main and mizzen masts could be chopped down. At the same time, the heavy iron starboard anchor was dumped onto the reef.

Flinders was standing high on the sloping deck observing these activities and trying to establish the outline of the reef around them. While doing so, he came up with a worrying theory. If the hulk was made light enough to move across the coral, and if stormier seas arrived, the ship might be washed all the way to the other side, which he could just make out in the distance, and sink into the depths of the ocean. The plan to lighten ship was instantly abandoned.

Flinders was aware that the waters on the downwind side of the reef were calm enough for *Bridgewater*'s rescue boats to approach in safety and pick up the survivors. He could see the glimmer of *Bridgewater*'s masthead lantern not far away, which could only mean that Captain Palmer was standing by and preparing to mount a rescue attempt as soon as the conditions allowed. It was, therefore, imperative that all possible information regarding the condition of the ships and the men, and the safest approach to the wrecks, be conveyed to *Bridgewater*. Flinders knew that 'something speedily' needed to be done to save the men; after consulting with Fowler, he took it upon himself to board the gig and be transported into the night and towards *Bridgewater*. He later wrote:

> The boat being obliged to lie at a little distance from the ship, to prevent being stove, I jumped over-board and swam to her; and we pushed through the breakers to the smooth water, receiving two or three surfs by the way, from which we hardly escaped sinking. On examining into the condition of the boat, I found nothing to bail out the water ... and instead of the proper crew of four men, there were only three [plus] the armourer, a cook, and a marine, who did not know how to handle an oar. These last were set to bailing with their hats and shoes, and we rowed towards *Bridgewater*'s light, keeping under the lee of the breakers.

Before long, Flinders realised that his effort was destined to be fruitless: they were struggling to make headway, and the chances were that *Bridgewater* would soon tack, sail further away and be impossible to reach. Reluctantly, he pushed the tiller across and turned the gig back to the smoother water in the lee of the reef, the whereabouts of which could be identified by the blue lights shining from lanterns that were burning aboard *Porpoise*. This was being done both as a guide for Flinders and to signal to *Bridgewater* that there were survivors.

> I determined to remain under the lee of the breakers until [*Bridgewater*] should approach, and to lie near the *Porpoise* in case of her going to pieces before morning, we might save some of the people.
> I wished to have got on board the ship to let them know of the boats being safe and what we had discovered

of the reef; but the breakers between us, and the darkness of
the night cut off all hope of communication before
morning. They burned blue lights every half hour, as a
guide to the *Bridgewater*, but her light was no longer seen
after two in the morning. At that time it appeared to be low
water, and the ship lay so much more quiet than before,
that the apprehension of her going to pieces before daylight
had much subsided; to be prepared, however, for the next
flood, Mr. Fowler employed his people during the night in
making a raft of the spare top masts, yards, etc., with short
ropes all round it, by which the people might hold on; and
a cask of water, with a chest containing some provisions, a
sextant, and the *Investigator*'s log books, were secured upon
the raft.

It was another cold, wet and miserable seven hours for those aboard
the gig before first light arrived, a period made all the more difficult
by their uncertainty about the loss of life aboard *Cato*, which by
then was all but broken up, and about the whereabouts and fate of
Bridgewater, the lights of which had not come back into view. As it
was, just before *Cato* smashed onto the reef *Bridgewater* had gone
frighteningly close to colliding with her. This came when both
ships were executing unnerving manoeuvres in desperate bids to
avoid being wrecked; had there been a collision, there was no
doubt there would be three ships lying decimated on the reef.

While Flinders was in the gig and standing off in the lee of the
reef, there was added drama aboard the now heavily heeled
Porpoise. A candle had fallen from its holder below deck and started
a fire, and for a short time it appeared that those on board would
more likely burn to death than drown. It was only through quick
action by the crew that the flames were doused.

Even without the threat of fire, it had already been an exhausting evening for all on board, as Westall explained:

> During the dreadful scene, after the first confusion had
> subsided, all was coolness and prompt obedience. Many
> though drenched with the sea, and exhausted with fatigue,
> would only accept with moderation the spirits served out to
> recruit their strength.

The men aboard the gig had a near-sleepless night. Flinders spent much of the time contemplating the magnitude and consequences of the events that had occurred. Ultimately, he accepted that no plans for rescue could be based on the assumption that *Bridgewater* remained safe at sea, and that she would come to their aid:

> My thoughts were principally occupied in devising plans for
> saving ourselves, under the apprehension that we might see
> no more of the *Bridgewater*; but not to discourage the people,
> I spoke of everybody getting on board that ship in the
> morning, and of continuing our voyage to England. Of the
> poor *Cato*, we could neither see nor hear anything.

It would later be learned that *Cato* had struck the point of a ledge of rock-hard coral, which was like the corner of a plateau, the face of which descended vertically to the ocean floor. The impact was so great that the ship's forward sections literally burst open and the hull was engulfed by a raging torrent of water. In no time, *Cato* was capsizing to windward. With her decks exposed to the explosive power of the waves, she was being smashed to pieces.

Inevitably, the ship was soon threatening to break in two, so those on board rushed to the only relatively safe place – the foredeck – and crowded behind whatever they could for protection from the waves. Before long, they were facing annihilation and the only spot to hide was behind the forecastle. Should that break apart, it would be every man for himself.

When first light eased its way into the new day, what was left of *Cato* came into view for those aboard *Porpoise*. There was little more to be seen than the outline of the bowsprit, which was pointing skyward. As the day continued to emerge, survivors could be seen waving – but how many had survived would not be known for some time.

Flinders had, by then, decided that there was enough daylight for him to safely guide the gig across the shallow but surging waters that covered the reef and return to *Porpoise*. Unbeknown to him, he and his men had been given up for dead by the crew of *Porpoise*.

> At the first dawning of day, I got on board the *Porpoise* by the help of the fallen masts. Everybody was in good spirits at seeing the ship hold together so well, and finding the boats safe; for the gig, with all in her, had been given up for lost, someone having thought he saw her sink in the breakers.

As Flinders was helped back aboard, an observation was made that eased everyone's fears somewhat. Nature had provided a lifeboat of sorts – a chance to survive – in the form of a barren sand cay. It lay within an achievable distance from the location of the wrecks, and plans were immediately initiated to move people there:

> With the daylight appeared a dry sand bank, not more than half a mile distant, sufficiently large to receive us all with what provisions might be got out of the ship; and the satisfaction arising from this discovery was increased by the

Bridgewater being perceived under sail, and though distant,
that she was standing towards the reef. On the other side, the
appearance of the poor *Cato*, with the people waving to us
from the bowsprit and fore castle, the only parts above water,
was truly distressing.

While Fowler coordinated the assembly of water and provisions
on deck, Flinders returned to the gig and was rowed to the cay so
he could assess what it offered. With *Bridgewater* returning and
appearing certain to anchor in the lee of the reef, Flinders planned
to go aboard 'and point out to Captain Palmer the means by
which he might take on board the two crews and what else might
be saved'.

To Flinders' horror, however, and to the shock and disbelief
of all, *Bridgewater* was seen to tack and then sail away from them,
eventually fading into the haze on the northern horizon. It was as
if Palmer was taunting the damned. Surely he knew there were
survivors – lanterns had been lit throughout the night to indicate
that – and surely he or his subordinates must have confirmed
through the use of looking glasses that there was activity on both
ships.

While the shipwrecked sailors watched *Bridgewater* leave,
Flinders returned his mind to the precautionary thought he had
while in the gig overnight: what could be done if *Bridgewater* was
wrecked and could not return to rescue them? His fear was rapidly
evolving into reality.

Flinders' first priority, though, was to get a boat to *Cato* and
convey its men to *Porpoise*, but it was to be an effort burdened with
danger – and death. With the surf still raging, *Porpoise*'s cutter was
unable to get alongside the shattered ship, so for Captain Park there
was only one alternative:

Captain Park and his men, throwing themselves into the
water with any pieces of spar or plank they could find, swam
to her through the breakers; and were then taken to the
Porpoise where they received food and some clothing. Several
were bruised against the coral rocks, and three young lads
were drowned. One of these poor boys, who, in the three or
four voyages he had made to sea, had been each time
shipwrecked, had bewailed himself through the night as the
persecuted Jonas who carried misfortune wherever he went.
He launched himself upon a broken spar with his captain;
but having lost his hold in the breakers, was not seen
afterwards.

By nightfall, all the men and as much water and provisions as
possible had been transferred to the sand cay, including the fresh
meat supplies that the ships carried – 'the pigs and sheep that had
escaped drowning', as Flinders wrote. Much to his pleasure, Trim
had also survived the night of mayhem and waited dutifully aboard
Porpoise for his master to take him to shore.

The initial task for the first group to reach the sandbank was to
take a salvaged topsail yard and set it up on the highest point of
land; then they hoisted 'a large blue ensign ... to it with the union
downward, as a signal to the *Bridgewater*'. This was done because
the survivors simply could not believe that *Bridgewater* had
deliberately abandoned them; she had sailed away while waiting for
better wind and sea conditions to develop, they felt sure, so that a
full-scale rescue effort could be mounted in safety. While Flinders,
too, wanted to believe this, he thought it more prudent to 'act as if
we had no such resource'. It was a theory that would prove to be
well-founded, as he later described.

Captain Palmer had even then abandoned us to our fate, and was, at the moment, steering away for Batavia, without having made any effort to give us assistance. He saw the wrecks, as also the sand bank, on the morning after our disaster, and must have known that the reef was not all connected ... He bore away round all; and whilst the two hapless vessels were still visible from the mast head, passed the leeward extremity of the reef, and hove to for the night. The apprehension of danger to himself must then have ceased; but he neither attempted to work up in the smooth water, nor sent any of his boats to see whether some unfortunate individuals were not clinging to the wrecks, whom he might snatch from the sharks or save from a more lingering death.

Incredibly, it was later confirmed that Captain Palmer – although he suspected that there were survivors – had decided, in a cowardly and callous act, to abandon the crews of both *Porpoise* and *Cato*; on his arrival in India, he declared that both ships and all hands were lost. An account of his claims appeared in the *Calcutta Orphan* newspaper on 3 February 1804. In this article, Palmer admitted seeing the wrecks – although he had confused one ship for the other – but prefaced his reasons for not rendering assistance and sailing on with these words: 'Finding we could not weather the reef, and that it was too late had it been in our power to give any assistance; and still fearing that we might be embayed or entangled by the supposed chain or patches ...'. Palmer never mentioned the sandbank that became the sanctuary for the shipwrecked sailors.

Flinders later obtained a copy of a journal written by *Bridgewater*'s third mate, Mr Williams, and it was damning of the captain.

At half past seven a.m. (Aug. 18) saw the reef on our weather bow, and from the mast head we saw the two ships, and to leeward of them a sand bank. The weather abated much, we set all our sails, and every man rejoiced that they should have it in their power to assist their unfortunate companions; as there was every probability of our going within two miles of the reef. The morning threatened; but before the wind increased we had time to satisfy ourselves if there were any still in existence; we had nothing to apprehend but what could be seen before we approached so near. The ships were very distinctly to be seen from aloft, and also from the deck; but instead of rendering them any succour, the captain ordered the ship to be put on the other tack, and said it was impossible to render them any relief. What must be the sensations of each man at that instant? Instead of proceeding to the support of our unfortunate companions, to leave them to the mercy of the waves, without knowing whether they were in existence, or had perished! From the appearance of the wrecks, there was every probability of their existing; and if any survived at the time we were within sight, what must have been their sensations on seeing all their anxious expectations of relief blasted.

Until our arrival at Bombay, nothing particular occurred, except my being sent on shore at Tellicherry [on India's west coast] with the account of the loss of the *Porpoise* and *Cato*; an account that served for the moment to blind the people. In executing this service, I did, for the first time to my knowledge, neglect my duty, and gave a contrary account; but for this reason – I was convinced that the crews of those ships were on the reefs, and that this was an erroneous account made by Captain Palmer to excuse his own conduct.

I left it on shore for the perusal of the inhabitants, after
relating the story as contrary as possible. This was the cause
of many words; and at length ended with my quitting the
ship, and forfeiting my wages and a part of my clothes.

Flinders realised that *Cato*'s Captain Park had actually saved *Bridgewater*
from meeting the same fate as the other ships: he had bravely and
unselfishly taken action to avoid a collision with *Bridgewater*, and that
gave the big ship enough sea-room to sail clear of the reef.

Bridgewater subsequently disappeared with all hands, having
departed Bombay. Flinders commented somewhat sardonically that
'Captain Palmer and the Bridgewater, who left Bombay for
Europe, have not been heard of, now for many years. How
dreadful must have been his reflections at the time his ship was
going down!' He added: 'Lieutenant Tucker of the navy, who was
first officer of the Bridgewater, and several others as well as
Mr Williams, had happily quitted the ship in India.'

Various tasks were allocated to individuals and groups of men
when they reached the safety of the sand cay that first afternoon;
one of those tasks unearthed a maritime mystery that remains
unsolved to this day. The men sent in search of driftwood washed
up on the shore discovered, to their amazement, the worm-riddled
and weather-beaten timbers of another wreck. It was obviously a
sternpost from a large ship, and calculations made by the master of
Porpoise, John Aiken, showed that it was from a vessel of around
400 tons – one-third larger than *Porpoise*. This led Flinders to
suggest that they had found wreckage from one of the two French
expedition ships – *La Boussole* and *L'Astrolabe* – that had departed
Botany Bay, south of Sydney Town, on 10 March 1788 under the
leadership of Jean-François de Galaup, Comte de Lapérouse, and
were never seen again.

However, the wrecks of both these ships were later found on reefs in the Santa Cruz Islands, so the origin of the sternpost on the cay remains unknown. There have been suggestions that it came from an American whaler, as they were known to have operated in that part of the Pacific in the second half of the eighteenth century. Searches in recent times have found no evidence of an unknown wreck on the fringes of what is now known as Wreck Reefs. At the time, though, the castaways of *Porpoise* and *Cato* weren't concerned with history: they had found an excellent piece of firewood that would burn for days.

Still uncertain whether or not they had been left for dead by *Bridgewater*, the sailors faced more adversity during the first night they were ashore. *Porpoise*'s two cutters and the gig had been hauled up the sand cay and secured at a point where they were above the obvious high-water mark, but when the men awoke the next morning the gig was gone. It had not been properly secured, and a high tide had floated it off the cay, claiming an irreplaceable asset.

That same morning, some of the men hoped they would wake to see *Bridgewater* nearby, but it wasn't. They expressed great concern that it, too, had been lost on a nearby reef; as seafarers, they could not accept that Captain Palmer had left them for dead.

With the two crews living as one on the cay, along with many of the crew of *Investigator*, who had sailed as passengers, it was paramount that a level of authority and discipline be established to ensure that their chances of survival and rescue were maximised. As the most senior officer, and with the support of Lieutenant Fowler and Captain Park, Flinders took charge. From then on, it was as if they were aboard a landlocked ship.

By 23 August *Cato* was 'a few scattered fragments', but *Porpoise* remained mostly intact due to the relatively benign weather. Yet Flinders knew all too well that a tropical storm could easily tear the wreck asunder, so it was imperative that her timber carcass was emptied of the things most important to survival as quickly as possible. When the salvaged items had reached the beach and been listed, it was confirmed that there was sufficient water and provisions to support the 94 survivors for three months at full allowance. All the sails, rigging and spars that could be recovered were also brought ashore.

Under the circumstances, it was a satisfying situation and the hopes everyone held that they would escape this tiny patch of sand seemed justified. But Flinders was disappointed about the state of his own valued treasures:

> My books, charts, and papers had suffered much damage, from the top of the cabin being displaced when the mizzen mast fell; all such papers as chanced to be loose on the night of the shipwreck were then washed away by the surfs, and amongst them a chart of the west side of the Gulf of Carpentaria and part of the North Coast, upon which I had been occupied in the afternoon. Part of my small library shared the same fate; but the rest of the charts, with my log and bearing books and astronomical observations were all saved, though some of them in a wet and shattered state. The rare plants collected on different parts of the south, the east, and north coasts of Terra Australis, for His Majesty's botanic garden at Kew, and which were in a flourishing state before the shipwreck, were totally destroyed by the salt water; as were the dried specimens of plants.

The cay that was their lifeline was in the middle of what Flinders had already named Wreck Reefs, which he calculated was between five and six miles in circumference. At low tide it was approximately 300 yards by 100 yards, and its highest point was between two and three feet above the average high-water mark. Fortunately, the reef formed a protective bastion that dissipated the swells as they crossed the coral and surged towards the cay. However, when the wind and seas were up, the men were continually peppered by salt spray; this explained the absence of vegetation on the cay, except for 'a few diminutive salt plants'.

The stores that had been salvaged were placed in a tent made from spars and sails. The same materials were also used to create tents for each mess of officers and men. Still, it was the yard that carried the inverted ensign that dominated the scene. It would soon have another use as well.

> One of the men whose liberty governor King had granted at my request, being guilty of disorderly conduct, the articles of war were publicly read, and the man punished at the flag staff. This example served to correct any evil disposition, if such existed; the men worked cordially together, and in all respects we preserved the same discipline and order as on board His Majesty's ships.

With everyone having now abandoned all thoughts of salvation coming from the return of *Bridgewater*, Flinders called a meeting of the officers to consider every conceivable means of escape 'from the precarious situation in which our misfortune, and captain Palmer's want of energy and humanity, had left us exposed'. The eventual conclusion was that there were two options open to them: one was for an officer and crew to man the larger of the two six-oared cutters and attempt the dangerous passage of more than 700 nautical miles to the nearest centre of civilisation, Port Jackson; once there, they could arrange with Governor King for a vessel or vessels to rescue the men. The alternative plan was precautionary, in case the cutter was lost while sailing to Sydney – which was highly possible at that time of year:

> ... it was resolved that two decked boats, capable of transporting every person remaining on the bank, except one officer and boat's crew, should be immediately laid down by the carpenters, to be built from what was already and might be still further saved from the wreck; and that, if the officer in the cutter did not return with assistance in two months, the boats should then, or as soon after as they could be ready to sail, proceed to Port Jackson.

As an extension of the latter plan, it was also decided that the second, smaller cutter – along with an officer, a second officer and a boat's crew – should remain at the sand cay, in case it were necessary for the two boats that were being built to set sail for Port Jackson. That crew would be responsible for Flinders' charts and books, remaining under orders from him to wait 'a few weeks longer than the two months; and then go to Port Jackson also, should no vessel arrive before that time'. Flinders explained: 'This precaution was necessary, lest any unforeseen occurrence should delay my return to the bank beyond two months, though not prevent it altogether; that the charts, journals, and papers might still be found there, to be taken on to England if wanted.'

It was no surprise when Fowler proposed that Flinders – the one man in their group who, through his extensive exploration, held an intimate knowledge of the east coast of Australia – should captain the large cutter on its voyage to Sydney. It was also agreed that Captain Park should be the second officer aboard the cutter, and that two crews of six capable oarsmen be selected so they could rotate between rowing and rest periods whenever the boat was not under sail. With a total of 14 men aboard, plus supplies, the cutter would be overloaded and would have considerably reduced freeboard, but Flinders believed that the cutter's ability to make the journey more swiftly outweighed its chances of being swamped by large waves.

Even so, Flinders was apprehensive. His experiences along this sometimes rugged coast left him in no doubt that the voyage would be perilous, even for a man of his ability. They would cross an often unforgiving ocean, where there were few places to hide from storms; in fact, if a storm should arise on the first stage, there would be absolutely nowhere they could find shelter. This would be an open ocean passage of 60 leagues – 180 nautical miles – to a place he knew well, Sandy Cape, the northernmost point of the world's largest sand island, Fraser Island. He had sailed past this island in 1799, and had landed near the cape in 1802.

Once the coast had been achieved, however, the tough times could well be just beginning. In gentle or following winds the cutter would make good speed, with the assistance of sail and the south-flowing coastal current, which often ran like a river at up to two knots. But Flinders also knew that this same current could create insurmountable conditions should one of the frequent blusterous storms rampage out of the south: a strong wind opposing a strong current would create breaking seas that could easily erase from existence a small and vulnerable vessel like the cutter.

During these considerations, Flinders' mind would no doubt have harked back to the lengthy discussions he had enjoyed with Captain William Bligh aboard HMS *Providence*, during Bligh's second mission to transfer breadfruit plants from Tahiti to the West Indies. Bligh was a legend in the Royal Navy, and with the British public, all because of the mutiny aboard his previous ship, HMS *Bounty*.

After the ship was overrun by its rebel crew, Bligh and his loyalists had been forced to board an open 23-foot launch in mid-ocean, and were left for dead. Inevitably, Bligh would have explained to Flinders and others that he could well have tried to cross the Tasman Sea, from where they were drifting aimlessly near Tonga, and endeavour to reach Port Jackson, but such a passage would almost certainly have delivered fatal consequences: the tempestuous Tasman spared no one when it was in its foulest moods and could easily have claimed the launch and all 18 men on board. Instead, Bligh opted for an incredible 3600 nautical mile course to Timor – a 47-day voyage that stands to this day as the greatest feat of seafaring and survival in maritime history.

Flinders realised that he was in a somewhat similar situation to Bligh's: an open boat of slightly greater length (around 29 feet) and a considerable complement of men – 14 in all. The big difference was that he had no option but to take on the Tasman, and he stepped up to the challenge like a man who knew no other way. If he had one twinge of disappointment, it was that there was no place for Trim in the crew. He would have to wait with the others on the sand cay.

Nine days after *Porpoise* and *Cato* had plunged onto Wreck Reefs, the cutter had been thoroughly checked and prepared for its epic undertaking. It was given a name: *Hope*. At eight o'clock on the morning of 26 August, everything was in readiness. *Hope* was ready to go, with three weeks of supplies aboard. But while this mission was critical to the survival of all 94 men, many of the well-weathered seafarers who were staying behind were actually discouraging their leader from departing: it was a Friday, and one of the more powerful superstitions among mariners is that you never set sail on that day. Friday was seen as symbolising death: it was the day of the week on which Christ had been crucified.

Regardless of this, all 14 men boarded the cutter without hesitation. Once the bow was turned towards its initial course, to the west, the men onshore gave three rousing cheers for Flinders, *Hope* and her crew, and this gesture was returned with great passion. Simultaneous to the departure, a barefoot sailor sprinted to the spar flying the ensign, which still had the canton carrying the union in the lower corner. He hauled it down and immediately re-hoisted it right-way-up. This action was not lost on Flinders: 'This symbolic expression of contempt for the *Bridgewater* and of confidence in the success of our voyage, I did not see without lively emotion.'

It was a day of clear skies, a light breeze from the south and smooth seas. The men who had been steadying *Hope* in the water released her, and she pulled away from the beach to the sound of cheering and waving. It wasn't long before the gentle thud of timber that came each time the men pulled on the oars had faded into silence. Those left behind willed Flinders and his crew fair winds and smooth seas as they watched the cutter's outline, by then with sails set, become a mere speck on a wide expanse of ocean, before it evaporated into the horizon, headed towards a fate that might never be known.

As it would turn out, Flinders' long-yearned-for reunion with his wife, Ann, which he still hoped was just months away, would not happen for another six tormenting years.

CHAPTER TWO

Cook, Bligh and Flinders

Perhaps incongruously, Matthew Flinders' life was set on a clearly defined course by a fictional character in one of the world's best-known adventure books and was subsequently influenced by two of the most acclaimed master mariners of the late eighteenth and early nineteenth centuries.

As a young boy, Flinders devoured every one of the near 110,000 words in Daniel Defoe's *Robinson Crusoe*, an exciting, adventure-laced tome first published in 1719. The story of the sole survivor from a ship that foundered in a savage storm in 1659, it is sometimes considered to be the world's first true work of fiction. After his shipwreck, Robinson Crusoe made his way to the shore of a deserted island, where he remained marooned for many years. The book's colourful 65-word original title was virtually an abridged version of the story. It read in part: 'The Life and Strange Surprizing Adventures of Robinson Crusoe, of York, Mariner: Who lived Eight and Twenty years, all alone in an un-inhabited Island'.

Typically of the era, the publication was not divided into chapters, so it was seemingly endless, breathtaking reading for the young lad. The turn of every page accelerated his desire for the excitement that came with sailing beyond distant horizons and on to unknown foreign shores. The young Matthew Flinders wanted to be Robinson Crusoe.

As he progressed through his early teenage years, his desire for sea-borne adventure did not diminish, so he chose the one obvious career path available to him. In 1789, when aged 15, his name first appeared on the books of the Royal Navy.

As Flinders later explained, he did this against the wishes of family and friends. In particular, his father, a highly respected doctor, was very much opposed to it; he wanted his son to tread the family path. However, the lure of adventure on the high seas was far stronger than human bonds. Later in life, Flinders would confirm the influence that *Robinson Crusoe* had had on him: 'I burned to have adventures of my own. I felt as I read that there was born within my heart the ambition to distinguish myself by some important discovery.' Indeed, there were some eerie similarities between Flinders' and Crusoe's lives. A paragraph in Defoe's book described Crusoe going against his father's desire for him not to go to sea:

Being the third son of the family, and not bred to any trade,
my head began to be filled very early with rambling
thoughts. My father, who was very ancient, had given me a
competent share of learning, as far as house education and a
country free school generally goes, and designed me for the
law; but I would be satisfied with nothing but going to sea,
and my inclination to this led me so strongly against the will,
nay, the commands of my father, and against all the entreaties

and persuasions of my mother and other friends, that there
seemed to be something fatal in that propension of nature
tending directly to the life of misery which was to befall me.

In the decades ahead, Flinders' achievements would come through
a life of challenge, daring and adventure that was not dissimilar to
that experienced by his fictional hero. In reality, though, he became
such a successful seafarer, explorer and cartographer that history
would see him as part of an illustrious triumvirate, the other two
members being Captain James Cook and Captain William Bligh.

The common thread linking this trio of exceptional mariners
was the famous naturalist and patron of science Sir Joseph Banks, a
man whose great influence in English society extended through to
King George III. Banks, who was with Cook on HMS *Endeavour*
in 1770, on the first British voyage of discovery into the South
Pacific, was the president of what is today the world's oldest
scientific organisation, the Royal Society, from 1778 to 1820.
When in 1775 he became aware of the 21-year-old Bligh's
emerging talents as a seafarer and cartographer, Banks recommended
him to Cook as sailing master aboard HMS *Resolution* for what
would be Cook's third and final voyage into the Pacific. Then, in
1793, after Flinders sailed as a midshipman with Bligh aboard
Providence on its successful voyage to Tahiti, it came to Banks'
attention that Flinders was emerging as a man of similar ilk to Cook
and Bligh. This would eventually lead to Banks recommending to
the Admiralty and the King in late 1800 that Flinders be given
command of a ship so that he could circumnavigate New Holland
and explore its entire coastline.

The proposal for this expedition came just 12 years after the
King and the British parliament had acceded to Banks's suggestion
and established a penal colony at Port Jackson in New South

Wales, the territory claimed for Britain by Cook in 1770. Banks had noted:

> We have now occupied the country of New South Wales more than ten years, and so much has the discovery of the interior been neglected that no one article has hitherto been discovered ... It is impossible to conceive that such a body of land, as large as all Europe, does not produce vast rivers capable of being navigated into the heart of the interior ...

Banks wanted Flinders to search for those mighty rivers along the coastline of this newly claimed British outpost, and Flinders could not have asked for a better commission. It was one that would present him with all the challenges and excitement that his childhood ambitions had sought.

His life's journey had its genesis in a small and somewhat insignificant market town named Donington, in the midst of the swampy and foggy (but by then primarily drained) Fenlands of Lincolnshire. This centuries-old town was located about 100 miles directly north of London, and was a ten-mile horse ride inland from the black mud shores of the Wash, a large, square-shaped bay on England's east coast that opens to the North Sea.

The man who would become Donington's most famous son was born on 16 March 1774 to Mathew and Susannah Flinders. The family home was a modest dwelling on the edge of the town's market square. A small surgery stood as an extension on one side of the residence, and it was here that Flinders senior practised as a doctor; in fact, he was a third-generation doctor in the town. Not surprisingly, it was expected from the outset that young Matthew would study law or enter the medical profession and succeed his father in the family practice.

The origin of the Flinders lineage in England almost certainly dates back to the very early years of the twelfth century, when, as an article on the history of the region in the Holinshed's Chronicle in 1807 confirmed, a major part of Flanders, on the opposite side of the North Sea, was 'being drowned by an exudation or breaking in of the sea, [and] a great number of Flemings came into the country, beseeching the King to have some void place assigned them, wherein they might inhabit'.

The majority of those who fled the flood and migrated to England moved into the middle counties, and as they were from Flanders it is easy to understand how the name Flinders emerged into the local society. For that reason, it is highly likely that Matthew Flinders' family tree was firmly planted in the Donington region centuries earlier.

Matthew is known to have had several sisters and brothers. The diaries of his father, Dr Mathew Flinders, reveal that the first of Matthew's sisters, Elizabeth, was born on 24 September 1775. John (Jackey) Flinders, born 28 September 1776, lived for only six weeks. Sister Susannah was born 22 May 1779 and another brother, again named John, was born two years later – 5 April 1781 (he is believed to have been committed to a mental asylum at age 19). Samuel, born 3 November 1782, went on to join his eldest brother in the Royal Navy. The doctor's diaries also reveal that at least four other children (two sets of twins) were born and died within 24 hours of birth. Matthew's mother, Sussanah, died aged 31, when Matthew was just nine years old. Dr Flinders subsequently remarried and as a result Matthew had two step-sisters, Hannah and Henrietta.

Matthew displayed a remarkably fertile and inquisitive mind at a very young age, especially when it came to the unknown in the world of nature. One day, he disappeared from his home for some hours; only after anxious scouting was he found, wading in one of the shallow marshes nearby. He had a pocket full of pebbles – his 'instruments' – which he dropped into the flowing water at selected points so he could watch the flow of the current and discover the source of the water.

Flinders commenced his schooling at Donington Free School, an institution founded in 1701 by the philanthropist Thomas Cowley so that the children of local families facing financial hardship could learn to read and write. After some years it became a fully fledged school, yet through to Flinders' time it remained free for all children to attend.

At the age of 12, Flinders moved on to the nearby Horbling Grammar School, and it was there that one teacher, Reverend John Shingler, had a significant influence on his education. It was through Shingler's efforts – which Flinders would recognise later in life – that he excelled in reading, writing and mathematics, all subjects that would greatly assist his rise through the ranks of the navy. In particular, it was his ability to master mathematics that allowed him to teach himself the essential science for maritime explorers: navigation.

Flinders was always aware that his deep desire to join the navy would one day clash with the plans his parents had long held for him. As his mother had by then passed away, he knew he faced a difficult confrontation with his father – one that he was in no hurry to have. Instead, the teenager came up with another strategy for presenting his case. His father had a slate hanging on the back of a door in the surgery – a type of eighteenth-century diary, on which he wrote himself reminders about patients and appointments – and Matthew would leave messages on it for his father to read, all relating to his passion for a seafaring life.

The youngster also believed that his uncle, John Flinders, who was in the navy, would support him when it came to the unavoidable discussion with his father, so he wrote to him asking for guidance. Unfortunately, Uncle John was of little help: he had been in the navy for 11 years and was still waiting to achieve the rank of lieutenant. Because of this, his comments to his nephew were little short of damning. For him, favouritism almost always overrode talent within the navy.

John Flinders' letter, however, did tender one piece of practical advice: he suggested that, should Matthew remain determined to pursue a career under sail, he should study several valuable works: Euclid's *Elements*, a mathematical and geometrical thesis written by the Greek mathematician around 300 BC, along with two other publications dealing with navigation. For Matthew, this suggestion far outweighed his uncle's negative comments, so the 13-year-old set about finding and buying the books and applying himself to a year of solid study at home. (His uncle waited another two years for a posting as a lieutenant. When it came, it was with HMS *Cygnet* in the West Indies, but a severe bout of yellow fever claimed his life soon after.)

By the end of these 12 months of study, the self-taught Matthew had acquired a remarkable knowledge of the subjects that would matter most to his career. He was now 14, and inevitably, while studying at home, he would have learned of Captain Cook's much-heralded discovery in 1770 of the coast of what could well prove to be the 'Great South Land'. He would also have been aware that the famous explorer had subsequently been murdered by natives in the Sandwich Islands (now Hawaii) in 1779, a year after he became the first European to visit them. News of his death would not reach England for another two years.

While confident that his studies had prepared him well for a naval career, Flinders realised that his knowledge and enthusiasm would not necessarily secure him an entrance into the navy. A direct link, particularly through family ties, to a senior officer who could nominate him for service was far more likely to win him a position, but there were no such opportunities immediately available to this lad from rural Donington.

However, as fate would have it, a circuitous link soon presented itself. A cousin, Henrietta Flinders, was employed as a governess for the family of the commander of HMS *Scipio*, Captain Thomas Pasley, and she was aware of Matthew's determination to join the navy. She mentioned her cousin's ambitions to the captain, who was immediately impressed by the thought of a 15-year-old who was apparently gaining a wealth of knowledge without the benefit of a tutor. He was so impressed, in fact, that he asked to meet Matthew so he could decide for himself if he had the mettle to make a sailor.

The meeting at Pasley's residence turned out to be as embarrassing as it was encouraging for the aspiring seafarer. Such was the rapport he enjoyed with Captain Pasley and his family that he was invited to stay the night, and he accepted the offer without hesitation, even though he did not have a nightshirt with him. That concern was quickly allayed when he went to his room and found that his hosts had, very considerately, placed night attire on the bed for him. He took the nightshirt and put it on, only to realise that he had made a terrible mistake – he was wearing a young woman's nightdress, one featuring frills, lace and ribbon. It turned out that the captain's daughter, who had given up her bed for the guest, had forgotten to take her nightdress from the room. At breakfast the next morning, Matthew was the source of considerable mirth as, somewhat embarrassed, he related what he had done.

Regardless of his *faux pas*, Flinders had left a good impression on Captain Pasley, because within weeks – on 23 October 1789, to be precise – he had arranged for Matthew to be placed on the naval register as a lieutenant's servant for HMS *Alert*, a two-masted, 14-gun brig-sloop.

From the moment he set foot on the ship's deck, he was in an almost overwhelming new world. His eyes and mind were full of wonder as he tried to absorb his surrounds: the height of the masts and complexities of the rig. He scanned the deck and did his best to understand which feature played what role in the operation of the ship. It was an awe-inspiring moment for a 15-year-old from the English countryside.

This initial stage of his naval apprenticeship lasted seven months. Then, in May 1790, Pasley's influence emerged once more. The captain now held no doubt that his initial faith in the young man was justified, so he had Flinders join his crew aboard *Scipio*, which was lying at the Royal Navy Dockyard at Chatham, in the River Medway, east of London.

Scipio was a 64-gun third-rate ship of the line, a design considered to be the best configuration for modern-day battle: fast and manoeuvrable under sail and well-armed, with cannons mounted on two decks – an impressive step up from *Alert*.

Sailing under Pasley's command would prove to be invaluable for Flinders. He would 'learn the ropes' on deck and, through hands-on experience, put into practice the knowledge he had gained through his home studies. Again he must have impressed, because his Pasley-assisted progress continued. The following year, when the captain was transferred to the command of the 74-gun third-rate ship of the line, HMS *Bellerophon*, he asked Flinders to join his crew as a midshipman.

This was a move to a 'real' ship for Flinders. Launched only four years earlier, *Bellerophon* – known as *Billy Ruffian* or *Ruff'n* by her crew – would become one of the most famous fighting ships in the Royal Navy. Her war record included the Battle of the Nile and the Battle of Trafalgar. On 15 July 1815, she would come to great prominence when Napoleon Bonaparte, who had appointed himself Emperor of the French in 1804, was escorted as a defeated man onto her main deck, where he surrendered to Captain Frederick Maitland. This was in the aftermath of the Battle of Waterloo, when the Emperor had been forced into submission after 25,000 of his men were killed or wounded and another 8000 taken prisoner. Napoleon had planned to escape France by sea to the United States but was intercepted by *Bellerophon*. Following his surrender to Maitland, Napoleon was held aboard the ship for three weeks, before being sent into exile at Saint Helena, where he died six years later.

When Flinders joined *Bellerophon* in 1790 he was just 16, and his youthful exuberance had him wanting to cross oceans and touch foreign shores. He was ready for high adventure but it wouldn't materialise in the short term. While recognising that he was learning much by being aboard *Bellerophon* and under the tutelage of a well-recognised master, the lack of actual sea time made him feel as though his career was marking time. This belief was compounded when he was suddenly transferred to a 64-gun ship, HMS *Dictator*, which was not likely to be going anywhere soon.

However, although Flinders didn't know it, it appears that this move had been made simply to protect the continuity of his time in service. It is possible that his superiors had transferred him in order to enhance his chances of promotion, as they considered that the young man held the potential to be a true leader. He was in a holding pattern, but not for long.

Much to Flinders' delight, the frustration he had harboured for months disappeared very quickly: he was advised that he had been posted to *Providence*. It was a move that would bring him everything he wanted. It meant he would soon be heading offshore to a destination on which fantasies were created: the tropical paradise of Tahiti in the South Pacific. Equally satisfying was the knowledge that his captain would be none other than William Bligh, a national hero in England, and a man whose vast experience as a commander, navigator, cartographer, seafarer and explorer would bring a sizeable benefit to Flinders' own career.

Flinders knew, of course, that Bligh had lost his ship, *Bounty*, to 21 mutinous crewmembers after it had departed Tahiti in April 1789. It was bound for the West Indies, where the more than 1000 breadfruit plants that it carried would be unloaded and then cultivated, so they could provide cheap food for the slave population of the islands.

The consequences of the mutiny had brought hero status to Bligh right across English society. This even extended to the King, whom he had been honoured to meet. During the overthrow, the mutineers had had the opportunity to kill Bligh and the 22 men who remained loyal to him; instead, the leader of the uprising, Fletcher Christian, showed a modicum of remorse by allowing the captain and 18 of his supporters to board a small and completely open launch mid-ocean.

For Christian and his bunch of rogues, this was, in reality, little more than another way of taunting Bligh and his men: they could be seen to be giving their former shipmates a fighting chance of survival, but deep down they knew that this chance was next to nothing. There is no doubt that they fully expected Bligh and his men to succumb to the elements soon after the launch was cast adrift.

With the 19 men aboard, plus a miserly amount of provisions, the launch was grossly overloaded and in immediate danger of capsizing: the freeboard, which represented the distance between safety and sinking – the measurement between the gunwale and the surface of the sea – was less than a couple of hand-spans.

Christian's plans were to see *Bounty*, himself and the mutineers also disappear, but theirs would be a well-contrived and deliberate exit. They intended first to return to the romantic charms of the hazel-skinned, barely clad beauties they had come to love on the shores of Tahiti's Matavai Bay, and eventually to a new life on a remote and rocky outcrop virtually unknown to the outside world: Pitcairn Island.

Yet the mutineers did not take into consideration Bligh's remarkable seafaring and navigational skills, and the never-say-die determination that was held by all aboard the launch. Bligh rallied his men and managed to reach the small island of Tofua, which lay 30 nautical miles north-east of the location of the mutiny. For four days they tried to find food and water, before finding themselves surrounded by several hundred intimidating islanders, who left no doubt that they saw the Englishmen as invaders and were determined to slaughter them there on the rugged and rocky beach. In a manner for which the English are renowned, Bligh – who had just four cutlasses for defence – did the only thing he could: he all but ignored the threat, and with a stiff upper lip and a focus that was nothing but forward, he moved his men to the launch, which was anchored in shallow water just a few yards away from the shore. They rowed away, but not before one man was stoned to death in an horrific and bloody scene on the beach.

Those aboard the launch looked back in horror, knowing they could do nothing to help their comrade: they had to make good their escape. Bligh called on those at the oars to straighten their backs and pull as hard as they could. The islanders weren't done yet: some piled rocks aboard their canoes and set off in pursuit of the Englishmen, whose overladen launch was labouring through the ocean swells. Inevitably, the swiftness of the canoes soon allowed them to surround the launch, whose occupants were bombarded with stones. It was only through Bligh's presence of mind, which allowed him to orchestrate a remarkable escape, that he and his men survived.

It was evident to the Englishmen that they were traversing a part of the world where cold-blooded killers, and possibly cannibals, were resident on the islands. They knew that, if they wanted to have any chance of seeing Mother England again, they could not safely go ashore anywhere in the region.

Bligh put it to the men that there was just one strategy to be considered. Having sailed with Captain Cook, he knew that there was a European settlement somewhere in Timor, to the north of New Holland, and it represented their only chance for salvation. It meant they would have to attempt an extremely perilous voyage of more than 3600 nautical miles across an always threatening ocean that could claim their launch at any moment. There was no doubt that they would face storms, calms and unforgiving seas, and accordingly they had to accept there was little in favour of them achieving their goal. Additionally, apart from the considerable dangers they faced from the elements, they had only very basic navigational equipment available to them – they didn't even have charts. They would also have to find their way through the bastion of coral reefs that lined the northern coast of New Holland, but before they got there they might be confronted by starvation, dehydration and fatigue. Beyond that, swamping, capsize or equipment failure could quickly and easily end their days.

These were odds no man would ever want to face, but Bligh and his men knew it was Timor or termination. After a brief discussion, the men universally agreed that their decision was obvious, and with that they turned the launch's bow towards the setting sun and on a course that would take them into the unknown.

Forty-seven days later, 18 emaciated men saw Kupang, Timor, come into view. They had survived 3618 punishing nautical miles. Much of the time had seen them battling gales and life-threatening seas, and they were constantly bailing water. Their food was generally rationed to one and a half ounces of bread and a quarter-pint of water – about a cupful – per man, per day. The little cured pork they had was treated as an occasional delicacy, while most of the alcohol was used in small quantities to help men who were losing their grip on life.

Little wonder, then, that when Bligh returned to England on 15 March 1790 and word spread of the mutiny and his remarkable voyage to liberation, he was lauded by King and commoner alike.

Now Matthew Flinders was to sail as a lieutenant with the great man – a true master mariner. Maritime history was being written; the trio of great mariners and explorers that would be hailed in later centuries was about to be formed: Cook, Bligh and Flinders. Cook was the grand master, Bligh the diligent and dedicated young sailing master who thrived on every lesson Cook passed down, while Flinders would benefit greatly from both. All three would hold some form of affiliation with maritime exploration in Australia, and with the establishment of the British colony there.

Right then, though, a very excited young Matthew Flinders could not gather his slops soon enough. He packed and headed for Deptford, where the recently launched 107-foot sloop-of-war, *Providence*, was being fitted out under Bligh's direction.

CHAPTER THREE

To Paradise with Bligh

Flinders probably travelled to the dockyard at Deptford aboard a naval pinnace or launch, although he could have gone by a horse-drawn coach. If he did, he would have traversed the rolling green hills and farmlands on the outskirts of the village before the coach turned into Butt Lane and arrived at the sprawling facility that stood boldly on the banks of the Thames, just four miles downstream from London.

It was 8 May 1791, and one can only imagine the adrenaline that was pumping through the veins of the 17-year-old as he tried to determine which three masts among the many he could see in the distance at the dock belonged to *Providence*. He would not have had to wait long to find out, because soon after entering the 30-acre site he would have been escorted through the maze of solidly built stone warehouses and workshops, then on to where his ship was moored. From there, it was only a steeply angled wooden plank leading to the ship's main deck that remained between him and his first big ocean adventure, and it would have taken him just a few energetic strides to make that transition from shore to ship.

For almost every sailor joining a new ship, the first 24 hours were the 'time to swing one's hammock': this was when they could acquaint themselves with the vessel, both above and below deck, and meet their shipmates. With *Providence* still being prepared for her long voyage to Tahiti and back, there's no doubt that Flinders would have grabbed this opportunity. At the same time, he would have looked across the dockyard and appreciated some of the history the famous facility – England's first Royal Dockyard – had seen since 1513, when it was established by order of King Henry VIII. This was where Queen Elizabeth I knighted Sir Francis Drake on the deck of *Golden Hind* in 1581, and where Sir Walter Raleigh had supposedly laid down his cape to protect the same queen's shoes. It was the port from which Captain Cook had departed aboard *Resolution* on his tragic final voyage; and more recently, from which Bligh had set sail aboard *Bounty*.

Providence had been in the water just two months, so everything about her was new. Flinders would have savoured the rich smell of newly sawn timber and that of the pitch used to seal the deck. He would also have watched with great interest as riggers working aloft attached the standing and running rigging to the ship's three masts and spars. At the same time, on deck and below, shipwrights were busy completing the fit-out. While ship design and construction had changed little in two centuries, *Providence* displayed the latest technology, being essentially a multi-purpose vessel – one that lent itself both to battle and to exploration. There was certainly no reason for her to be part of the Royal Navy's battle fleet at that time, however, because England was enjoying a respite from its feuds with the French and other European nations. The 406-ton *Providence* was 107 feet and ten inches overall, flush-decked, and had a beam of 29 feet and one inch. One hundred sailors were required to man her, and her protection came in the form of ten cannons and 24 smaller swivel arms.

Early in Flinders' time on board – possibly even on that very first day – he would have met his captain, William Bligh, and when he did he would have doffed his hat in salute, in line with naval tradition at the time. The hand salute, as seen today, was not introduced to the Royal Navy for at least another 50 years; it was instituted by Queen Victoria because she did not approve of men in uniform being hatless.

Flinders would have learned from his master that there was to be considerably more to this voyage than collecting the breadfruit plants in Tahiti and transferring them to the West Indies. An important and challenging exploration was also to be undertaken, and the young man would be very much a part of it.

After deciding that there should be another attempt to get breadfruit to the Caribbean, and having purchased *Providence* for the project, the Admiralty had met to formulate its orders for Captain Bligh. This naval hierarchy comprised both 'sea lords' and 'civil lords', although the naval representatives were always in the majority. They met regularly in the same boardroom at Whitehall, in London, that is used to this day: an ornately decorated room, panelled with dark oak, with tall windows that reach from near the floor to the ceiling. The lords had agreed that they should also commit the breadfruit expedition to an important new task: Bligh would 'make a complete examination of Torres Strait'.

Their reasoning was simple. The strait was known to comprise an extremely dangerous cluster of reefs and islands that were strewn across the 90-mile-wide expanse of ocean stretching between the north-eastern tip of New Holland and the southern coast of New Guinea, and raging tidal currents boiled through there. Should a safe channel be found through the middle of the strait, then the time taken for a voyage from Great Britain's new outpost in Port Jackson to home ports in England would be considerably reduced. Such a maritime track would mean that for the majority of the year – excluding the cyclone season – ships would no longer have to undertake the arduous and often dangerous voyage home to the east, across the Southern Ocean and through the 'sailors' graveyard', the waters around Cape Horn. This was the worst place on Earth to be, should Poseidon become outraged by a ship's presence. Over the centuries, his malevolent moods had created gargantuan breaking seas, screeching winds, potent currents, even icebergs, which had led to countless men and ships being 'buried' at the Horn without trace.

History records that the first European to guide a ship through Torres Strait was the Spanish pilot whose name it carries, Luis Váez de Torres, in 1606. He had sailed along the southern coast of New Guinea, while in 1770 Captain Cook – after he had discovered the east coast of New Holland – had probed the strait from east to west aboard *Endeavour*, close to the shores of Cape York. Now it was Bligh's turn, but his commission was far more difficult, even though he had the advantage of knowing something of the strait. He had become aware of its dangers when in discussion with Captain Cook aboard *Resolution*, and he had navigated *Bounty*'s launch through it following the mutiny in 1789.

If Bligh was successful in charting the strait, then ships bound for India and England would sail north from Sydney, ride the south-east trade wind through the strait, enter the Indian Ocean, then sail on to either India or return to the Atlantic via the Cape of Good Hope. The Admiralty's directive to Bligh also meant that *Providence* would be making a west-about passage to the Caribbean once she had departed Tahiti.

But first, before any of this could be achieved, Bligh had to prepare *Providence* to the best of his ability, and that related to every facet of the mission. From the moment the *Bounty* mutiny was ignited, Bligh knew that it would not have occurred had he had a complement of marines aboard the ship to back his command; had there been a small tender sailing in support of *Bounty*, his authority would have been even more secure. So, for this second breadfruit voyage, he requested both these from the Admiralty, via Sir Joseph Banks, and its board agreed.

This time, however, the importance of having a support ship had as much to do with the order to explore the uncharted waters of Torres Strait as it did with preventing a mutiny. Bligh explained this in his letter to Sir Joseph: 'A small vessel with about 30 men would be of use and may enable me more effectually to render the navigation of Endeavour Straits less hazardous ... an expeditious help for ships home from Botany Bay.' (Bligh sometimes referred to Torres Strait as Endeavour Straits; this was the name given to the passage to the south-west – close to Cape York and leading into the Gulf of Carpentaria – which Captain Cook had taken with *Endeavour* in 1770.)

The chosen vessel was a stout little brig aptly named *Assistant*. Her overall length was 51 feet; she displaced 110 tons and was manned by 27 men. With this decided, Bligh then had the pleasure of appointing a friend, Lieutenant Nathaniel Portlock, as *Assistant*'s captain. He was an experienced officer and man of the sea who was well aware of the responsibilities that came with being the master of a support vessel on such an extensive voyage; he had served as master's mate aboard *Discovery*, which had been the tender for *Resolution* on Cook's third voyage.

While *Providence* was only a few feet longer than *Bounty*, she had twice the tonnage, and this meant that Bligh's militia could include a lieutenant, a sergeant, two corporals, a drummer and fifteen marines. When it came to the rest of the crew, Flinders found comfort in the knowledge that two *Bounty* crewmembers – the sailmaker, Lawrence Lebogue, and a steward, John Smith – would be aboard: this was surely testament that Captain Bligh was not the harshest of taskmasters, as some were quick to suggest. Also, Flinders had friends who knew Bligh, and they did not speak badly of him. Even more importantly for Flinders, Bligh would pass on his wealth of knowledge to the young man, whose evolving talents were similar to his own at the same age.

Captain Pasley also retained a keen interest in his 'naval son'. Two months before *Providence* departed, he wrote to Flinders requesting that they stay in contact.

Bellerophon, Spithead, June 3rd, 1791.
Dear Flinders,
I am favoured with your letter on your return from visiting
your friends at the country, and I am pleased to hear that you
are so well satisfied with your situation on board the
Providence. I have little doubt of your gaining the good
opinion of Capt. Bligh, if you are equally attentive to your
duty there as you were in the *Bellerophon*. All that I have to
request in return for the good offices I have done you is that
you never fail writing me by all possible opportunities during
your voyage; and that in your letters you will be very
particular and circumstantial in regard to everything and
place you may chance to see or visit, with your own
observations thereon. Do this, my young friend, and you
may rest assured that my good offices will not be wanting
some future day for your advancement. All on board are
well. Present my kind remembrances to Captain and
Mrs Bligh, and believe me, yours very sincerely,
    Thomas Pasley.

Unfortunately, some of Flinders' communiqués and notes from this voyage have been lost, but sufficient information can be retrieved from a number of sources, such as journals created by his fellow *Providence* crewmen, including that of 23-year-old George Tobin, a third lieutenant. They provide a detailed picture of the voyage, and of what Flinders and all the crew experienced on what was his first passage to the Southern Hemisphere and its distant destinations.

Providence and *Assistant* left Deptford on 22 June and eased their way downstream on the ebb tide to Galleons Reach, where they anchored and took on guns and ammunition. When that task was complete, the anchor was weighed and the sails set for the remainder of the voyage down to the mouth of the Thames, then out onto the open waters of the English Channel. Their intended course from there was to the anchorage at Spithead, off Portsmouth, but that had to change – and rather rapidly. As *Providence* sailed down the Thames and out to sea, Bligh and his senior officers became concerned: the ship was exhibiting an undesirable trait, one that would make her unsafe in heavy weather. She was, in naval jargon, 'crank' – unstable and difficult to handle – so they headed for nearby Sheerness, where, after the ship was moored, an additional 20 tons of iron ballast and some shingle was placed in the bilge for added stability.

Once at Spithead, the day of departure from English waters approached all too quickly; not surprisingly, there was the usual air of anxiety among the crew, especially those whose sailing experience had never extended beyond the mouth of the Thames. But even the most seasoned sailors felt a twinge of trepidation. They knew that if everything went to plan, they could expect to return home in two years, but there were no guarantees. They would be sailing into an unknown world that harboured an inordinate number of hidden dangers. Tobin wrote:

The day approached fast for our departure from the British
Shore and civilized society, to mingle with the uncultivated
children of nature – in more distant countries. He must
indeed be destitute of reflection and sensibility who has not
<u>some</u> connexions or attachments to bind him to his native
Isle; particularly happy in my relatives and friends. I sorely
felt the separation, nor did I look to this voyage of anxious
uncertainty, without some unpleasant thoughts; but they
were soon dissipated; it was a Voyage I had eagerly courted
and volunteered, and my profession taught one that repining
was wrong, and would avail naught.

For the teenage Flinders, mystification, apprehension and an overload
of eager anticipation could only have created a fast-changing tide of
emotions.

Early in the afternoon of 2 August 1791, the anchors were
hauled up to the end of the cathead and secured for sea.
Simultaneously, the sheets, braces and buntlines were manned so
that the designated sails could be set to catch the favourable breeze
that would propel *Providence* through the large fleet of ships
anchored at Spithead, past the Isle of Wight and out into the
English Channel, where she would be set on a west-south-west
course, towards the Atlantic Ocean.

For the next five days the wind remained fair but fickle, so it
wasn't until their sixth day at sea that the southern coast of England
had finally set below the horizon in *Providence*'s wake. Tobin recalled
that, as the coast disappeared, many of the crew were 'anxiously
casting the last look on the hills of our native isle as it receded from
the view, until the wat'ry horizon bid the prospect die'.

The ship's crew was divided into the relatively new Royal Navy
program of three watches. The captain insisted that, when it rained,

a 'good fire' should be lit in the galley below deck – with a sentinel standing by to prevent accidents – so the members of the off-watch could remain warm and dry their clothes. Tobin noted that this custom 'was observed throughout the voyage; as well as enforcing the people to dry their wet clothes, which at length became habitual to them. Too much attention cannot be paid to it, as nothing generates sickness so much on board ship, as wet or damp clothes.'

Progress was not fast on this first stage of the voyage: the ship was never put under any great test by wind or sea, so the crew had ample time to become acquainted with their new vessel. Not even the often ugly Bay of Biscay challenged *Providence* as she headed south towards her first stop, Tenerife, the Spanish protectorate off the coast of Africa.

Soon after a hazy first light emerged on the morning of their twenty-fifth day at sea, the lookout shouted from high above that he could see land ahead. It was Pico del Teide, the snow-capped volcanic peak that stands 12,198 feet above sea level – Tenerife's highest point, and the highest point among all the islands of the Atlantic. Before long, the eager eyes on deck spotted the peak, which was quickly becoming visible as the rising sun caused the snow to become a brilliant white. Less than 24 hours later, *Providence* had slowly clawed her way over the 20 nautical miles that separated her from land and was at anchor just off the city of Santa Cruz.

With the ship settled and rolling gently in response to the Atlantic's swells, a senior crewman was sent ashore by Bligh to inquire whether the island's governor would accept a traditional Royal Navy cannon fire salute from *Providence*. This offer was graciously declined, for the reason that the expense for the Spanish government to respond with a similar salute would be very great.

Over the following days, those crewmembers not on anchor watch or committed to working aboard the ship took the opportunity, when they were permitted, to go ashore. Flinders was among them and was able to send his first letter to Captain Pasley. It was, as requested, full of observations.

Not a large town; streets wide, ill-paved and irregular. The houses of the principal inhabitants large; have little furniture, but are airy and pleasant, suitable to the climate. Most of them have balconies, where the owners sit and enjoy the air. Those of the lower classes ill-built, dirty, and almost without furniture. In the square where the market is held, near the pier, is a tolerably elegant marble obelisk in honour of our Lady of Candelaria, the tutelary goddess of the place. The Spaniards erected this statue, calling it Our Lady, keeping up some semblance of the ancient worship that they might better keep the Tenerifeans in subjection.

We visited a nunnery of the order of St Dominic. In the chapel was a fine statue of the Virgin Mary, with four wax candles burning before her. Peeping through the bars, we perceived several fine young women at prayers. A middle-aged woman opened the door halfway, but would by no means suffer us to enter this sanctified spot. None of the nuns would be prevailed upon to come near us. However, they did not seem at all displeased at our visit, but presented us with a sweet candy they call Dulce, and some artificial flowers, in return for which Mr Smith [the botanist] gave them a dollar. In general these people appear to be a merry, good-natured people, and are courteous to and appear happy to see strangers. We found this always the case, although they said we were no Christians: but they generally took care to make us pay well for what we had. They live principally upon fruits and roots, are fond of singing and dancing, and upon the whole they live as lazily, as contentedly, and in as much poverty as any French peasant would wish to do.

Although the stop was scheduled to last for a week, after only a couple of days the majority of the crew was eager to get under sail again so they could enjoy some cooling sea breezes, as Tobin explained:

The weather during our stay was uncommonly sultry and oppressive; nor did the night air at all make amends for our sufferings in the day. The Land breeze which in most warm Latitudes is eagerly courted, is here as much to be dreaded, the rocks acquiring such a degree of heat from the day's sun as to render the air passing over them almost insupportable. The Thermometer in the shade was at 89° which was higher than it ever rose in the subsequent part of the voyage.

The 'first-timers' aboard *Providence* had never experienced such stifling heat and humidity, but there was worse to come. They were yet to enter the tropics – the Tropic of Cancer was still another 250 nautical miles to the south.

Wish as they did for cooler weather, it wasn't to come for some time. Once *Providence* sailed from Tenerife and began closing on that defining line of latitude, the situation on board became increasingly unbearable. Existence below deck was so clammy and airless that wind sails were fitted above hatchways to force air into the hull, and each evening the main deck was sluiced with a considerable amount of water in order to lower the temperature below. Actually, there were two reasons for this washing down: it also helped preserve the deck timbers, which were being dried out by the savage heat from the sun during the day.

The ship's journey from Tenerife to the Cape Verde Islands proved to be an endurance-testing, sluggishly slow passage in light weather: 900 nautical miles in nine days meant that the average speed was only four knots.

During this time, there was great concern for Captain Bligh. He became seriously ill and experienced what he described as 'violent headaches' – possibly a recurrence of the medical conditions that came as a consequence of his body being ravaged by starvation and dehydration during the launch voyage that followed the *Bounty* mutiny. The concern for him was such that, after anchoring in the bay at Porto Praya in the Cape Verde Islands, Tobin was immediately sent ashore to meet with the governor and ask whether the captain could take up residence there until he regained his health.

Much to Tobin's amazement, the governor's recommendation was that the captain be kept on board and *Providence* put to sea immediately: there was an unidentified fever running rampant through the community and causing the deaths of five or six people every day. Tobin returned to the ship and reported this to Captain Portlock, who had taken command while Bligh was ill. Portlock had no hesitation in making the call: *Providence* would set sail for Cape Town as quickly as possible.

This, however, was easier said than done. When it came time to weigh anchor, no amount of effort by the men manning the capstan bars could lift it from the bottom. It had obviously fouled on something. Every conceivable manoeuvre was tried, in order to get it free, but none was successful. Eventually, the strain on the bower cable was such that it exploded at the point where it passed through the hawse hole, near deck level. With the breeze being offshore, *Providence* was now adrift, so the crew immediately turned their attention to setting the sails.

The loss of the bower anchor was costly, as anchors came at a premium for ships on voyages such as this. They were a vital piece of insurance for the safety of the vessel, and every time one was lost a mission was a step closer to being abandoned. Portlock hoped a replacement anchor could be found in Cape Town. Interestingly, it was later deduced that the anchor was probably hooked on one of the bowers lost by a ship engaged in the Battle of Porto Praya in April 1781. This was a clash between a British squadron led by Commodore George Johnstone and a French squadron led by the Bailli de Suffren, which saw neither side claim an outright victory.

By this time, Flinders was becoming increasingly comfortable in his position aboard the ship. He assisted with, among other things, the navigation, where his most challenging task was to be able to hold the heavy brass sextant steady enough while standing on the pitching deck so he could 'shoot the sun'. Then he would take that information and 'prick the chart' – place *Providence*'s position on the chart. If he was unable to get a sun sight then dead-reckoning, a method based on the course and distance sailed in a given time, would apply. Also, by being one of the most junior of the six midshipmen aboard *Providence* he would almost certainly have been given the duty of winding the chronometers and recording the times at noon each day so a correction could be made for a loss or gain.

He was intrigued by the many facets of nature that he observed, the likes of which he had never seen before. He saw large pods of dolphins that surrounded the ship and swam alongside it, often surfing on the bow wave and always showing off. He and other crew were in awe of their aerial antics; often they would leap up to six feet in the air before making a perfect re-entry into the sea.

Much to the delight of the crew, the captain was slowly returning to good health – so much so that on 3 October he was able to enjoy the high-jinks and entertainment associated with the great maritime tradition of 'crossing the line'.

Flinders was one of a considerable number amongst the crew who were at the centre of this celebration. For the first time in his life, he was about to travel from the Northern Hemisphere into the Southern Hemisphere. Soon after the equator was crossed, King Neptune, bearing a trident, and his not so pretty 'wife' emerged from *Providence*'s forecastle. They approached the quarterdeck on makeshift 'thrones', mounted on a gun carriage that was rolled along the deck. Once there, they set about inducting everyone who had previously only voyaged in the Northern Hemisphere. An apprehensive Flinders, like every other victim, had to pay a fine based on his rank before he was unceremoniously 'baptised' in a large tub containing 'sufficient filth' for the occasion.

Since leaving England, it had become increasingly apparent that *Assistant* was not the ship that had been hoped for. Despite the best efforts of her captain and crew, she did not sail anywhere near as fast as expected; because she was frustratingly slow, *Providence* often had to proceed under reduced sail so that the two ships remained in visual contact. This problem was addressed as soon as the vessels arrived in Cape Town. Portlock had *Assistant*'s rig and sails modified, and she was a considerably faster boat as a result.

As the two ships continued south down the well-travelled course to Cape Town, Mother Nature was always presenting something new that could be appreciated by Flinders and others who had not previously ventured into these climes. There was the inexplicable luminescence they observed so often in the water at night, something science would eventually reveal to be 'ocean phosphorescence' – forms of plankton that briefly emit a bright light when the water is disturbed. On some nights this phenomenon could be seen in *Providence*'s wake for more than a mile. Then there was the flight of the magnificent albatross, which always glided serenely on the updraughts that came with the ocean swells. Most intriguing of all, though, were the 'blubbers' – jellyfish. Everyone struggled to comprehend their existence, the most mystifying thing about them being, as Tobin noted, that when they were cut in half 'there was no spasm or convulsion taking place'.

During the first week of November, for the first time since the ships had left England, a strong gale moved in from the north-west. With the wind increasing in strength, men were sent aloft to reef and furl the sails, but even under reduced sail the ship was averaging more than eight knots and surging down the waves at more than ten. As the seas rose and became more turbulent, so the phosphorescence in the ocean came to life in the most spectacular fashion. According to Tobin, *Providence* seemed to be sailing 'in a sea of liquid fire' for as far as anyone could see. For those on the quarterdeck, it was a very eerie sight; when looking forward, the bow wave was so large and powerful that the luminescence it created was enough to illuminate the high-angled bowsprit and the sails set from it. It was a ghostly image.

On 6 November, after more than six weeks under sail, *Providence* anchored a mile offshore in Cape Town's Table Bay – a setting that left the adventurous Flinders and his shipmates in awe. The backdrop to the scene was one of the most beautiful in the world: the 3500-foot Table Mountain, named for the two-mile plateau that is its crown. However, as beautiful as the setting was, Flinders was not overly impressed by the Dutch colonialists he met in Cape Town, as he described in a letter to Captain Pasley:

> The Dutch, from having great quantities of animal food, are rather corpulent. Nevertheless they keep up their national characteristic for carefulness. Neither are they very polite.

A stranger will be treated with a great deal of ceremony, but when you come to the solid part of a compliment their generosity is at a stand. Of all the people I ever saw these are the most ceremonious. Every man is a soldier and wears his square-rigged hat, sword, epaulets, and military uniform. They never pass each other without a formal bow, which even descends to the lowest ranks, and it is even seen in the slaves.

Providence and *Assistant* had to be substantially overhauled in preparation for the next stage of their journey, one that would see them confronted by the impulsive perils of the bitterly cold Southern Ocean, en route to Van Diemen's Land. From there, it would be a sweep across the similarly challenging Tasman Sea, before the warm reprieve that would come in the South Pacific as they closed in on Tahiti.

After six weeks in Cape Town the work was complete. Fresh food and water, plus some chickens and livestock, had been taken on board, and everything was in readiness for departure. Once the anchor was weighed and the sails clewed down and set, both ships would be heading towards the 'Roaring Forties' in search of the westerly winds that would carry them on their course. There was still a long way to go: Tahiti was around 10,000 nautical miles to the east. The crew's morale was high. Flinders and his shipmates had come to know each other well on the voyage from England, and during the valuable time they had ashore in Cape Town they had taken every opportunity to explore the city known as 'the Tavern of the Seas'.

The remoteness that comes with a voyage into the Southern Ocean became apparent 48 hours after the ships' departure from Cape Town, when the coast of Africa disappeared from view. It was Christmas Eve, and plans were well in place for a considerable celebration the following day, where they would enoy sea-pie of mutton washed down with copious quantities of grog.

A few days later, the much desired strong westerlies arrived – accompanied by unsympathetic seas – and in no time everything was being put to the test. As the wind strength increased, so the sail area was reduced; a third reef went into the main topsail and a fourth reef into the fore topsail, while the other sails were completely furled. It might have been summer in that part of the world, but there was nothing summery about the environment that was being endured. It was a bleak existence under a lead-grey sky.

When the bad weather passed, leaving a calm sea in its place, Captain Portlock had a gig launched so he could be rowed to *Providence* and report to Captain Bligh. He wanted to satisfy himself that Bligh was pleased with the modifications made to his ship in Cape Town: it was now faster and more manageable.

Westerly fronts were continually catching up with *Providence* and passing her, so sails were reefed and unreefed around the clock. The worst gale came on Friday, 13 January. The ship's log reveals that she was 'rolling very deep and taking water over the gunwales'. At times the seas were so large that they burst into the main cabin and damaged timberwork.

Both ships were then on a course that would take them to Saint Paul Island, and for good reason. With dead-reckoning always playing a major part in navigation, this island had become an important waypoint for seafarers – a signpost that confirmed on voyages from Cape Town to Van Diemen's Land that a ship was on track.

This part of the voyage was providing an exceptional education in seamanship for Flinders, as well as lessons in how to keep a ship clean and its crew healthy. Bligh was one of the greatest exponents of both these skills, so the youthful student could not have wanted a better mentor. Flinders, on every one of his watches, would have been actively involved in the process of navigation, particularly with the sextant. This innovation had come into use in the mid-eighteenth century; it accurately measured the angle of a celestial body above the horizon, which meant that a navigator could calculate his ship's position at sea with considerable precision. Throughout each watch, Flinders plotted *Providence*'s course towards Saint Paul Island, which was shown on charts to be at approximately 77 degrees, 30 minutes east longitude and 38 degrees, 50 minutes south latitude. Sure enough, as *Providence* closed on that position, the conical shape of Saint Paul began appearing above the horizon to the north-north-east. The ship's course was changed so that she cruised six nautical miles to the south of the landmass, before turning east once more.

Several weeks later, early on 8 February, those on deck peered through the dimness of first light and began to decipher the hazy profile of the high hills some 12 nautical miles to their north. It was Van Diemen's Land.

The following day *Providence*'s sails were clewed up and neatly furled, and the ship's boats were launched so she could be towed to a safe anchorage in the sheltered and crystal-clear waters of Adventure Bay, south of where Hobart lies today. The hands on deck who were tidying the ship could take some time to appreciate the bold, natural beauty of this remarkably remote region, around 14,000 nautical miles by sea from home.

Adventure Bay was well known to Bligh. He had been there with Captain Cook in 1777, and aboard *Bounty* four years prior to this visit. The bay, which was first sighted by the Dutch explorer Abel Tasman in 1642, was known to be a perfect place to collect water and gather wood. Facing east, it was well protected from the worst of the weather, and because the sea was deep, even close to the shore, it gave ideal shelter to weather-beaten Southern Ocean mariners en route to the Pacific.

Bligh ordered a group of men to go ashore and find out whether the apple trees he had planted four years earlier had survived. One was still there, healthy but smaller than could have been expected after such a time. The other trees had probably been destroyed by a bushfire, Bligh decided. A few days later, he had the botanists go ashore and plant another seven trees. Just as Captain Cook had done when he was there, Bligh had a message carved into a tree trunk: 'Near this tree Captain William Bligh planted seven fruit trees 1792: – Messrs S and W, botanists'. Alongside a nearby stream, he had the botanists plant some quince, strawberry, fig and pomegranate plants, and then decided to introduce a cock and two hens to Van Diemen's Land by releasing them into the wild. While Bligh was enthusiastic about the establishment of foreign fauna in this environment, the crew was puzzled: they were certain the natives would be soon eating chicken, terminating the captain's experiment.

Bligh knew there was a lake immediately behind the beach, so he ordered that the small boat that was aboard *Assistant* be taken ashore and carried there so he could explore it. As it turned out, the venture became a highly successful fishing expedition – the lake turned out to be teeming with bream.

Throughout their two-week stay, Bligh, Flinders, Tobin and others were often in the longboat carrying out an extensive reconnaissance of what we know today to be Storm Bay. Incredibly, though, these excursions never led them to realise that Adventure Bay was on the eastern shore of a small island – they assumed it was part of the landmass that surrounded them to the west. However, it was only eight weeks later that this fact would be revealed. It came when a French rear admiral, Antoine Raymond Joseph de Bruni d'Entrecasteaux, stopped in a beautiful inlet on the south-eastern tip of Van Diemen's Land, which he named Recherche Bay after one of his two expedition ships. From there, d'Entrecasteaux took a longboat and explored the coastline directly north, an exercise that soon confirmed that the region around Adventure Bay was separated from Van Diemen's Land by a significant waterway. The waterway is now named D'Entrecasteaux Channel, and the small island Bruny Island.

The Bligh expedition concentrated on regions to the north of Adventure Bay. During their excursions, Flinders and other 'first-timers' continued to be amazed by the sight of kangaroos, which were abundant. There was ample evidence of the presence of local Aboriginals – their bark canoes were plentiful, most about 12 feet long and made from layers of bark from the peppermint gum or stringybark trees. Yet much to everyone's surprise, the English had virtually no contact with them. Most of those who were seen were extremely timid and ran away whenever the foreigners, in their colourful 'skins', made an approach.

Years later, when Flinders was penning *A Voyage to Terra Australis*, he recalled a 'remarkable circumstance' during one encounter with the Adventure Bay natives. Flinders wrote that 'when presents wrapped up in paper were thrown to them, they took the articles out, and placed them on their heads'. He noted that this act was also recorded by Burgomaster Nicolaes Witsen, the mayor of Amsterdam, when he wrote in 1705 of encounters the Dutch explorers had had with natives on the eastern side of the Gulf of Carpentaria, 2000 miles to the north. He had written that 'the people swam on board of a Dutch ship; and when they received a present of a piece of linen, they laid it upon their head in token of gratitude'.

Bligh's stopover in Adventure Bay proved to be successful, but when it came time to prepare to set sail there were two unexpected disappearances. The nanny goats, which had been taken ashore to graze, made good their escape into the wild, but more disconcerting was the desertion into the bush of one of the crew from *Assistant*. Tobin explained the circumstances in his journal:

> Several parties were sent in the morning to beat the woods in search of one of the Assistant's people who had deserted his boat. Throughout the previous night a light had been kept at the Mast head and guns fired at intervals, supposing he had lost himself. After some time he was discovered by Pearce concealed in such a manner as left no doubt it was his intention for the vessels to proceed without him. He assigned as a reason for his absence being unjustly accused of the theft, which determined his taking this desperate step. The poor wretch must in all probability have soon perished, not having the smallest portion of food with him, or anything to produce a fire with. When taken, he declared he preferred the risk of starving in this distant country, or meeting its natives, to remaining on board under such an accusation.

When *Providence* and *Assistant* weighed anchor and cruised out of Adventure Bay on 22 February, Bligh decided to sail to the extremities of the exceptionally large sound. He had hoped to find the entrance to Frederick Henry Bay, which he had seen to the north from the hills behind their anchorage, but that effort brought no reward; the wind direction was unfavourable. As fate would have it, Flinders would return to these waters before the turn of the century as an explorer under sail.

By the time Bligh decided to abandon the search for the entrance to the bay, the wind had changed direction and it was proving difficult for both ships to hold the easterly course that would see them weather Cape Pillar before entering the Tasman Sea. They could sail no closer to the wind – they were close-hauled with the wind two points forward of abeam – and were barely above the lay-line to the headland when it all became too much for *Assistant*'s foreyard. The ship was being pressed so hard the solid timber spar splintered, causing the sail to flog wildly and dangerously while crew tried to contain it. Given the magnitude of the problem and the voyage that lay ahead, Bligh immediately signalled for a return to the anchorage in Adventure Bay so that repairs could be made.

It took only 24 hours to replace the broken spar, but in that time Bligh, Flinders and others were rewarded with another discovery. In the distance, just to the west of north, they saw for the first time – possibly because it was continually enveloped in cloud – a high, flat-topped summit that was capped in snow. They named it Table Mountain – although forty years later it would be renamed Mount Wellington, in honour of the Duke of Wellington and his role in the defeat of Napoleon at the Battle of Waterloo in 1815. The city of Hobart now sits proudly between the mountain and the Derwent River.

Adventure Bay and its surrounds gave Flinders his first true taste of the life he had wanted since childhood. He loved every moment of it – the exploration and navigation, the preparation of charts and sketches, and the logging of information. Flinders was keen to record as much detail as possible for future reference. In fact, his logbook entries often carried more detail than those of his captain. Yet this was only the start. A few weeks later, *Providence* and *Assistant*, having crossed the Tasman Sea, would have rounded the southern cape of New Zealand and be bound for Tahiti. That was where the real adventure would begin.

It took about seven days for *Providence* and her consort to reach New Zealand. Once there, they were hauled onto a more northerly course for what was the start of the final 2300 nautical miles to Tahiti. Flinders was forever gaining knowledge from his highly experienced captain, such as how in misty weather it was beneficial to have a crewman stationed forward of the bow, on the jib boom, as a lookout, instead of aloft because his range of vision through the fog was better.

When the captain had previously sailed through this region aboard *Bounty*, he had happened upon a small island that, being so low, was barely visible and could therefore have easily claimed his ship. This time, then, as a precaution, Bligh ordered that every evening the sails would be reduced on *Providence* and *Assistant* to slow their progress. This would then allow the ships' course to be changed far more quickly, should there be cause for alarm with the sighting of breakers during the night. Bligh also directed that a lookout was to be stationed aloft on *Providence* all night, as well as during the day.

Each day while at sea, the crew carried out numerous routines, some designed to keep the ship clean and the air below deck as fresh as possible, and others to ensure that the ship was well maintained. Fresh water was flushed through the bilge on a regular basis and then pumped out, while at night fires set below deck also ensured that there was a flow of dry air, which helped eliminate dampness. The sailmakers were forever busy on deck, repairing damaged sails and making new ones, while an equally important task was to grease the masts regularly so that abrasion from the spars rubbing against them was minimised.

Maintenance checks of the mast and rigging were seemingly endless during the voyage – but even so, this did not mean calamity was always avoided. At first light on 13 March, *Providence* went very close to losing her main topmast. Flinders noted in his log: 'At daybreak, found the main topmast trestle trees broke – took in the sail, sent down the yard and secured the mast.' The trestletrees are vital to supporting the topmast at the point where it is attached to the lower mast. The topmast has its heel located between the trestletrees, which are timbers that run fore and aft at the top of the lower mast.

Flinders also noted his captain's determination to ensure that the crew remained as healthy as possible. The regular diet was 'thick potable soup gruel for breakfast. Krout and sweet wort as customary ... it is nearly a copy from Captain Cook, whose attention in preserving the health of his men was unremitted.'

As the two ships sailed into the higher latitudes, so the weather became more tropical. There were the occasional thunderstorms and hailstorms to contend with, and the temperature during the day progressively increased. Most notable, though, was the colour of the sea, which became a more vivid shade of blue. One night the heavens exploded into bright light when 'a blazing meteor fell in the SW not far distant from the ship which for a few seconds enlightened the whole atmosphere', Flinders recorded.

Flinders regularly noted how *Providence* was forced to reduce sail so that the smaller *Assistant* could stay in visual contact with her, particularly when the winds were strong. He also described a rare occasion when *Assistant* was directly ahead of the larger and faster *Providence* – the two ships went close to colliding. 'The Assistant about three cable lengths ahead was suddenly taken aback [i.e. the sails were back-winded by a rapid change in wind direction]. Providence eased off ... and went to leeward of her. [The captain] ordered her to keep always abaft the beam.'

Another regular exercise for the crew was target practice: 'the boat crews exercised at small arms' and 'exercised great guns and marines at platoon firing'.

While the weather became increasingly pleasant, the men soon realised that this brought some unpleasant and unwanted guests. Tobin explained:

> Other visitors tempted by the change of climate from their lurking places, gave us considerable trouble. The ship swarmed with cockroaches. To destroy them the beams and carlings were frequently washed with boiling water. Many methods are practiced to get rid of these troublesome – and destructive – insects, but hot water thrown with force into their hiding holes seems to be the most effectual; yet to arrive at it altogether is impracticable. The increase of the Cockroach is astonishing; by exposing the Egg in a phial to the sun, after detaching it from the female, above sixty young ones were counted on the shell bursting.

Flinders turned 18 on 16 March, a day that saw *Providence* and *Assistant* charging east on the face of a strong gale. It was an unpleasant day, and while he would not have been the recipient of any particular birthday gift, a more than appropriate present – being part of a history-making discovery of a new South Pacific atoll – came little more than two weeks later. On 5 April, the lookout at the masthead shouted that he had spotted breakers off to port. The man on the helm was directed to change course so that the sighting could be confirmed and observed from the deck.

A few hours later, *Providence* was sailing three nautical miles off the outer edge of a reef that formed part of a previously undiscovered atoll, some 500 nautical miles south-east of Tahiti.

Fortunately, because it was near noon, Bligh was able to get the best possible sun sight to chart the discovery accurately. Flinders remarked that:

> The sight of land after being so long from it, could not be
> but a pleasant one, especially as we perceived it to be covered
> with trees ... The lowness of the land would make it difficult
> to discover it at night 'till very near it. The interior part of
> the island is entirely occupied by water, leaving scarcely
> more than a ridge which a frightful surf in some places nearly
> breaks over. We saw no sign of inhabitants.

While the discovery of this low-lying atoll – now known as Tematangi – was an exciting moment, it also confirmed the wisdom of Bligh's decision to proceed prudently, especially at night, in these essentially uncharted waters.

At this time, *Providence*, having sailed a circuitous course through the southern latitudes of the South Pacific, began being headed – as Bligh had hoped – by the arrival of the south-east trade wind. Soon after, she was on a rollicking run north, with every stitch of sail set, and was closing in on Tahiti at between eight and ten knots. The sea and sky were blue, and the bow wave and wake snow-white – a magnificent site, and the ultimate experience for any sailor.

It was 10 April when the crew on deck heard the eagerly awaited call from the lookout, who was stationed near the topgallant yard on the foremast, that he could see Point Venus, the headland at the eastern end of Matavai Bay, their ultimate destination.

Life for the Tahitians at this time was relatively carefree; they did not need to know if it was a weekday or weekend. Suddenly, there was a stirring among those on the beach: a sailing ship was emerging from behind Point Venus. After holding a safe offing from the reef, which fanned out from the headland, the ship turned towards the bay. The sails were progressively being clewed up and furled to slow her progress.

Bligh quickly realised that the welcome being shown them was nowhere near as boisterous as he had experienced when he'd first anchored there with *Bounty*, and there was a simple explanation for this: the people at Matavai were at war with their neighbours. Even so, considerable exuberance was shown by some islanders, who had taken to their canoes and paddled out to welcome their visitors.

As *Providence* glided towards her anchorage, Flinders and the others who had not previously been to these shores were in a state of disbelief as they watched the canoes surging towards the ship. It was as if *Providence* was under attack, but fortunately these 'attackers' were friendly. Flinders took it all in, observing: 'Immediately we put into the bay, the natives began to come off in their canoes – they presently found out that Captain Bligh was on board, which seemed to give them much pleasure – for they were not positively certain whether he was alive.'

In reality, there was almost too much happening for Flinders to absorb. This was most definitely paradise, beyond the most fertile images any individual could have conceived. In the white wake of the canoes was the beach, where other islanders waited anxiously to greet the Englishmen. The crew could not help but be amazed by the vista of the beautiful beach, with coconut palms that leaned at alarming angles out over the sand – which, incredibly, was black. Then there were the islanders' huts on the beach, and the rolling hills beyond, many of which had waterfalls streaking down from their summits. Finally, they took in the distant backdrop of ancient, jagged volcanic peaks, the lava from which had created the island and its fine black sands. Equally amazing was the thought that this utopia had remained unknown to the rest of the world until just 25 years earlier, when, on 18 June 1767, the Englishman Samuel Wallis had sailed over the horizon and discovered 'Otaheite'.

It had been 252 days since *Providence* set sail from England when the bosun made the announcement that all on board had been waiting to hear: he informed the officers on the quarterdeck that the anchor was set and the ship was secure. It was midday, and *Providence* was in nine fathoms just half a mile from the beach – an ideal, sheltered location – while *Assistant* was anchored inshore of her.

By then, both ships were completely surrounded by a flotilla of canoes, some laden to the point of almost sinking under the weight of hogs, fruits and other things, which the islanders hoped they could trade for much-prized items made from iron, especially hatchets. However, the presence of a whaleboat manned by white men inspired surprise and intrigue in *Providence*'s crew. It would soon be learnt that these men were some of the 21 survivors from the wreck of an English whaling ship, *Matilda*. She had been lost only weeks earlier on an atoll nearly 700 nautical miles south of Matavai Bay. Survivors in four of the small whaling boats had taken nine days to reach Tahiti.

The locals, on the water and ashore, became increasingly excited as word spread that the 'king' of *Providence* was their great friend Captain Bligh – 'Brihe' – a man whom they had grown to respect when he was there for five months aboard *Bounty* in 1788–89, and who knew their idol, Captain Cook, extremely well. With that knowledge, there was no holding them back: the locals hurriedly clambered up the steps on the side of the ship and onto the deck so they could welcome the captain and his crew. As this invasion occurred, the crew was quickly realising that every word they had heard about the welcome that came on arrival in Tahiti – and about the alluring beauty of the near-naked Tahitian women –

was true. There was no holding back from either side: the women wanted to be the *tayo* – or friend – of their chosen ones from the outset, and all the evidence indicates that the 18-year-old Flinders was one of the chosen.

As a mark of respect for 'Brihe', the queen of the village and the village chiefs also came aboard, bearing special gifts for him, including hogs, cloth and fruit. This interlude gave Bligh the perfect opportunity to inquire if they knew the whereabouts of any of the *Bounty* mutineers, and if the crew of HMS *Pandora* had managed to take any into custody. Much to the captain's pleasure, the islanders told him everything they knew, including the fact that some who had decided to stay in Tahiti when *Bounty* returned there had been found and taken aboard *Pandora*.

The valuable lessons learned during *Bounty*'s mission to Matavai Bay led to this current operation running remarkably smoothly. With the breadfruit plants almost ready to be collected and potted, the botanists set about establishing an area on the beach that would become the nursery until it was time to transfer the plants to the ship. That would happen just prior to departure.

For Flinders and many of the younger members of the crew, the navy learning process continued aboard the ship, while lessons about life took place in a most satisfying way ashore.

With there being no dissent or disobedience of any significance within the crew, Bligh was a happy man. This was a far cry from what he had experienced when he was there with *Bounty*. That time, some men had deserted and others had demonstrated a total disregard for authority. There was no doubt that having marines on board to enforce the Articles of War was making a difference, even though the lure of the Tahitian lifestyle was just as strong for his men. Still, there was one odd moment for Bligh. The only man who had to be punished for failing to follow orders since leaving

England was the marines' own drummer, who felt the flay of the tails a dozen times.

Bligh's biggest concern during the fourteen weeks they were anchored in Matavai Bay was his continuing health problems. At times, his headaches and nausea meant he was completely incapacitated and unable to leave his cabin.

The collection of the breadfruit plants went to schedule, although the search for suitable saplings forced the men to travel up to eight miles into the tropical forests. On 14 July the islanders began helping the crew to load the plants onto the ship, and little more than two days later the job was complete. There were more than 2100 breadfruit plants, plus around 500 other plants the botanists decided would be of interest to Sir Joseph Banks and their associates at Kew Gardens.

While all this activity was happening, Flinders was helping prepare charts for what he expected to be the most challenging and rewarding part of the voyage: the exploration of Torres Strait. But he soon found out that Bligh had decided they should also explore some more islands en route to the strait – Fiji, or Bligh's Islands, as they had become known. Bligh had discovered a number of islands in the southern part of this archipelago during his legendary launch voyage from Tofua to Timor. This news excited Flinders: it was as if he would be delving even deeper into Robinson Crusoe's world.

Before dawn on 18 July, the Tahitians were already arriving and going aboard *Providence* to say a final farewell to their friends. The strong bonds the sailors had established with their respective *tayos* were about to be severed, and all struggled with the associated emotion.

Eventually, amid scenes of unbridled affection and animated farewells, the captain had no option but to call time. He ordered that the launch be brought aboard and the sails be prepared, and that the anchor be weighed.

'Aye aye, Captain,' was the response.

Sailors quickly climbed the ratlines to the yards and began releasing the lines that held the sails in a tidy furl. On deck, other crew took the braces, sheets and lines off their belaying pins and uncoiled them so they were ready for use, while on the foredeck men began preparing the capstan so the anchor could be raised. With great reluctance, the islanders started to climb down the side of the ship to their canoes.

This was a deeply moving time for sailors and islanders alike, after so many wonderful weeks in paradise, but for the crew of *Providence* there was important work elsewhere that had to be done.

CHAPTER FOUR

A Mission
Accomplished

While *Providence* was being steered away to the west on a larboard tack, and the serrated mountain ridges of Tahiti began to blur with the increase in offing, the yardmen in the rig began unfurling the sails in the usual orderly fashion. The ship's speed gradually increased as each sail that had been called for was sheeted home and trimmed to best capture the freshening south-easterly trade wind, and before long *Providence*'s bold and buxom bow was parting the waves with a surging sound. The course that lay ahead – to the West Indies via Torres Strait, the Indian Ocean and the Cape of Good Hope, and then home – was near 20,000 nautical miles.

Bligh had agreed to take 15 of the crew from the wrecked *Matilda* with him so they could be repatriated to England: 13 were aboard *Providence* and two on *Assistant*, which once again was sailing in company like a faithful servant. Five other *Matilda* survivors, plus a convict 'lifer' who had conned his way aboard the whaler and used it as a means of escape from Port Jackson, chose to stay in Tahiti. An islander named Mydiddee had willingly joined *Providence*. He was carrying his superior's hopes that he would meet King George III and learn much about England, before returning home some day on another ship.

A few days after the ships' departure, another islander, who had worked closely with the botanists, emerged from below deck. A stowaway! The captain decided that this man should be allowed to remain on board, as he might be of assistance to the botanists once *Providence* reached the West Indies.

These were ebullient days for Midshipman Flinders. He had experienced paradise, a place where natural beauty was unspoiled through a lack of contact with the outside – in particular, European – world. This lad from the marshlands of England had seen the South Pacific at its best, but even so, he could once again feel the acceleration of adrenaline in his veins: the considerable challenge of grand exploration through uncharted waters continued to generate a sense of wonder in him. Next it would be Fiji, then the shallows and dangerous tide rips of Torres Strait – and of course, anything unknown they might happen upon along the way.

Initially, *Providence*'s course was influenced by the captain's considerable desire to learn what he might of *Bounty*, the mutineers and the ship sent in search of them, *Pandora*. He decided the first place of call would be Whytootackee (now Aitutaki) in the Cook Islands, a supremely beautiful island ringed by an atoll that he had discovered only a matter of days before the mutiny in 1789. Once there, Bligh ordered that the ship sail right around the ten nautical miles of reef encompassing the island and magnificent lagoon, searching for a wreck. Later, after conversing with the natives, he concluded that *Bounty* had not made landfall there, but *Pandora* most certainly had.

As beautiful as Whytootackee was, the weather that accompanied *Providence*'s departure was nowhere near as appealing. As the ship sailed away from the lee of the atoll, so conditions deteriorated. 'Fresh gale and cloudy with a troubled sea,' Tobin's log entry stated. Before long, the powerful following seas had increased in size so greatly that *Providence* was rolling heavily from gunwale to gunwale. Men were sent aloft to reduce sail and lower yards to the deck to reduce windage and improve stability, but they couldn't get to the fore topsail soon enough and it blew apart as if a cannonball had gone through it. The sailmakers were kept busy repairing it over the next few days.

The immediate destination was Fiji. As there was so little information regarding the threats to navigation in the region, an 'anxious lookout' was maintained at all times. Flinders noted that this included having 'a hand kept at the bowsprit end to look out', and once again Bligh reverted to having sail greatly reduced at night to slow the ship and thus reduce the risk of being wrecked on a coral reef or small island.

By day, when all possible sail was set, the speed of the two ships was at times more than double the rate of their progress at night. For the crew, the daylight hours provided a far more interesting environment: whales, dolphins and a wide array of seabirds were often their escorts, and tropical storms that delivered rain that pelted down like musket balls were also regular occurrences.

By the first week of August, *Providence* was amid the islands in the southern region of Fiji. The sailing was now more treacherous than ever, and the highest level of prudent seamanship was necessary for safe passage. Bligh ordered that the smaller *Assistant*, because of her shallower draft, should lead and probe the waters ahead. Within a day, the ships were surrounded by so many magnificent islands that Bligh and the entire crew realised they could easily take months to fully explore them, but the demands placed on the captain to clear Torres Strait before the cyclone season caused him to make only slight deviations from his desired course to the northern tip of New Holland. Because of this, he adopted a simple way of identifying each island or atoll the ships passed: they were identified by letters of the alphabet, and when he had applied all 26 letters he used numerals.

Flinders was very much a part of this surveying procedure, sometimes standing a watch from the masthead, where he could record observations. This is evident from his log:

[Island] P from the masthead ¾ past 6 am August 7th ...
    This island was a greater distance from us than the other two, when we were nearest it. I cannot pretend to say of what size it is, but I think it could not be bigger than L or M ...

Two days later, the young midshipman had found an island worthy of Robinson Crusoe:

V at 10 am August 8th Distant 7 or 8 Leagues
    This is the most beautiful island we have yet seen.
We were near enough to distinguish a village about half way
up the hills surrounded with cocoa nut trees with which the
island abounds and the houses were built. The situation is
romantic and truly delightful. All parts of the island we saw
were surrounded by a reef. From one to two miles distant we
saw a small bay on the SW side where we fancied there was
an opening in the reef but I am not certain ... This was
thought worthy to be called Paradise Island.

It was also noted with interest that at night, after the ships had been observed by natives from shore during the day, fires were lit on high points of the land, which, as Tobin assumed, was 'probably to alarm the neighbouring isles of our approach'.

When island number two was reached, it was obvious that there were no more to be seen to the west, so *Assistant* was ordered to make full sail and press on.

In the days leading up to the two ships reaching Torres Strait – which was downwind on the course they held – *Assistant* remained in the lead, sometimes keeping up to two miles ahead. She carried a bright lantern at night so *Providence* could follow her, while her crew was always at the ready to signal *Providence* – via musket or cannon fire, and flags during the day – should any navigational hazard be sighted. Captain Portlock often took it upon himself to go to the masthead and scan the horizon to confirm that his ship was on a safe track.

Surprisingly, Bligh never published a narrative of this expedition, but Flinders did so some 20 years later, using his own notes. He acknowledged his captain's approval: 'Having had the honour to serve in the expedition, I am enabled to give it from my own journal, with the sanction of Captain Bligh.'

The first sign of a serious navigational danger came on 1 September, when breakers were 'thundering on the reef'. The scene – a massive expanse of surging white water – was little short of alarming, and over the following 24 hours the magnitude of the challenge and the associated dangers they were about to face became brutally apparent to Flinders.

Flinders' log revealed how, from that moment, they were constantly avoiding danger:

4 pm: *Assistant* made the signal to denote danger – saw a shoal bearing SWbyW to WSW about 2 miles – hauled to the wind on the starboard tack

6 pm: In 1st reefs and shortened sail

12 mid: The *Assistant*'s signal to tack, answered, tacked and stood after her

2 am: ... tacked ship per signal

4 am: Tacked per signal

6 am: At ¾ past 6 bore away – the *Assistant* leading – saw the shoal from the masthead WbyN

8 am: At 8 the shoal from the masthead bore WNW 2 or 3 leagues – not seen from the deck ½ past 8. Spoke the *Assistant* per signal

9 am: At 9 more breakers from the masthead on the lee bow and beam – ¼ past 10 southernmost point of the breakers in sight SbyW¼. Squall – tacked per signal and spoke the *Assistant*

12 noon: The breakers just in sight from the topmast head NNW about 6 miles. The *Assistant* in company leading.

It was little different the following day:

In keeping to the northward we had expected to have gone clear of the many rocks and shoals, which extend out to some distance all along the northeast coast of New Holland, but it appears those from the south coast of New Guinea are equally troublesome and dangerous ... we find ourselves hemmed in so that our situation appears to be rather doubtful. Should they extend all along to Endeavour Straits, thro' which our passage lies, the prospect before us is not the most desirable ... but we trust the abilities of our Captain, which I believe we may safely rely upon, will extricate us from all difficulties and bring us safe thro' the strait in which case we should consider all the dangers of our voyage at an end.

Torres Strait was already living up to the widely held belief that it was a near impassable stretch of water. Fortunately for the crews of both ships, the first sighting of sandbanks and reefs came in daylight. Had this happened at night, the ships could well have foundered. Bligh decided that the best way to stay on the safest possible course at night was to have *Providence* and *Assistant* short-tack through the dark hours. This involved the ships sailing across the wind over a short distance then tacking and sailing back on a reciprocal course for a similar distance so that they remained in water that was free of danger. While this was happening, the leadsman was regularly heaving the lead to sound the depths. The lump of metal he used weighed about ten pounds and was attached to a line that could confirm a depth of more than 100 fathoms.

Because of the fast-flowing currents, and the shallows and reefs that had already been observed, it was evident that there would be times when it was too dangerous even for *Assistant* to be the lead vessel. Each time this situation arose, Bligh had men take a smaller cutter and the whaleboat so they could search for a passage to the west, a task that was far from easy. All too often, when the men in the small boats were becoming confident that they had found a safe passage to the next area of deep water, they would be confronted by yet another impassable barrier – a coral reef or sandbank. Their only option was to abandon that particular probe and start again.

As if the natural dangers being faced were not enough, on 5 September the captain's worst fears became reality when the explorers came under attack by natives of the islands. This is how Flinders saw the situation unfold:

> Boats were again sent to sound the passage. Several large
> sailing canoes [about 50 feet in length] were seen; and with
> the cutter making the signal for assistance [by firing a musket],

the pinnace was sent to her, well manned and armed. On the return of the boats in the afternoon, it appeared that, of four canoes which used their efforts to get up to the cutter, one succeeded. There were in it fifteen Indians, black, and quite naked; and they made signs which were interpreted to be amicable. These signs the officer imitated; but not thinking it prudent to go so near as to take a green cocoa-nut, which was held up to him, he continued rowing for the ship. A man, who was sitting upon the shed erected in the centre of the canoe, then said something to those below; and immediately they began to string their bows. Two of them had already fitted arrows, when the officer judged it necessary to fire in his own defence. Six muskets were discharged; and the Indians fell flat into the bottom of the canoe, all except the man on the shed: the seventh musket was fired at him, and he fell also. During this time, the canoe dropped astern; and the three others having joined her, they all gave chase to the cutter, trying to cut her off from the ship; in which they would probably have succeeded, had not the pinnace arrived, at that juncture, to her assistance. The Indians then hoisted their sails, and steered for Darnley's Island.

No boats could have been manoeuvred better, in working to windward, than were these long canoes by the naked savages. Had the four been able to reach the cutter, it is difficult to say, whether the superiority of our arms would have been equal to the great difference of numbers; considering the ferocity of these people, and the skill with which they seemed to manage their weapons.

Over the next 48 hours progress was slow, methodical and extremely cautious. Finally, the ships anchored in the lee of Dalrymple's Island, which was the westernmost island they had sighted. Flinders noted that canoes had been seen on the beach, and when the ship's boats were sent ashore – the crew having been advised to approach with caution – they were openly welcomed by the natives, who were 'waving green branches and clapping upon their heads, in token of friendship'. The two sides exchanged gifts, the natives being extremely enthusiastic to get anything made from metal.

While the ships were at anchor, the cutter and whaleboat were sent to the west once again to take soundings and determine the most suitable course for the ships to follow. Flinders, however, who was thriving on his increased workload, was convinced that the navigational hazards were becoming even more threatening: 'The strait, instead of becoming clearer, seemed to be more and more embarrassed with dangers, as the vessels proceeded westward.' As if that wasn't enough, the next islanders they encountered were far less cordial than those of Dalrymple's Island:

There were many natives collected upon the shore of Dungeness Island, and several canoes from Warriors Island were about the brig [*Assistant*]. Presently, Captain Portlock made the signal for assistance; and there was a discharge of musketry and some guns, from his vessel and from the boats. Canoes were also coming towards the *Providence*; and when a musket was fired at the headmost, the natives set up a great shout, and paddled forward in a body; nor was musketry sufficient to make them desist. The second great gun, loaded with round and grape, was directed at the foremost of eight canoes, full of men; and the round shot, after raking the whole length, struck the high stem. The Indians leaped out, and swam towards their companions; plunging constantly, to avoid the musket balls which showered thickly about them.

The squadron then made off, as fast as the people could paddle without showing themselves; but afterwards rallied at a greater distance, until a shot, which passed over their heads, made them disperse, and give up all idea of any further attack.

In passing the deserted canoe, one native was observed still sitting in it. The other canoes afterwards returned to him; and, with glasses, signals were perceived to be made by the Indians, to their friends on Dungeness Island, expressive, as was thought, of grief and consternation.

No arrows fell on board the *Providence*; but three men were wounded in the *Assistant*, and one of them afterwards died. The depth to which the arrows penetrated into the decks and sides of the brig, was represented to be truly astonishing.

Here, and in many other situations, the attention to detail the 18-year-old Flinders showed in his observations was commendable. His notes presented impressive 'word images' of his surrounds, and of the natives who were part of the region:

Upon the whole, the arms of these people bespeak then ingenious and warlike, and their appearance perfect savages. Whether they have the custom of devouring their fellow creatures as some of the inhabitants of New Guinea are said to have, we had no opportunity of informing ourselves ... In their persons we observed that the cartilage of the nose was entirely cut away and the lobes of their ears slit like the inhabitants of Bligh's Islands. In speaking to each other their language was very distinct – they wore ornaments of small shells strung like beads.

The exploration was halted for three days on 12 September by a howling south-easterly gale, which forced the ships to hold hard at anchor. When the storm abated and anchors were weighed, an ever-increasing number of islands and reefs were sighted. The location of each new find was carefully recorded on charts, as was the depth of water that the lead lines were revealing. On 16 September a cluster of three more small islands was sighted, and it was here that Captain Bligh decided it was time do something on behalf of Mother England: he sent the second lieutenant to the most north-western of the isles 'for the purpose of taking possession of all the islands seen in the strait, for His Britannic Majesty George III', as Flinders noted. The appropriate ceremony was conducted ashore; the name bestowed on the region was Clarence's Archipelago. This particular island was named Possession Island (although later it became North Possession Islet).

Torres Strait was proving to be a maritime minefield for the explorers, but there was no turning back. Naturally, every man aboard *Providence* and *Assistant* was hoping by this time that the worst was behind them, but that wasn't so. The entire expedition almost came to grief a few hours later in what would prove to be the most dangerous part of the maze – a situation that became more life-threatening with the arrival on the scene of some aggressive islanders. Flinders detailed the events:

Sept. 17. The boats led to the westward, steering for a
passage between Mulgrave's and Jervis' Islands; but seeing it
full of rocks and shoals, the vessels anchored a little within
the entrance, in 10 fathoms, coarse ground; until the boats
should sound ahead. The flood tide, from the ENE, was
found to set through between the islands, at the rate of

four miles an hour; and the breeze being fresh, and bottom bad, the situation was considered to be very unsafe.

Whilst the boats were sounding, several Indians in three canoes, were perceived making towards them; but on a swivel shot being fired over their heads, they returned to Mulgrave's Island, on the south side of the passage. On the signal being made for good anchorage further on, the *Assistant* led to the WbyS.; but on reaching the boats, the bottom was found much inferior to what had been imagined; the approach of night, however, obliged Captain Bligh to anchor, soon afterward, in 8 fathoms. In this situation, the vessels were so closely surrounded with rocks and reefs, as scarcely to have swinging room; the bottom was rocky; the wind blowing a fresh gale; and a tide running between four and five knots an hour.

It was an incredibly anxious night for all on board: should anything go wrong, there would be no opportunity to save the vessel. If the anchor had dragged or the cable parted in those testing conditions, the jagged coral and rocks making up the reefs would have claimed a ship in an instant. This was, as one crewman suggested, 'Hell's Gates'.

Through exceptional seafaring and navigation, and with an element of luck thrown in, *Providence* and *Assistant* were eventually extricated from this predicament, and entered open water where everyone could finally breathe easy: they were now clear of all obstacles, as the log revealed: 'in the western half of the compass, no danger was visible'.

It had taken 19 sometimes anxious, often threatening and torturous days to successfully transit Torres Strait. 'Perhaps no space of 3½ degrees in length presents more dangers than Torres Strait,'

Flinders wrote, 'but with caution and perseverance the captains, Bligh and Portlock, proved them to be surmountable, and within a reasonable time.'

The point where the two ships finally exited this contorted mass of maritime obstructions was appropriately named 'Bligh's Farewell'. Once they were in safe water, the timoneer aboard *Providence* was ordered to take up a course towards Timor. Flinders explained in his log entry for Wednesday, 19 September 1792 that, with the danger of Torres Strait behind them, the crew then had to turn their attention to a task they'd had little time to consider in the previous few weeks – the survival of the plants.

> As we have all the appearance of being clear of the dangers
> attending these straits ... our principal concern now is the
> preservation of the plants. It is certain that not only salt water
> but the air which passes over it is highly prejudicial to
> vegetation. At this time there are about 200 dead pots nearly
> the whole of which were those that stood in the remote parts
> of the greenhouse below, yet even this must be thought a
> small proportion out of the pots, when it is considered that
> we have been near 9 weeks at sea.

The young midshipman also noted that a strict system of rationing water had been introduced aboard *Providence* while the ship was negotiating Torres Strait. This was done because it was not known how long it would take to clear the shallows and reefs and reach a point where their course to Timor would be unimpeded; it seemed quite possible that they might be forced to backtrack before reaching the Indian Ocean. To run out of fresh water would not only create a dire situation for all on board, it would also mean that the plants – the very reason for this voyage – would die:

> We were not suffered to drink at any time, but were never at
> any regular allowance till now – at present each man is
> allowed a pint of water per day, exclusive of his grog, pea
> soup and water gruel, in the two last the water has been
> reduced more than half some time[s].

This strict but understandable regulation inevitably caused disharmony amongst the crew, and some anger towards the captain. It was even suggested that some of the highly prized plants on board had already died because a rascal in the crew had been watering them with seawater. Bligh was unable to find the culprit, so the cat-o'-nine-tails stayed in its place. However, it is known that the strict rationing of water forced Flinders and others to lick the droplets of fresh water that came from the base of the pots after the plants had been watered.

At five a.m. on 1 October, while *Providence* and *Assistant* cruised to the north-west before a light following breeze, the island of Timor began to loom large ahead. Twenty-four hours later, they were riding comfortably at anchor off the town of Kupang. It was then that both crews received some distressing news, which only confirmed how dangerous it was for vessels traversing these waters. It was learned that *Pandora*, the ship sent to the Pacific by the Admiralty in search of the *Bounty* mutineers, had been wrecked on a reef near the northern tip of New Holland while approaching Torres Strait. The loss of life had been considerable: 31 of the crew of 120 had perished. Four of the 14 mutineers who had been arrested had also gone down with the ship. 'On mature consideration we may think ourselves very fortunate in getting through [Torres Strait] so well as we did,' was Flinders' summation.

While the first priority in Kupang was to replenish the ship's water casks, a routine maintenance check aboard *Providence* revealed that the gammon ring, which attaches the rope bobstay to the stem just above the waterline at the bow, had parted. The bobstay is a vital piece of rigging that prevents the bowsprit from lifting skywards and breaking when the sprit comes under any load created by the foresails. Fortunately, the approach to Kupang had been all downwind, so the bowsprit had not come under any duress of consequence. But had *Providence* been close-hauled at any stage, the bowsprit could well have been ripped from its mounting in dramatic fashion, causing a dismasting.

By late October *Providence* and *Assistant* were back on the high seas, surging south-west through the Indian Ocean towards the Cape of Good Hope, before entering the South Atlantic and turning towards their next port of call, Saint Helena. Flinders was continuing to excel in taking observations, recording detail and assisting with the navigation. He knew he could not be better placed when it came to building a foundation for his naval career. Captain Cook had been Flinders' hero, and he had mentored Bligh. Now the unparalleled seafaring knowledge of both men was there for him to draw on.

While the actual sailing through the tropics had been stimulating and relatively easy, the crew of *Providence* was quickly reminded of the rough weather that can come in the southern climes. Flinders' log entry for 24 October described the reefing procedures that were undertaken when a powerful gale descended on them:

1 pm: Strong gales and thick cloudy weather.
    2 pm: Squally with small rain at times – third reefed
the topsails and got down top gallant yards.
    5 pm: Strong gales high sea. Ship rolling considerably
and shipping some water – stowed the whale boat in the

starboard waist – struck top gallant masts handed the
main sail – reefed the fore sail – close reefed the fore
and 3rd reefed the main topsail at 8 handed the mizzen
topsail.

On 6 November the crew had to hold a burial at sea. One of the
marines, Thomas Lickman, died as a consequence of a severe bout
of flux (dysentery), which he contracted in Timor.

After filling his first logbook with notes, Flinders started a new
one on 20 November. His first entry showed that, while he was
detailing his many and varied experiences, he was also thinking
about being home.

I cannot but reflect on the pleasing prospect we have of
bringing the voyage to a happy conclusion, a voyage, the
intention of which will ever rebound honour to the
benevolent promoters of it and to the English nation, who so
generously put it in execution. The discoveries we have
made and dangers we have passed tho' perhaps not of the
greatest consequence to us as a trading nation, will yet add to
our well established name as discoverers, increasé
geographical knowledge in general and to the cause of
navigation they will be an acquisition.

Captain Bligh, as the immediate agent, will no doubt
receive the honour and recompense equal to the task he has
performed and I as an actor tho' in an inferior station, shall
have the satisfaction, of having served my King in a cause he
has so much at heart, my country by assisting to put in
execution its benevolent intentions and myself by gaining
some knowledge of navigation, the universal diffusion of
which is one of our best national characteristics.

Having cleared the Cape of Good Hope, *Providence* and *Assistant* were set on a north-westerly course towards Saint Helena, 1700 nautical miles away. When they arrived there on 17 December, it became apparent to the crew that, barring some unforeseen disaster, they would get a substantial number of breadfruit plants to the West Indies. More than 800 of the saplings had survived so far.

This stopover presented the crew with an opportunity for some well-deserved respite in a pleasant climate. In fact, the isolation of Saint Helena appealed so much to one *Providence* crewmember that he decided to stay. It turned out that there was an underlying reason for his decision: 'Thomas Mathers (Gunners Mate) discharged his affairs,' Flinders noted. 'Being in an embarrassed situation in England he preferred staying here.' What caused Mathers to be 'embarrassed' is unknown but what is known is that he was encouraged to stay on the island by the locals.

The crew held a low-key celebration on Christmas Day. Two days later, after a 'tolerably fine bullock' had been ferried to the ship, hoisted aboard and then slaughtered for fresh meat, the time for departure had arrived.

After drifting free of the lee of Saint Helena, both *Providence* and *Assistant* began to benefit from the South Atlantic's south-easterly trade winds, which had, from time immemorial, defined the course to the north that sailing ships should take. It would be more than 4000 nautical miles before the expedition reached the West Indies, their penultimate destination prior to England, and home.

The voyage to the West Indies proved to be a superb, almost carefree downwind passage, during which full sail was set more often than not. New Year's Eve – 'a beautiful moonlight night', as Flinders recorded – was especially memorable. Nineteen days later, the Northern Hemisphere was beckoning.

Steady fresh trade and fine clear night it was with some
satisfaction we saw the North Pole Star, a sight we have been
deprived of now about 15 months ... these little
circumstances, are well known to arise from natural causes,
yet when observed, insensibly lead one to reflect on our
native shore – a pleasing thought after two years absence.

The only drama of sorts on this leg of the voyage came when the
main topgallant mast carried away, apparently because of 'the
Captain's ordering too many hands on the halyards'. The ship's
carpenters immediately got to work making a new one, and within
48 hours Flinders could report that they had 'Got the old main top
gallant mast down and got up the new one, slung the top gallant
yard and set the sail again'.

On 22 January the crews of both ships could take pride in the
fact that they were about to accomplish the prime objective of their
voyage: to transport breadfruit plants from Tahiti to the West
Indies so that a new and inexpensive food could be grown to feed
the slave labourers on the English plantations there. First they
anchored off Kingstown, Saint Vincent, and delivered 300 healthy
plants – some already 11 feet high, with leaves three feet long.
After that, they sailed 1000 nautical miles downwind to Kingston,
Jamaica, where a similar number of plants was transferred ashore.

The delivery of the breadfruit plants was completed by mid-
February, and from that moment the entire crew turned their
attention to home, which was just eight weeks away. Bligh
planned to depart as soon as possible, but within days that plan was
shattered under a cloud of bitter disappointment. A packet, the
passenger and cargo ship *Duke of Cumberland*, arrived from England
with 'news of war having been declared against Great Britain by
the French Nation'.

It was not until the middle of June that *Providence* was able to sail for home, and on 7 August she finally reached her dock at Deptford. What would not be known for some time was that the breadfruit mission, successful as it was, had been futile. When the trees matured and the breadfruit was first harvested, the slaves refused to eat it – they detested the taste.

The ships had been away from home shores for almost two years on what had been a remarkable voyage, and the entire crew could take great pride in what they had achieved. Not surprisingly, they were well praised by their captain, as well as by the extremely proud patron of the voyage, Sir Joseph Banks, to whom Flinders was finally introduced. It was a meeting that would prove to be extremely valuable to Flinders' later life.

Midshipman Flinders, then 19 and bearing a world of stories for his family, was eager to return to Donington. But the reunion would have to wait. England and France were at war, and the young man would soon be called into battle.

CHAPTER FIVE

To the Battlefront

In just two years, Matthew Flinders went from being a 17-year-old country boy from the fenlands of Lincolnshire to being an aspiring cadet seafarer in the Royal Navy. The promise his young mind had demonstrated and his enthusiasm for his job hadn't gone unnoticed by his legendary captain. Bligh, a man not known for lavishing praise, certainly recognised Flinders as a respected assistant during *Providence*'s voyage. This was confirmed a few years later in an article published in the *Naval Chronicle*, which reported that Bligh had been very impressed by Flinders' skill in preparing charts and making astronomical observations: as 'a juvenile navigator, the latter branch of scientific service and the care of the timekeepers were principally entrusted to him'. This also confirmed that the scientific aspects of a naval career were preferred by the trainee.

Being part of Bligh's mission to the South Pacific would prove to be of considerable value to Flinders' career. *Providence* had successfully transferred the breadfruit plants to the West Indies, new islands had been discovered, and Torres Strait had been successfully negotiated and charted. It was an all-round historic achievement, one that put more of the unknown world on the map. Even so, the voyage meant much more to Flinders, for he had experienced almost every dream that his mind had yearned for when breezing through the pages of *Robinson Crusoe* all those years before – adventure, foreign shores, tropical islands, native warriors, breathtaking scenery, beautiful women, romance, exploration and discovery.

Regrettably, though, the crew of *Providence* had little time to reflect on their successful venture. They had returned to a very different England, which was being prepared for a major confrontation with the French. The uprising that drove the French Revolution was pumping shockwaves across Europe, but more so in England, which sat as a prime target for conquering.

In France the revolutionaries were using the guillotine mercilessly on their opponents. Just four months after the French Republic was declared, in September 1792, King Louis XVI had his head locked into the guillotine's lunette, having been found guilty of high treason – he became the only French monarch ever to be executed. Ironically, just months earlier the same king had signed the document that made the death penalty 'by mechanical decapitation' law in the kingdom of France. This came after the French National Assembly agreed that the guillotine was the only 'humane' form of execution – one that ensured death was swift and painless.

The reign of terror that came over the ensuing 18 months saw more than 40,000 'enemies of the revolution' executed across France. Some 16,594 were killed by guillotine – then known as the 'national razor'.

Around this time, there was also a small, deep-seated stirring of discontent among the middle class in England, one based on a desire for democratic reform. It was, however, short-lived: the call to prepare the country for war numbed the faction's restlessness by turning the nation's attention towards a commitment to the fastest possible expansion of the Royal Navy – its frontline defence on the English Channel, the massive moat that separated it from France.

From the moment this expansion program was initiated, forests across England were filled with the sound of axemen felling huge oak trees. After being trimmed into logs, they were transported to the numerous Royal Dockyards on the south coast, where shipwrights took to them with saws, adzes and broad axes, carving the timber into keels, stem and stern posts, ribs, frames, knees, deck beams and planking. Fir, spruce or pine was used for the masts and spars. In the three years following *Providence*'s return to England, near 150 ships were added to the Royal Navy's register, and every one of them required crew.

The threat of invasion saw the legendary 69-year-old Lord Howe, known among sailors as 'Black Dick', take to the high seas once again, leading the 22 ships of the Channel Fleet on a search for any enemy ships that they could capture or destroy. Flinders would soon learn that his great friend Captain Pasley, who had enthusiastically supported his entry into the service, was leading missions as commodore aboard *Bellerophon* under Howe's orders.

Within weeks of stepping ashore from *Providence*, Flinders seized the opportunity to 'report in' to Captain Pasley, who had returned from patrol. When that meeting took place he no doubt went into great detail about his experiences aboard *Providence*; this information, along with Bligh's positive reports on how well the young man had performed his duties, was enough for Pasley to invite Flinders to join him aboard *Bellerophon* as an aide-de-camp, or personal assistant.

Yet again, the Pasley magic was guiding Flinders on a course that would bring nothing but good. This included some hard-learned lessons from the commodore himself, who was also making an impressive climb through the ranks. In seemingly no time,

Pasley had his newly appointed aide-de-camp with him on the deck of *Bellerophon* with the ship under sail and a crew of some 600 officers and men on board.

Flinders' journal from this period still exists, and while much of it has been ruined by seawater and the ravages of time, the pages relating to his service aboard *Bellerophon* are intact and legible. Interestingly, despite experiencing many dramatic events that left indelible impressions on his mind, Flinders compiled this journal with the blandness and brevity one would expect of a midshipman writing from notes and memory for his superiors. The pages are almost devoid of real colour, high drama, hypothesis and hyperbole. Instead, they take the reader onto *Bellerophon*'s quarterdeck via unemotional, hard facts. Regardless, it is wonderful reading that provides great insight into Flinders' character and experiences.

The first entry of note comes on Wednesday, 11 September 1793 – a month after *Providence* reached port and four days after Flinders joined *Bellerophon*, which was then being prepared to go in search of enemy ships on the English Channel (and possibly in the North Atlantic). Flinders recognised that it was a proud moment for all aboard *Bellerophon* when she set sail and the evidence of Pasley's promotion was raised for all to see: 'Hoisted a broad pennant by order of Lord Howe, Capt Pasley being appointed a commodore of the fleet. Weighed and anchored in our station in Torbay.'

This day signalled the start of an era in Flinders' life that was in direct contrast to what he had experienced with Bligh aboard *Providence*. The ships of the fleet were patrolling the seas with the sole intention of protecting England, and Flinders had to wait only a week before *Bellerophon* came into contact with enemy vessels:

Saw nine or ten sail, seemingly large ships, standing towards us. The Admiral made the *Russell* and *Defence* signals to chase, also the *Audacious*; and soon after ours. By this time the strange ships had brought to, hull down, to windward, seemingly in some confusion ... At 9 the Admiral made the sign for the strange fleet being an enemy, and for our sternmost ships to make more sail. At 10 the signal to engage as the other ships came up was made. The enemy had now hauled their wind, and standing from us with as much sail as they could carry. Split one jib; got another bent as fast as possible. We were now the headmost line of battle ship and gaining fast upon the enemy ... Ship all clear for action since 9 o'clock.

19 November: Judge six of the enemy's ships to be of the line, two frigates and two brigs ... tacked, as did the *Latona*, which brought her near the rear of the enemy's ships, at which she fired several shot; she tacked again at 5, and fired, which the sternmost of their ships returned. At dark ... set top-gallant-sails, but obliged to take them in again for fear of carrying away the masts. Sundry attempts were made during the night to set, but as often obliged to take them in. At 12 lost sight of all our ships except one frigate. Very thick and hazy, with much rain. Made the signal that the enemy had bore away. Saw the *Latona* and *Phoenix*, who seemed suspicious of each other, but on discovering they were friends both bore away after one of the enemy's ships ... About 9 the *Phoenix* and *Latona* being the only friends in sight, the latter made the signal for the enemy being superior to the ships chasing. Soon after we made the signal to call the frigates in ... In the firing the preceding evening the *Latona* received a shot between wind and water in the breadroom, and another in the galley; but happily no one was hurt and but little injury received.

There was still no direct action for *Bellerophon* in this encounter, but on 27 November Flinders saw firsthand how an enemy ship might try to make an attack by hoisting false colours:

Hazy weather. Squadron in company. Saw a strange ship to the southward, who hoisted a Union Jack at the main topmast head and a red flag at the fore. The *Phoenix* being ahead made the private signal, but the stranger not answering she made the signal for an enemy. We immediately made the general signal to chase. At 10 the *Phoenix* and *Latona* fired a few shots at her, upon which she hoisted French colours, discharged her guns, and struck. She proved to be *La Blonde* of 28 guns and 190 men. The squadron brought to. The French captain came on board and surrendered his sword to the commodore. Separated the prisoners amongst the squadron. An officer of the *Phoenix* sent to take charge of the prize and a party of men from each ship.

While some patrols continued through the bitterness of the Northern Hemisphere winter, it would not be until May of the following year, 1794, that Flinders would find himself in the cauldron of a true naval battle. It would be officially recognised as the Battle of Brest, but British naval history would more often than not refer to it as 'the Glorious First of June'. It was the first major naval battle between the English and Revolutionary France in a period of war that would span 22 years and later involve Napoleon Bonaparte.

History reveals that the Glorious First of June was a battle where neither side could claim outright victory, but, as the name suggests, the British won the conflict between the respective navies. However, the convoy of ships carrying desperately needed grain to France from America – which the British were trying to intercept – managed to elude them and reach port. Its arrival brought considerable relief for the French people, who were facing a major food shortage due to poor crops, a dislocated economy and the turmoil that came with the revolution.

Early on the morning of 28 May, the British fleet, then some 400 nautical miles into the Atlantic, sighted 26 French ships of the line under the command of Rear-Admiral Villaret-Joyeuse. Flinders' journal takes us into the bloody battle; his first reference comes on the morning the French were spotted:

Saw two strange sail, one of which the *Phoenix* spoke, and soon after made signal for a strange fleet south-south-west. About 8, we counted 33 sail, 24 or 25 of which appeared to be of the line, and all standing down towards us. At 8.30 our signal was made to reconnoitre the enemy – as we were now certain they were. A frigate of theirs was likewise looking at us.

Thursday, 29 May: Fresh gales with rain at times, and a swell from the westward. Repeated the general signals for chase, battle, etc. Kd [tacked] ship occasionally, working to windward under a press of sail, our squadron and the frigates in company, and our fleet a few miles to leeward.

It appears that Flinders made special note of the fact that they had tacked *Bellerophon* – a 168-foot, 1643-ton full-rigged ship – through the eye of the wind more than once, which was a grand display of ship handling and seamanship in the rough conditions. One mistake under the 'press of sail' that *Bellerophon* had set could easily have led to her being dismasted.

To execute a tack, the ship had to 'haul up' so she was sailing at good speed and as close to the direction of the wind as possible.

Then, with the necessary crew tending the sheets and braces controlling the sails that were set, the call to 'tack' would come from the quarterdeck. The ship had to be steered on an arc to windward until she passed through the eye of the wind and beyond, so that the wind was coming at a broad angle across the deck from the opposite side. Each sail had to be trimmed perfectly to help the ship through the manoeuvre, and quite often the jib and foresails had to be back-winded to help blow the bow downwind so *Bellerophon* was not 'caught in stays' – stopped head-to-wind. Once the ship was well beyond the eye of the wind, the sails had to be trimmed to suit the new course. The other, less challenging option – one which resulted in the loss of a lot of ground to leeward – was to turn the ship downwind and 'wear round'.

Bellerophon was eventually tacked into a position where she was at the rear of the French fleet; once there, she was steered towards a point from which she could mount an attack. The moment the French were in range, the air erupted with the sound of man-made thunder. Cannonballs blasted through clouds of dense smoke and smashed into the French hulls, while chain shot ripped through their spars, sails and rigging. This was the start of a brutal, unrelenting attack and counter-attack. Each time a ship either fired or received a direct hit it shuddered as if struck by a mighty earth tremor.

Pasley had as his primary target one of the largest and newest French ships, the 110-gun *Révolutionnaire*. This is how Flinders saw the conflict unfold:

About 3 the *Russell*, being a mile or two to windward of us, began to fire on the enemy's rear, as they were hauling on the larboard tack, and continued to stand on with the *Thunderer* and frigates, to get into their wake. We tacked a little before the rear ship was on our beam, which enabled us to bring them to action a considerable time before the other ships could come up to our assistance. Our first fire was directed on a large frigate which brought up the enemy's rear, but she soon made sail and went to windward of the next ship [*Révolutionnaire*] on whom we immediately pointed our guns. In a few minutes she returned it with great spirit, our distance from her being something more than a mile. My Lord Howe, seeing us engaged with a three-decked ship, and the next ahead of him frequently giving us a few guns, made the *Russell* and *Marlborough*'s signals to come to our assistance, they being on the weather quarter. About dusk more of the fleet had got up with us, the signal having been made to chase without regard to order [in the line]. The *Leviathan* and *Audacious*, particularly, passed to windward of us, and came to close engagement; the first keeping as close to him to leeward as she could fetch, and the latter fetching to windward of him, laid herself athwart his stern and gave a severe raking. The headmost of the French fleet were apparently hove to, but made no effort to relieve their comrade.

One direct hit into *Bellerophon*'s rig almost dismasted her: the main cap shroud was hit and close to parting, and the main topmast was bending to within inches of exploding into splinters. Men rushed to ease the pressure on the rig by easing the sheets and taking in the main topsail – an action made doubly difficult by the rough seas and strong wind. When that was done, and with projectiles still hurtling through the air, men scampered aloft to lower the topgallant yard and topmast to the deck so they could be saved.

The damage to *Bellerophon* made her difficult to manoeuvre, so Pasley had the signal for 'inability' made for Admiral Howe to see.

With that noted, the Admiral 'called us by signal into his wake', and *Bellerophon* took up a position immediately astern of *Queen Charlotte*. The crew then busied themselves making repairs.

Things weren't going well for the three-decked *Révolutionnaire*, as Flinders described:

> The enemy's rear ship about 9 [at night] had his mizzenmast
> gone and he bore down towards us, the *Russell* and *Thunderer*
> striking close to his weather quarter and lee bow, keeping up
> a severe fire, but he scarcely returned a shot. Having got
> clear of them he continued coming down on us, apparently
> with the intention of striking to our flag [surrendering], but
> firing a shot now and then. He was intercepted by one of
> our ships, who running to leeward of him soon silenced his
> guns, and, we concluded, had obliged him to strike.

By last light – around ten o'clock – the once proud *Révolutionnaire* was drifting aimlessly, a smashed, splintered and defeated hulk. She could take no more. Her colours were lowered but the British chose not to claim her as a prize. Instead, they left the wreck to be ignominiously towed home as clear evidence of British naval superiority. Howe then signalled for his ships to move on and prepare for the inevitable second round of the battle that would come the next day.

Throughout the night, every available man aboard *Bellerophon* was carrying out repairs and getting the ship ready for that next encounter.

> At daybreak the enemy's line was formed about 2 miles
> distant, and our commander in chief made the signal to form
> the line of battle, and take stations as most convenient. We

bore down and took ours astern of the *Queen Charlotte*, the *Marlborough* and *Royal Sovereign* following. About 8 our fleet tacked in succession, with a view to cut off the enemy's rear, the *Caesar* leading and my Lord Howe the 10th ship. As soon as our van [squadron] were sufficiently near to bring them to action, the enemy's whole fleet wore in succession, and ran to leeward of their line in order to support their rear, and edged down van to van. At 10 the firing commenced between the headmost ships of both lines, but at too great a distance to do much execution, and the Admiral made the signal to tack in succession in order to bring the enemy to close action, but not being taken notice of, about noon it was repeated with a gun.

At this time Flinders and others aboard *Bellerophon* noted that *Audacious* was no longer with the squadron. Unaware that *Révolutionnaire* had not been claimed as a prize, they assumed that *Audacious* was towing her back to England. In fact, *Audacious* was limping home to Plymouth after being so badly damaged in the previous day's battle that she was of no further use to the campaign:

Friday, 30 May: fresh breezes and hazy weather. The Admiral made signal to cut through the enemy's line. We luffed up as close to them as possible. The enemy were now well within point-blank shot, which began to fall very thick about us, and several had passed through our sails before we tacked. Immediately we came into the *Queen Charlotte*'s wake we tacked, lay up well for the enemy's rear, and began a severe fire, giving it to each ship as we passed. My Lord Howe in the *Charlotte* ... cut through their line between the 4th and 5th ship in the rear. We followed, and passed between the 2nd and 3rd. Their third ship gave us a severe broadside on the bow as we approached to pass under her stern, and which we took care to return by two on her quarter and stern. Before we had cleared her, her fore and maintop masts fell over the side, and she was silenced for a while, but it was only till we had passed her.

It was as *Bellerophon* steered through her nominated gap in the French line that one of the more colourful episodes in the life of Matthew Flinders occurred – one that probably came as a consequence of the young man's fervour in the heat of his first fight. At the time, Pasley had 14 nine-pounder guns mounted on the quarterdeck, loaded and ready for action, but they were not to be fired until an enemy ship was in a highly vulnerable position. Flinders was oblivious to this strategy, so when a French three-decker came within 'musket shot range' – about 300 yards – and as there were no men at the cannons on the quarterdeck, he took it upon himself to inflict all possible damage on the opposition. He lit a match and set off as many of the cannons as he could.

It was an act that saw the French ship hammered in spectacular fashion, so much so that Flinders was feeling very proud of himself – until Admiral Pasley rushed up, grabbed him by the collar, shook him sternly and bellowed, 'How dare you do that, youngster, without my orders?' Flinders' response came without hesitation: 'Thought it a fine chance to have a shot at 'em.' It appears that, deep down, Pasley was impressed by the impetuosity of his aide-de-camp, because nothing more came of the incident. There's no doubt, though, that Flinders learned a valuable lesson.

Lord Howe wanted to continue his pursuit of the French but only a few of his ships remained seaworthy enough to follow his orders. The damage on *Bellerophon* was considerable. Much of the rigging on the foremast had been cut to pieces and needed to be repaired or replaced, and new braces had to be reeved. The foresail had been shredded and the mainsail had to be deep-reefed, as the pressure from a greater sail area would almost certainly have caused the cap shroud to part and the topmast to break. The sailmakers were plying the needle as fast as they could; almost every sail on the ship had taken more than one hit and needed to be repaired.

By 5.30 p.m. *Bellerophon* was back in battle mode, and soon after she rejoined *Queen Charlotte*. Howe, using the flag signal system he had devised four years earlier – which would ultimately be introduced to the Royal Navy in 1800 as the *Telegraphic Signals of Marine Vocabulary* – ordered that a line of battle in two divisions be formed, in preparation for the resumption of hostilities. However, it would be more than 24 hours before the torrid conflict resumed.

Sunday 1 June: Moderate breezes and foggy weather.
[Two p.m.] Saw the enemy to leeward, 8 or 9 miles
distant ... edging away from the wind, and several of their
ships were changing stations in the line; some of them
without topmasts and topsail yards. About 7 the Admiral
made the signal to haul to the wind together on the larboard
tack, judging we should not be able to bring on a general
action to-night ... At daybreak the enemy not in sight. A
little before six saw the enemy in the north by east about 3
leagues. Made the signal to the Admiral for that purpose,
who by signal ordered the fleet to alter the course to
starboard together, bearing down towards them. At 8.10 the
signal was made to bear up and each engage their opponent.
We accordingly ran down within musket shot of our
opponent, and hove to, having received several broadsides

from their van ships in so doing. We now began a severe fire
upon our opponent, the second ship in the enemy's van,
which she returned with great briskness. The van ship
likewise fired many shot at us, his opponent the *Caesar*
keeping to windward, not more than two points before our
beam in general, and of course nearly out of point-blank
shot. About 9 the action became general throughout the two
fleets. A little before 11 our brave Admiral [Pasley] lost his
leg by an 18-pound shot, which came through the
barricading of the quarter-deck.

The incident came when *Bellerophon* was closely engaged with a
French ship, *Éole*. It had lasted three hours and *Éole*, although
severely battered, was still blazing away. This was when the horrible
blast smashed through the timberwork and catapulted Pasley across
the deck. Crewmen rushed to his aid but the magnitude of his
injury was immediately apparent as he lay sprawled on the deck,
stunned and in an expanding pool of blood.

While the battle continued to rage, Pasley was rushed to a
cabin below deck, where surgeons began operating on him – with
no form of anaesthetic, as it did not exist in those days. Command
of the ship was automatically transferred to Captain William Hope.
Flinders' journal describes the continuation of the battle.

It was now the heat of the action. The *Caesar* was not yet
come close to his opponent, who in consequence of that
fired all his after guns at us. Our own ship kept up a severe
fire, and by keeping well astern to let the *Caesar* take her
station, their third van ship shot up on our quarter, and for
some time fired all his fore guns upon us. Our shot was
directed on three different ships as the guns could be got to

bear. In ten or fifteen minutes we saw the foremast of the third ship go by the board, and the second ship's main-top-sail-yard down upon the cap. Otherwise the two headmost had not received much apparent injury, at least in the rigging. At 11 1/4, however, they both bore away and quitted the line, their Admiral being obliged to do the same sometime before by the *Queen Charlotte*.

On seeing the two van ships hauling upon the other tack, we conjectured they meant to give us their starboard guns. The *Caesar*'s signal was immediately made by us to chase the flying ships. On his bearing down they were put into confusion, and their ship falling down upon them they received several broadsides from the *Leviathan* and us, before they could get clear. And now, being in no condition to follow, we ceased firing; the main and foretopmast being gone, every main shroud but one on the larboard side cut through, and many on the other, besides having the main and foremasts with all the rigging and sails in general much injured. We made the *Latona*'s signal to come to our assistance, and got entirely out of action.

When the smoke cleared away, saw eleven ships without a mast standing, two of whom proved to be the *Marlborough* and *Defence*. The rest were enemy's, who, notwithstanding their situation, kept their colours up, and fired at any of our ships that came near them. The *Leviathan*'s opponent particularly (the same ship whose foremast we shot away) lying perfectly dismasted, the *Leviathan* ran down to him to take possession; but on her firing a gun to make him haul down his colours, he returned a broadside, and a severe action again commenced between them for nearly half an hour, and we could see

shot falling on the water on the opposite side of the
Frenchman, which appeared to have gone through both his
sides, the ships being at half a cable's length from each
other. The *Leviathan* falling to leeward, and, seeing his
obstinacy, left him, but not before his fire was nearly
silenced ... the French, having collected their best-
conditioned ships in a body, and being joined by two or
three other disabled ships, were making off, having
apparently given up all ideas of saving the rest.

This bitter, five-day opening round between these cross-channel
neighbours and long-time adversaries brought a heavy toll. For the
French, near 7000 men were killed, wounded or captured, while
the British had around 1000 killed or wounded.

Flinders, in recording the toll aboard *Bellerophon*, noted that
'fortunately no accident happened with the powder, or with guns
bursting':

We had but three men killed outright [a fourth died from his
wounds soon after] and about 30 men wounded, amongst
whom five lost their limbs, and the other leg of one man was
so much shattered as to be taken off some time after. Our
brave Admiral was unfortunately in this list. Most of our
spars were destroyed, and the boats [on deck] severely
injured.

One French ship, *Vengeur*, sank after an incredible four-hour duel
with HMS *Brunswick* that saw her blasted apart below the waterline.
Another six ships were captured; the men taken prisoner were
distributed among the British squadron. Flinders wrote an insightful
appraisal of the contingent that went aboard *Bellerophon*:

Their seamen, if we may judge from our own prisoners, are in a very bad state both with respect to discipline and knowledge of their profession; both which were evidently shown by the condition we saw them in on the 31st, many of them being without topmasts and topsail yards, and nearly in as bad a state as on the 29th after the action. 'Tis true they were rather better when we saw them in the morning of June 1st. Out of our 198 prisoners there certainly cannot be above 15 or 20 seamen, and all together were the dirtiest, laziest set of beings conceivable. How an idea of liberty, and more so that of fighting for it, should enter into their heads, I know not; but by their own confession it is not their wish and pleasure, but that of those who sent them; and so little is it their own that in the *Brunswick* [which was engaged yardarm and yardarm with the *Vengeur*] they could see the French officers cutting down the men for deserting their quarters. Indeed, in the instances of the *Russell* and *Thunderer* when close to the *Révolutionnaire*, and ours when cutting the line, the French do not like to come too close. A mile off they will fight desperately.

Admiral Pasley's injuries were so extensive that he would never sail again. This was an enormous loss for the Royal Navy: he was a fighting seafarer of exceptional talent who left no doubt that he was destined for great things. However, he remained in the service. In 1798 he became Commander-in-Chief, The Nore, and the following year Commander-in-Chief, Plymouth. Around this time he also became Sir Thomas Pasley after being awarded a baronetcy. He died in 1808.

The fact that Pasley would never again assume a sea command certainly affected Flinders' career. Had that enemy shot not blasted across the quarterdeck on that fateful day, there is no doubt this 20-year-old aide-de-camp would have stood by his captain in many future battles and enjoyed the promotion that came with it. However, as fate would have it, within two months of that fight with the French another exceptional opportunity presented itself, one that would see Flinders return to the fascinating challenges and excitement that came with exploration on the opposite side of the world. It would return him to the seafaring lifestyle he longed for, and would lead to his name being forever remembered in Australian history.

Interestingly, as the years would reveal, this change of course meant that the total time he would ever spend at the battlefront was just five days – in the Glorious First of June, from 28 May to 1 June, 1794.

CHAPTER SIX

Small Boats –
Big Challenge

Little more than two months after the horrific incident that ended Admiral Pasley's distinguished career as a naval seafarer, Matthew Flinders went ashore from *Bellerophon* for the final time. The date was 10 August 1794 – the same day he was commissioned to join His Majesty's Armed Vessel *Reliance* as master's mate, a posting that was an important step towards becoming a lieutenant.

In the ensuing weeks Flinders was able to return to Donington for a much anticipated and long overdue reunion with his family. No doubt he enthralled his relatives and friends with colourful, almost unimaginable, stories about his adventures into the South Pacific, Torres Strait and the Caribbean. However, those same stories were tempered by firsthand accounts of the brutality of war on the high seas, particularly after what he had seen happen to his captain.

Undoubtedly, while listening to these wonderful anecdotes, the dedicated Dr Flinders came to better understand why his eldest son had chosen life in the Royal Navy over the family medical practice in tiny Donington. Matthew was in his element – and, most importantly, he was doing his father proud.

When it came time for farewells after the all-too-brief visit, the family was aware that it would be many more years before they would be together again (as it happened, it would be five). The reason for this was simple: Matthew had told them in a most enthusiastic manner that his next assignment would see him returning to the Antipodes, where he hoped an opportunity would present itself for him to explore parts of the coastline of the great, unknown land of New South Wales. He could never have imagined the huge impact his expeditions would have on the contours of the world map, and Australian history.

Flinders had learned from conversations on the quarterdeck with a shipmate aboard *Bellerophon* – the 24-year-old Fifth Lieutenant Henry Waterhouse – that a 90-foot full-rigged 'discovery vessel', *Reliance*, was being prepared to sail to the new penal colony that had been established at Port Jackson, and that Waterhouse had been appointed by the Admiralty as the ship's captain. It was a conversation that would have immediately aroused in Flinders vivid thoughts of the opportunities that might come his way, should he be able to join the mission. The time he had spent in Van Diemen's Land had whetted his appetite for exploring this incredible southern landmass, and the voyage of *Reliance* would deliver even greater prospects for new discoveries. His desire was simple: to explore the region and go where no European had been before.

Adding to the appeal of the expedition was the knowledge that his younger brother, Samuel, who had also joined the navy, would be with him aboard *Reliance*. Even more noteworthy for Matthew was the news that *Reliance* would be conveying the colony's new governor, Captain John Hunter, to Port Jackson.

Hunter, who had also been part of the recent battle with the French, having sailed with distinction aboard Lord Howe's *Queen Charlotte*, was to become the second governor of New South Wales. It was a posting he had eagerly sought, having already been to the settlement with the First Fleet in 1788. At that time, he had served as captain of the fleet's flagship, His Majesty's Armed Vessel *Sirius*, which had transported the colony's first governor, Captain Arthur Phillip, to New South Wales. As the second-most senior naval officer with the fleet, he would have assumed the role of lieutenant-governor if Governor Phillip had died or been unable to carry out his duties in the outpost.

In *A Voyage to Terra Australis*, Flinders reported the circumstances surrounding the voyage in his own words:

In the beginning of 1795, captain (now vice-admiral) Hunter sailed a second time for New South Wales, to succeed Captain Phillip in the government of the new colony. He took with him His Majesty's armed vessels *Reliance* and *Supply*; and the author of this account, who was then a midshipman and had not long before returned from a voyage to the South Seas, was led by his passion for exploring new countries, to embrace the opportunity of going out upon a station which, of all others, presented the most ample field for his favourite pursuit.

As destiny would have it, both Waterhouse and Hunter would have considerable influence on Flinders' life for some time. Initially, it was Waterhouse who provided the first opportunity for advancement by including him in the complement of 59 who would crew *Reliance*. However, he obviously saw far more in Flinders than simply a young naval officer on the rise. He recognised that Flinders' character and experiences – such as his voyage with Bligh, his experiences in battle and his penchant for exploration – made him a valuable addition to this mission.

Fortunately for Flinders, the colony's next governor also had a deep-seated desire for exploration. Hunter became increasingly fascinated by the new settlement and the country surrounding it during the more than four years he had spent there with the First Fleet – so much so that he had carried out a considerable amount of exploration by sea of the nearby coastline, including Botany Bay to the south, Broken Bay to the north, Port Jackson itself and some of the Parramatta River, which meandered inland to the west of the settlement. An impression of the tiny community that was soon scattered along the shores of Sydney Cove can be gleaned from the details contained in Governor Phillip's first census, which he forwarded to Lord Sydney (whose name was given to the settlement after Phillip decided against his original preference, New Albion) back in England: a white population of 1030 (including 736 convicts), seven horses, seven cattle, 29 sheep, 74 swine and six rabbits.

These were humble beginnings for what stands as a proud nation today. Actually, the colony's stuttering start over its first decade was due primarily to the soil around Sydney Cove, which proved to be far from suitable for farming. It was a problem made worse by a series of droughts that caused crop failures and drove the settlement to the brink of famine.

Governor Phillip realised that the only way to ensure relief from the looming food crisis was to look to foreign shores, so in February 1790 he ordered both *Sirius*, under the command of Captain Hunter, and *Supply*, captained by Lieutenant David Blackburn, to sail to China and Batavia respectively to secure food and other supplies. However, with the crisis compounding by the day, more immediate action had to be taken if the colony was to survive.

The governor was decisive. To ensure the pressure was taken off the dwindling food supply as quickly as possible, he directed that the two ships, while en route to Asia, should transfer as many convicts as space would allow to Norfolk Island, a 14-square-mile subterranean mountain peak that protruded above the surface of the Tasman Sea some 900 miles east-north-east of Port Jackson. It had been discovered and named by Captain Cook in October 1774, and knowledge of its existence had caused Lord Sydney to issue an order to Governor Phillip before he departed England with the First Fleet: 'send a small establishment thither to secure the same to us and prevent it being occupied by subjects of any other European Power'. Accordingly, within a few weeks of the establishment of the colony in Sydney Cove, Governor Phillip had directed Lieutenant Philip Gidley King to take eight free men, nine male convicts and six female convicts 'whose character stood fairest' to claim the island under the British flag. King had done just that, arriving on the island on 6 March 1788.

When *Sirius* and *Supply* cleared Sydney Heads on 7 March 1790 and sheeted home their sails to suit the course towards the island, they had on board more than 130 crew, two companies of soldiers, five free women and their children, 183 convicts and 27 children of convicts. The passage across the Tasman Sea was relatively straightforward but there was no safe harbour on Norfolk Island where the ships could shelter, so they had to stand off on the open sea while the convicts were unloaded into small boats and rowed ashore. Having been forced offshore by bad weather while this was taking place, Hunter managed to sail *Sirius* back towards the island on 19 March, positioning her just off a reef in Slaughter Bay on the island's southern side.

Once there, the crew began unloading the remaining cargo so it could be transferred to a nearby beach, when suddenly an unexpected change in the direction and strength of the wind brought havoc to the scene. While the smaller and more manoeuvrable *Supply*, which was nearby, was able to sail to safety, *Sirius* was trapped on a lee shore with nowhere to go; there was no time to set the sails so she could claw her way to windward and clear the reef.

It was a helpless and hopeless situation. Those on shore and on deck could only watch in dread as the howling wind drove the 540-ton ship stern-first onto the reef. The surf then became the aggressor, turning *Sirius* beam-on to the reef, before beginning the agonisingly slow process of pounding her to bits. For a shocked Hunter, the horrifying experience rekindled childhood memories of being wrecked on the coast of Norway when sailing with his father.

All possible cargo that floated was tossed into the sea, in the hope it would be washed to shore, and those on board were saved by a lifeline – a long rope was attached to a barrel, which was thrown overboard so the surf could carry it to the beach. Once secured on shore, the crew was then able to jump into the turbulent sea and work themselves along the rope to safety. No lives were lost.

Incredibly, two convicts took it upon themselves to swim out to the ship to release the livestock still corralled on deck. With that task completed, they decided to see what else remained aboard the abandoned ship – and they found the grog locker, which they raided. In little to no time they were completely inebriated. They then decided they should accelerate the demise of *Sirius* by setting fire to the wreck. As soon as smoke was seen, a marine swam out to the ship, put out the fire and dragged the two stupefied men ashore.

The next day, *Sirius*'s crew began salvaging what they could of their ship, while *Supply* returned to Sydney Town with the news that the ship that was so vital to the security of the colony and its first inhabitants had been wrecked. A stunned Governor Phillip wrote: 'You never saw such dismay as the news of the wreck occasioned amongst us all; for, to use a sea term, we looked upon her as our sheet anchor.'

As it turned out, it would be 11 months before another ship could be sent to Norfolk Island to repatriate Hunter and his men to Sydney Cove. Following discussions, Governor Phillip decided that, as Hunter no longer had a ship to command, he should return to England. The first available ship was the Dutch vessel *Waaksamheyd*, and Hunter and some of his crew began the arduous 13-month passage home to England aboard it. There, he was commissioned by the Admiralty to join two friends, Lord Howe and his commander, Sir Roger Curtis, aboard Howe's flagship, *Queen Charlotte*, for patrols on the English Channel and out into the Atlantic.

Back in Australia, Governor Phillip was struggling with ill health. In December 1792 he was repatriated to England for treatment. When it became clear that Phillip would not be returning to his post – he resigned on 23 July 1793 – Hunter, then aged 56, immediately set about ensuring that his name was put forward most prominently as a candidate for the role of governor. He did that through two of the best possible proposers – Lord Howe and Sir Roger. Howe suggested that Hunter's appointment 'would be a blessing to the colony': he was a highly principled man of strong conviction, whose considerable understanding of the settlement and its surrounds was second to none.

It was also common knowledge among the Admiralty and government that Hunter held a deep and positive interest in the colonisation of Australia. Even though so little was known of the continent, he could see the immense benefits that a British presence in that part of the world might provide Mother England, strategically and through rural activities. Not surprisingly, Hunter was appointed to the position of governor.

When Phillip arrived back in England he had with him a journal that Hunter had written, which detailed many of his experiences in the colony and on the waters around it; in particular, it described his achievements as an explorer. Much to Hunter's delight, it was published in London in 1793, prior to his departure aboard *Reliance*. It was titled *An Historical Journal of the Transactions at Port Jackson and Norfolk Island, With the Discoveries That Have Been Made in New South Wales and the Southern Ocean Since the Publication of Phillip's Voyage.* Hunter's knowledge of the region and Flinders' enthusiasm for it most certainly made for vibrant conversation between the two men while aboard *Reliance*.

It was on Hunter's recommendation that Waterhouse was appointed captain of *Reliance*, which was scheduled to sail to Sydney Town in company with a tender vessel, HMS *Supply*, an American-built ship which had been recently purchased by the Royal Navy and named in honour of the famous, recently de-commissioned, *Supply*. Hunter wrote to the authorities that although Waterhouse was a young man and not a hardened officer, he was 'the only remaining lieutenant of the *Sirius*, formerly under my command; and having had the principal part of his nautical education from me, I can with confidence say that he is well qualified for the charge.'

By the time both ships were deemed ready for sea, the mission was six months behind schedule. During the delay, the governor-in-waiting spent much time pondering the challenges and threats that he might face during his term, particularly in light of the havoc the French were wreaking across Europe. The outpost, being small and so distant from Europe, was certainly vulnerable to attack by a foreign invader; should an attack come, it would almost certainly be from a fleet that was sailing into the Southern Ocean via the Cape of Good Hope. While much would depend on the outcome of hostilities in Europe, Hunter knew it would be foolish to wait until it was too late. It was clear to him that there was a way to prevent this potential threat: the British should hold sway over the Cape of Good Hope, which stood as a bastion between Europe and the remote outpost at Port Jackson. France was already occupying Holland, and the Dutch were in possession of the Cape. Logic dictated that the French would soon turn their attention in that direction. Hunter wrote to the Admiralty in January 1795:

I cannot help feeling much concerned at the rapid progress
of the French in Holland ... and I shall not be surprised if in
consequence of their success in that country they make a
sudden dash at the Cape of Good Hope, if we do not
anticipate them in such an attempt. They are so very active a
people that it will be done before we know anything of it,
and I think it a post of too much importance to be neglected
by them. I hope earnestly, therefore, that it will be prevented
by our sending a squadron and some troops as early as
possible. If the Republicans once get a footing there, we shall
probably find it difficult to dislodge them. Such a
circumstance would be a sad stroke for our young colony.

He also reminded the Admiralty that the Cape was of even greater strategic value to the British, given the influence and commercial interests they held in India. Later that year, much to Hunter's delight, a naval contingent was sent to the Cape, and in September the Dutch there accepted British protection.

Although *Reliance* and *Supply* were now ready to unfurl sails and start their 13,500-nautical-mile haul to Sydney Town, they had to wait − not for favourable weather but for a convoy to be formed. The French remained a threat to any ships sailing on the English Channel.

The much anticipated day of departure came on 15 February 1795. *Reliance* and *Supply* were included in a very large flotilla of naval and merchant ships sailing under the protection of Howe's Channel Fleet and were escorted to a point in the Atlantic where they would be beyond the range of the French warmongers. From there, the ships scattered across the Atlantic on their courses to destinations well beyond the horizon.

As master's mate, Flinders was a 'petty officer' – a rating or, in army jargon, non-commissioned officer. He dealt directly with the ship's master, Waterhouse, and was the only rating on the ship to have this authority. He was also authorised to command the vessel should the master be unable to do so, to walk the quarterdeck and to mess in the gunroom. At sea, one of his primary duties was to inspect the ship daily; after carrying out that task, he had to report to the master any problems with the sails, masts, spars or rigging. In essence, he made sure everything was shipshape.

Without question, the most interesting person among all aboard *Reliance* was a man simply known as Bennelong – the first Aboriginal to have been taken to England and presented to King George III. He had been captured in November 1789 by order of Governor Phillip, in the hope that the English might get an understanding of the native culture, customs and language. He learned to speak English and eventually became a colourful and well-respected member of the settlement, living in a 12-foot-square brick hut the governor had granted him on the eastern point of Sydney Cove. (The site, on which the Sydney Opera House now stands, is today named Bennelong Point.)

Bennelong had sailed to England with Governor Phillip in 1792. He was scheduled to return home aboard *Reliance* in 1794, but the six-month delay meant he had to endure the worst of an English winter while on board the ship, and it took a debilitating toll on him.

Governor Hunter, who was most concerned for Bennelong's health, wrote that, prior to leaving, the cold, homesickness and frustration that the delay caused had 'much broken his spirit'. There was another contributing factor for this man who was accustomed to wide open spaces – claustrophobia. He spent more than half of the nearly three years he was away from home aboard ships, either at sea or in port.

Sadly, the emotional stress Bennelong experienced while he was away from Sydney Town was compounded on his arrival home, when he learned that a member of the Cadigal tribe had wooed his wife in his absence. His gifts of a petticoat and a gypsy bonnet he had brought her from England did not convince her to return to him.

The first leg was a 1400-nautical-mile stretch almost due south to Tenerife, off the coast of Africa, and during the near four weeks it took to get there Hunter considered which course they should take when they weighed anchor and sailed on. His conversations with Waterhouse were influenced by the possibility that the French might have decided to take control of the Cape from the Dutch – was it worth the risk of stopping there and perhaps exposing themselves to danger? The alternative port of call was Rio de Janeiro, Brazil; from there, they could take a direct course into the Southern Ocean, bypassing the Cape and sailing directly to New South Wales. Favour fell that way.

From Rio, where they arrived in May 1795, Hunter penned a despatch to the government back in London. It outlined his reasons for not stopping at the Cape. '[I] conceive it safe from the uncertain state of the Dutch settlements in India to take the Cape of Good Hope in my way to Port Jackson,' he wrote, 'lest the French, following up their late successes in Holland, should have been active enough to make an early attack on that very important post.' In another note, to the Duke of Portland, he again aired his concerns about the security of the settlement in Sydney Town, should the French take the Cape.

Waterhouse had his own important decision to make in Rio regarding one of the key members of his crew, Second Lieutenant Nicholson, who had taken up that position eight weeks prior to the ships' departure from England. The captain was not impressed by the ability he had displayed since leaving home waters, and on 13 May he advised Nicholson that he was discharged as 'unserviceable'. Waterhouse elected not to elevate any of his existing crew into the position; instead, the ship would sail with the position vacant. This decision would prove fortunate for the 21-year-old Flinders. The dedication and professional manner he exhibited as master's mate had so impressed both the captain and commander that, in November, after *Reliance* had arrived in Sydney, he was promoted to second lieutenant.

No copy of Flinders' log for this voyage has survived, but some years later it was confirmed that while in Rio de Janiero he had displayed an inordinate talent for accuracy, detail and the recording of information, particularly for navigation. Sixteen years after being in Rio, Flinders became aware of the considerable debate that was flaring on both sides of the Atlantic as to the precise location of Cabo Frio, a dangerous cape 60 nautical miles to the east of Rio. An American mariner had declared that European charts were inaccurate, to a degree where ships might be wrecked on the cape as they made a dead-reckoning approach to the city. The seafarers' bible, the *Naval Chronicle*, drew attention to the matter.

After reading the article, Flinders weighed in most emphatically: he revealed the latitude and longitude for the cape that he had calculated from his own noon sun observations on 2 May 1795. The publishers of the *Naval Chronicle* were impressed and subsequently published the details Flinders had sent them. The article advised readers that this information – 'from a distinguished navigator' – was 'a valuable contribution towards clearing up the difficulty concerning the geographical position of that important headland'.

Although Flinders' brother, Samuel, was sailing with him aboard *Reliance*, he knew few others in the ship's complement, so from the time they sailed out of English waters new friendships were being forged. It soon became apparent to the master's mate that there was one individual with whom he had a lot in common. As Flinders later wrote:

> In Mr George Bass, surgeon of the *Reliance*, I had the
> happiness to find a man whose ardour for discovery was not
> to be repressed by any obstacles, nor deterred by danger; and
> with this friend a determination was formed of completing
> the examination of the east coast of New South Wales, by all
> such opportunities as the duty of the ship and procurable
> means could admit.

Bass, three years Flinders' senior, was also a Lincolnshire man. He was born the only child of a farmer, George Bass, and his wife, Sarah, in the tiny hamlet of Aswarby, just 12 miles west of Donington. After his father died when young George was just six years of age, his mother moved to Skirbeck, on the outskirts of the city of Boston, where he was enrolled at the Boston Grammar School. When he was 13 George was apprenticed to a local surgeon and pharmacist, Patrick Francis, and five years later he moved to London, having been accepted as a member of the Company of Surgeons.

Like Flinders, Bass had always harboured a love of the sea and the adventure it could bring, so it was no surprise when, just two months after he reached London, he was certified for the Royal Navy as a 'surgeon's mate any rate'. Just a week later he found himself at sea aboard HMS *Flirt*, a small and fast escort vessel. During several postings over the next few years, he learned navigational skills and the important fundamentals of seamanship. Bass was a prolific reader, and through this his fascination with explorers and the Pacific was somewhat sated – until he heard news that *Reliance* was being prepared for a voyage to New South Wales. He applied for a posting to the ship, and in April 1794 it was confirmed that he and his 'loblolly boy', a servant named William Martin, were to join the ship.

It appears that all aboard *Reliance* came to respect Bass, none more so than Flinders. He was an imposing young man, six feet tall, strong, handsome and with a flair for innovation. Governor Hunter was sufficiently impressed to write in an official despatch that Bass was 'a young man of a well-informed mind and an active disposition ... of much ability in various ways out of the line of his profession'. He was known as a determined individual who did not seek personal accolades as a consequence of his achievements.

The connection between Flinders and Bass was immediate, their common bond being a desire to explore what they could of New South Wales when their naval duties allowed. Flinders divulged all he had learned of the region through his studies and the frontline experience he had enjoyed when he sailed with Bligh. Before long, as Flinders wrote, the two were hatching some broad plans.

When writing *A Voyage to Terra Australis*, Flinders spelled out quite succinctly his theories about the need for maritime exploration of the regions north and south of Port Jackson:

A history of this establishment at the extremity of the
globe, in a country where the astonished settler sees

nothing, not even the grass under his feet, which is not different to whatever had before met his eye, could not but present objects of great interest to the European reader; and the public curiosity has been gratified by the perusal of various respectable publications, wherein the proceedings of the colonists, the country round Port Jackson, its productions, and native inhabitants, are delineated with accuracy, and often with minuteness. The subject to be here treated is the progress of maritime geographical discovery, which resulted from the new establishment; and as the different expeditions made for this purpose are in many cases imperfectly, and in some altogether unknown, it has been judged that a circumstantial account of them would be useful to seamen, and not without interest to the general reader.

After sailing away from Rio on a course that arced towards but bypassed the Cape of Good Hope, *Reliance* and *Supply* experienced a relatively uneventful passage across the Southern Ocean to Van Diemen's Land. From there, a course was plotted that ensured they passed well clear of Maatsuyker Island and the nasty, unforgiving reef eight nautical miles to its south-east. They continued sailing to the east until the coastline of the backdrop swept northwards. From that point, the two ships changed their course to parallel the shoreline and headed for Port Jackson.

One can imagine Bass and Flinders standing on the deck of *Reliance*, with Flinders indicating the points of interest he recalled from his voyage there aboard *Providence*. But neither man could have dreamed that the land they were observing would be the cause of a remarkable, history-making achievement that would permanently attach their names to it.

Only 630 nautical miles of the passage remained. Finally, on 7 September the monolithic, towering and rugged sandstone promontory that denotes North Head, at the entrance to Port Jackson, emerged through the distant haze, and soon after the two ships were entering what Flinders described as 'one of the finest harbours in the world'.

It had been just seven years since the First Fleet entered the same port and heralded the start of a new nation. And just as the ships of that fleet did, once inside the confines of the harbour *Reliance* was turned to port and headed upstream for the 10 miles remaining to what was now named Sydney Cove.

All the time, while *Reliance* made slow and cautious progress towards her destination, Flinders and the rest of the crew were on deck absorbing the unspoiled natural beauty that surrounded them: sandstone headlands capped in many places by a canopy of towering green eucalypts, rolling hills, a near countless number of inlets, bays and coves, many of which were backed by pristine beaches of golden sand.

After *Reliance* was anchored in Sydney Cove Governor Hunter was rowed ashore where he was welcomed by the men of the New South Wales Corps, but little did he know at the time he was already dealing with an 'enemy'. Driven by greed and opportunism, the corps – which became better known as the 'Rum Corps', because rum was effectively the local currency – had taken complete control of the colony in the period of no 'royal' rule, between the departure of Phillip and the arrival of Hunter. The men in uniform were running riot over the colony; as a result, the settlement was on the brink of chaos and collapse. Hunter said he found himself confronted by a 'turbulent and refractory colony [where] the whole concerns were taken into the hands of the military ... Had the original regulations of Governor Phillip, as things stood when I left the colony in 1791 remained ... I should have known what to do [however] the whole thing had been abolished'.

Within 24 hours, his long-held vision of being governor of a progressive, exciting and proud settlement was shattered. He now had a fight on his hands, and even if he could regain control, it was going to be a tough struggle for a man of his age when pitched against the much more energetic and younger corps members, led by Major Francis Grose – who had been appointed lieutenant-governor after Phillip's departure and was therefore being replaced by Hunter – and Lieutenant John Macarthur. Hunter endeavoured to gain the support of his superiors in England. Sending a replacement corps would have solved the predicament, but it was a case of 'out of sight, out of mind'. As a result, the 'war' with the New South Wales Corps would prove to be unwinnable for Hunter.

Meanwhile, Flinders, Bass and the remainder of *Reliance*'s crew continued working in their respective roles aboard the ship. However, the young would-be explorers were already contemplating their first adventure, as Flinders noted:

It appeared that the investigation of the coast had not been greatly extended beyond the three harbours; and even in these, some of the rivers were not altogether explored. Jervis Bay, indicated but not named by captain Cook, had been entered by lieutenant Richard Bowen; and to the north, Port Stephens had lately been examined by Mr C. Grimes, land surveyor of the colony, and by captain W. R. Broughton of H. M. ship *Providence*; but the intermediate portions of coast, both to the north and south, were little further known than from captain Cook's general chart; and none of the more distant openings, marked but not explored by that celebrated navigator, had been seen.

The fact that they were young and had not previously conducted any form of exploration meant there would be no official recognition – naval or otherwise – of their forthcoming expedition, a survey of Botany Bay and the major tributary that flowed into its south-western corner. However, the new governor did grant them a leave of absence for their undertaking. All that remained was to settle upon a vessel. As Flinders wrote, 'We turned our eyes towards a little boat which had been brought out by Mr Bass and others in the *Reliance*, and from its size had obtained the name of *Tom Thumb*.' It is highly unlikely that this was their vessel of choice, but there was little else available in the colony.

There was a considerable element of danger associated with the escapade, primarily because of the size of vessel they would be using, so it was not surprising that friends and associates did what they could to discourage them:

> Projects of this nature, when originating in the minds of
> young men, are usually termed romantic; and so far from any
> good being anticipated, even prudence and friendship join in
> discouraging, if not in opposing them. Thus it was in the
> present case; so that a little boat of eight feet long, called *Tom
> Thumb*, with a crew composed of ourselves and a boy
> [14-year-old William Martin], was the best equipment to be
> procured for the first outset.

Sadly, history has treated the maritime element of this remarkable undertaking with casual aplomb, yet from a sailing perspective it was an extraordinary achievement.

Tom Thumb was little more than a smooth-water rowing skiff that carried a small dipping lug sail, which could be set when winds were favourable. When Bass purchased the boat in England, he probably had visions of rowing it on Port Jackson and exploring its waterways. At just eight feet overall, *Tom Thumb* was not much longer than a bathtub; indeed, for the passage to Sydney it was stowed inside *Reliance*'s cutter, which was secured on deck amidships. The boat was also completely open and had very low freeboard, confirming that it was not designed for the open sea. When you add to the equation the two novice explorers and a young lad as crew, plus food, water, guns and ammunition, the fact that they completed the nine-day mission without major incident is quite astonishing.

They sailed from Port Jackson about a month after *Reliance* had delivered Governor Hunter to his new appointment. From the moment they turned south, the three intrepid sailors would have been left in no doubt that they were in a very tiny boat on the open sea. The notoriously turbulent backwash from the large and powerful ocean swells that crash on to South Head's bold and vertical cliffs would have tossed *Tom Thumb* around like a cork. It is unknown how long it took them to reach Botany Bay, but there's no doubt that the men felt great relief when they made their first stop, in the shallow bay where Captain Cook had dropped anchor for the first time after reaching the east coast of the continent in 1770. Cook had initially named the waterway Sting Ray Harbour, but later, as a tribute to the excellent achievements by the botanists aboard *Endeavour*, it became known as Botanist Bay, then, some time later, Botany Bay.

Depending on the conditions, and on whether they sailed or rowed, it would have taken the three adventurers all the daylight hours available to them – and possibly longer – to reach the craggy cliffs of Cape Solander, ten nautical miles south of Port Jackson. This cape, which stands at the entrance to Botany Bay, was named by Captain Cook in honour of one of the botanists aboard *Endeavour*, Daniel Carlsson Solander.

Flinders' note about the entire expedition was brief and unassuming:

> ... we proceeded round in this boat to Botany Bay; and
> ascending George's River, one of two which falls into the
> bay explored its winding course about 20 miles beyond
> where Governor Hunter's survey had been carried.
>
> The sketch made of this river and presented to the
> Governor, with the favourable report of the land on its
> borders, induced His Excellency to examine them himself
> shortly afterward; and was followed by establishing there a
> new branch of the colony, under the name of Banks' Town.

When their pioneering excursion to Botany Bay and beyond was completed, the trio returned to duties aboard ship, but their minds were as much on their next exploratory mission as on their jobs at hand. They would soon learn that their naval commission would curtail for some months their desire to be elsewhere: in December *Reliance* was scheduled to sail to Norfolk Island, carrying a judge advocate and an officer of the New South Wales Corps who were to take up postings there. The ship set sail in January 1796 and headed east across the Tasman Sea on a voyage that would take two months to complete.

Bass and Flinders spent much of their time at sea planning their next adventure, however, and seemingly the moment *Reliance*'s anchor had taken a bite on the bottom of Port Jackson on their return they were ashore and turning their plans into action. They wished 'to explore a large river, said to fall into the sea some miles to the south of Botany Bay, and of which there was no indication in captain Cook's chart'. Young Martin, who had enjoyed the *Tom Thumb* voyage immensely, would again be with them.

This new expedition would cover considerably more miles than their trip to Botany Bay and the George's River, so it was essential that they have a new boat. *Tom Thumb* would not have the capacity to carry the necessary food and equipment needed for this more extensive undertaking. Flinders wrote, 'As *Tom Thumb* had performed so well before, the same boat's crew had little hesitation in embarking in another boat of nearly the same size.'

It was fortunate for Flinders and Bass that a member of *Reliance*'s crew for the voyage from England was Daniel Paine, a young shipwright who had been appointed as the colony's first master boatbuilder. As there was no suitable small boat available for their proposed journey, they commissioned him to build one. However, it could be no more than 14 feet in length because of a regulation introduced to the colony by Governor Phillip, who feared that a private vessel longer than that would induce convicts to use it to escape from Port Jackson.

The new vessel was of a design similar to *Tom Thumb* and built using the clinker technique. When launched, she was appropriately named *Tom Thumb II*. Like her predecessor, she had a near-square dipping lug sail, was steered by a sweep oar, and was capable of being rowed.

When *Tom Thumb II* cleared the heads at Port Jackson around sunrise on 25 March, she was laden with the necessities for a substantial voyage. Water was stored in a small wooden cask fitted under the seat amidships, while food and firearms were stored in chests. Expecting a sea breeze from the north-east late in the morning, Bass and Flinders had decided to row the vessel offshore and so gain the maximum benefit from it.

What they didn't expect was the strong flowing current off the east coast of New South Wales, which took them south much faster than expected. As a result, when they closed on the coast in the early evening, instead of being off Cape Solander they were some 20 nautical miles further south. They soon realised from their very basic charts that the high hill they could see was Hat Hill, so named by Cook in 1770. (Today it is known as Mount Kembla, sitting five miles inland of Wollongong.)

The precipitous nature of the sandstone cliffs prevented them from landing during the night. Instead, they enjoyed a delightful sail south through to the morning, one filled with subtle sounds, like the regular churning of *Tom Thumb II*'s bow wave each time a swell built under the little boat's stern and sent her scurrying down its face. At the same time, off to leeward was the incessant muffled roar of the surf surging onto the rocks at the base of the cliffs, which stretched almost unbroken for nearly 20 nautical miles. Soon after sun-up, the weary sailors received some respite when the north-east sea breeze started to fan down the coast. As the light of day strengthened, they were heartened to see two small islets about six nautical miles to the south, which they were confident would offer them a landing spot.

A near calamity engulfed them before they got there. Flinders explained the circumstances in his journal:

... being in want of water, and seeing a place on the way where, though the boat could not land, a cask might be obtained by swimming, the attempt was made, and Mr Bass went on shore. Whilst getting off the cask, a surf arose further out than usual, carried the boat before it to the beach, and left us there with our arms, ammunition, clothes and provisions thoroughly drenched and partly spoiled. The boat was emptied and launched again immediately; but it was late in the afternoon before every thing was rafted off, and we proceeded to the islets. It was not possible to land there; and

we went on to two larger isles lying near a projecting point
of the main, which has four hillocks upon it presenting the
form of a double saddle, and proved to be captain Cook's
Red Point [Port Kembla].

As they continued their journey, the three spent hours trying to
dry out their clothing, muskets and gunpowder.

When they reached the isles, they realised there was nowhere
suitable to land. After dropping a stone anchor in the lee of one of
the rocky outcrops, they spent their second consecutive night
curled up in the cramped and narrow bilge of *Tom Thumb II*,
getting what little sleep they could. This was doubly difficult for
Bass, whose pale English skin had been badly sunburned. In
Flinders' words, he was 'one continued blister'. While there,
Flinders and Bass decided they should pay tribute to the dedication
of young Martin. 'We called these Martin's Isles after our young
companion in the boat,' Flinders wrote.

By now they were desperate for water, so when they saw two
obviously inquisitive 'indians' standing on the shore soon after sun-
up the next day, they rowed to the water's edge in the hope that
they might communicate with them. They learned that fresh water
could be found in a river a few miles to the south. As Flinders wrote:

We accepted their offer of piloting us to a river which, they
said, lay a few miles further southward, and where not only
fresh water was abundant, but also fish and wild ducks. These
men were natives of Botany Bay, whence it was that we
understood a little of their language, whilst that of some
others was altogether unintelligible. Their river proved to be
nothing more than a small stream, which descended from a
lagoon under Hat Hill [Lake Illawarra], and forced a passage

for itself through the beach; so that we entered it with difficulty even in *Tom Thumb*. Our two conductors then quitted the boat to walk along the sandy shore abreast, with eight or ten strange natives in company.

After rowing a mile up the stream, and finding it to become more shallow, we began to entertain doubts of securing a retreat from these people, should they be hostilely inclined; and they had the reputation at Port Jackson of being exceedingly ferocious, if not cannibals. Our muskets were not yet freed from rust and sand, and there was a pressing necessity to procure fresh water before attempting to return northward. Under these embarrassments, we agreed upon a plan of action, and went on shore directly to the natives. Mr Bass employed some of them to assist in repairing an oar which had been broken in our disaster, whilst I spread the wet powder out in the sun. This met with no opposition, for they knew not what the powder was; but when we proceeded to clean the muskets, it excited so much alarm that it was necessary to desist. On inquiring of the two friendly natives for water, they pointed upwards to the lagoon; but after many evasions our barica [cask] was filled at a hole not many yards distant.

Regardless of whether or not the natives were to become a threat to the Englishmen's security, many were fascinated by the muskets that Flinders and Bass had with them. Equally, the explorers were intrigued by the caution the Aboriginals showed towards these weapons: it appeared that word of the incredible noise that these contraptions emitted had travelled south from Port Jackson. Perhaps these Aboriginals had also heard that natives had been known to fall to the ground and die when the red-coated men pointed the

Courtesy SLNSW

This miniature watercolour portrait of Flinders on ivory (circa 1800) was backed by another thin piece of ivory and a metal 'ribbon', which held in place a lock of his hair.

Courtesy SLNSW

Courtesy SLNSW

Courtesy SLNSW

TRIM'S
SHORT CUT
(GLASS ALL SMASHED TO "FLINDERS".

Courtesy NLA

Items from an era: A sword, naval coat or sash badge and sextant believed to have belonged to Matthew Flinders. The drawing is of Flinders' loyal companion on land and sea, Trim, escaping a cloudburst by crashing through a closed window at his shore-side residence after arriving in England aboard *Reliance*.

The Providence and (her Tender) the Assistant. 1791   Page 3

HMS *Providence* and her tender, *Assistant*, by George Tobin (1791). Tobin was a third lieutenant aboard *Providence* for Captain Bligh's successful breadfruit voyage to Tahiti. Flinders served as a midshipman.

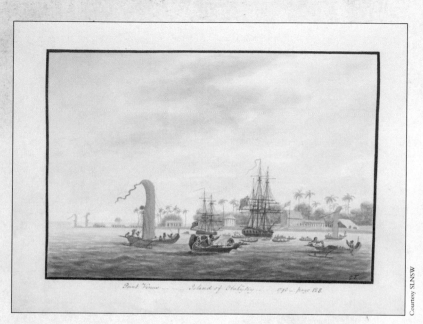

George Tobin's 1792 painting of HMS *Providence* and *Assistant* anchored near Point Venus in Tahiti.

At anchor in Adventure Bay, Van Diemen's Land, by George Tobin (1792).

View of Sydney Cove from 'The Rocks' area on the western shore of the inlet (1789).

A replica of Flinders' *Norfolk*, built for the re-enactment of the historic discovery of Bass Strait and circumnavigation of Tasmania exactly 200 years after the event.

A replica of *Tom Thumb*, the tiny vessel that took Matthew Flinders, George Bass and young William Martin on their voyage of discovery south from Sydney Town.

Bungaree, the Aboriginal Flinders had join him aboard *Norfolk* for the voyage north to Hervey's Bay in the hope he could communicate with local tribes.

H.M. Sloop INVESTIGATOR 1802

Sea Rivalry – HM Sloop *Investigator*. Etching by Geoffrey Ingleton.

On 24 March 1802 *Investigator* anchored at what would from then on be known as Kangaroo Island.

William Westall's *View of Port Jackson taken from the South Head* appeared in Flinders' *A Voyage to Terra Australis* along with Westall's etching above.

along the east coast — Cape Byron and Pt Lookout

The projecting heads near us at 2 o'clock had a tolerably fertile appearance. In the bight south of them, was a smoke close to the water side. The bight to the northward may probably afford shelter from winds at south. C. Byron makes like an island, the land immediately behind it being low, but it some rises towards that [way of] mountains at the top of which is Mt. Warning. — P.C. having passed this cape and as far as Point Lookout in the day time, I steered on all night towards E. Moreton; for the space from the point to the last cape had been previously examined in the Norfolk. — The hills about Mt. Warning are well covered with wood, and the country has a tolerable appearance even near the shore; but from hence to the northward, sand prevails more or less.

When Mt. Warning was seen it could not be less than twenty leagues distant & may certainly be seen some leagues further. — In the Norfolk sloop I laid down Pt. Lookout 20′ ″ to the south of capt. Cooks situation of it, and the observations this day at noon confirm the propriety of it. Our longitude gives much nearer with his

Cape Byron	N 5° W.
App.t time	2.57.41.7
... 543	16.31.43,2
☉ 736.40 3	24.54. 4
Longitude	153.39.55.5
E. 520	.41.57.
Mean	153.40.56.
	9.10
Noon back	153.31.38 E.
D.o forw?	153.37.30
Noon 25	153.34.34 E.

Pt. Lookout	S ... W. limit
App.t time	21.51.30,7
... 543	11.75.25,0
☉ ... 40 3	33.10.3 ...
Longitude	153.41.46.5
E. 520	39.21.
Mean	153.40.35 E.
by survey	.2.45
Noon 26	153.37.50 E.

Mer. alt. ☉	
☉ ... 60 3	} 42.46.46 ...
Latitude	27.10.3...

Courtesy SLNSW

A hand in history: A page from the journal Flinders kept aboard HMS *Investigator*.

muskets in their direction and the noise was heard. Bass had a red jacket with him; might the natives be anxious because they thought their visitors were some of these mysterious men in red?

This thought was compounded by the appearance of more equally apprehensive natives – soon near 20 were there – and they were beginning to surround the trio. Most disconcerting was the fact that, should the natives attack, they had no form of defence: they were still trying to dry their gunpowder. There was only one option: they should set about doing what they could to subtly expedite their departure back to sea.

Within minutes, however, good fortune was playing into their hands. The two natives who had come with them from Red Point were very proudly showing their fellow tribesmen how the visitors had clipped their hair and beards, and suggested that their friends follow their lead. Flinders took up his scissors and started trimming hair and beards, while Bass and Martin casually prepared the boat so they could leave. By the time Flinders had completed his tonsorial activities on a dozen highly amused and astonished Aboriginals, everything was in readiness for a retreat. While the locals became increasingly vocal about going further upstream to the lagoon, the explorers made good their getaway.

It was ten p.m. when *Tom Thumb II* cleared the entrance to the rivulet on what was a windless night. The crew rowed the boat until one a.m., when they were able to anchor close to the northernmost of the rocky islets they had seen on their way south. The following afternoon, they managed to get their little boat onto a beach north of Hat Hill. Much to their delight, they were able to cook food and relax without attracting attention from any Aboriginals. That night, Flinders noted, 'The sandy beach was our bed; and after much fatigue, and passing three nights of cramp in Tom Thumb, it was to us a bed of down.'

The following day, 29 March 1795, they continued on the return voyage. After rowing throughout the day and into the night, they were another 12 nautical miles closer to home. There was no beach to land on, only sheer cliffs, so they guided their little boat as close to the shore as cautious seamanship would allow, then lowered the block of stone which was their anchor over the side and settled in for the night.

Their respite was short-lived, as a sudden and violent southerly gale descended on them:

> At ten o'clock, the wind, which had been unsettled and
> driving electric clouds in all directions, burst out in a gale at
> south, and obliged us to get up the anchor immediately, and
> run before it. In a few minutes the waves began to break;
> and the extreme danger to which this exposed our little bark,
> was increased by the darkness of the night, and the
> uncertainty of finding any place of shelter. The shade of the
> cliffs over our heads, and the noise of the surfs breaking at
> their feet, were the directions by which our course was
> steered parallel to the coast.

It was a weather system referred to today as a 'southerly buster', and it created a dire situation for the adventurers because the boat was so small, the wind so strong and the seas increasingly threatening.

Their only option was to set the sail and try to run before the maelstrom. Bass took hold of the sheet controlling the sail, trimming it in a desperate bid to avoid capsizing. Flinders' role was equally harrowing. 'I was steering with an oar,' he wrote, 'and it required the utmost exertion and care to prevent broaching to; a single wrong movement, or a moment's inattention, would have sent us to the bottom.' The boat was also in danger of being swamped, so Martin's job was to bail incessantly.

Whenever possible, three sets of eyes peered into the rain-lashed darkness ahead, looking for surf breaking on any uncharted reef that would claim them in a trice, while hoping to find a headland they might be able to sail in behind, anchor and enjoy the refuge that the lee provided. Flinders later relived the drama:

> After running near an hour in this critical manner, some high breakers were distinguished ahead; and behind them there appeared no shade of cliffs. It was necessary to determine, on the instant, what was to be done, for our bark could not live ten minutes longer. On coming to what appeared to be the extremity of the breakers, the boat's head was brought to the wind in a favourable moment, the mast and sail taken down, and the oars got out. Pulling then towards the reef during the intervals of the heaviest seas, we found it to terminate in a point; and in three minutes were in smooth water under its lee. A white appearance, further back, kept us a short time in suspense; but a nearer approach showed it to be the beach of a well-sheltered cove, in which we anchored for the rest of the night. So sudden a change, from extreme danger to comparatively perfect safety, excited reflections which kept us some time awake: we thought Providential Cove a well-adapted name for this place.

This beautiful little haven, 20 nautical miles south of the entrance to Port Jackson, looks like it was created by driving a giant wedge into the immense cliffs. It was known to the natives as *Watta-Mowlee*. Today it is Wattamolla.

When the storm had blown through and the sea subsided, the three intrepid sailors rowed their skiff out onto the open sea once more and turned north. After covering less than five miles they came across a large bay with a river running into it, which would also have provided the protection they needed from the southerly gale. It was 1 April when they set about exploring the bay and the river system that twisted its way through the picturesque hills that lay to the west.

On the morning of 2 April they 'quitted' the bay, but before doing so they named it Port Hacking, in recognition of Henry Hacking, the colony's principal game hunter, who had first recorded its existence, having sighted the waterway during a kangaroo-hunting excursion.

Tom Thumb II then sailed north, her destination Port Jackson, just 15 nautical miles away. That evening, the little boat was secured snugly alongside *Reliance* in Sydney Cove, and its occupants were soon resting comfortably in their bunks.

CHAPTER SEVEN

South in Search of a Strait

When Governor Hunter arrived in Sydney Cove aboard *Reliance* in 1795 it soon became apparent to him and all aboard the ship that life was not easy for those who had preceded them from Mother England. They quickly learned that the settlement was experiencing severe growing pains due in no small way to a continuing drought, which was greatly impacting the nearby farms that were supposed to be providing essential crops. Additional pressure had been placed on the community by the arrival of two more fleets of convict ships. Those vessels had brought almost 3000 male and female prisoners to the colony, plus military personnel and a handful of pioneering free settlers – and every one of them had to be fed.

At that time there was only three months' supply of some staple foods remaining. With *Sirius* having been wrecked on Norfolk Island, it became even more imperative that *Supply* sail to Batavia as soon as possible so she could take on board the provisions and general supplies the colony so desperately needed. When she did eventually set sail on 17 April 1790, *Supply* left in her wake some very apprehensive settlers, many of whom were beginning to wonder if they had made the right decision in coming to the colony from England. There was even talk in some circles that the settlement might have to be abandoned.

The colony then had only two support vessels at its disposal. Both *Reliance* and *Supply* had, however, suffered from the ravages of time and tempest on the high seas, and consequently were on the verge of being deemed unseaworthy. Extensive repairs to both ships were the only solution. Captain Hunter wrote to his superiors in England that *Reliance* was 'so extremely weak in her whole frame that it is in our situation a difficult matter to do what is necessary'. *Supply* was in an even worse state – a near spent ship – primarily because she was built in America using birch, a material that deteriorated rapidly in the harsh conditions and warm waters that prevailed in New South Wales.

Hunter had an additional problem to consider. The Secretary of State in England had advised him that he should, as soon as practicable, purchase live cattle from the Cape of Good Hope, and with them establish a herd in Sydney that would guarantee a supply of meat. But the only two ships at the governor's disposal to make this voyage were *Reliance* and *Supply*.

At this time, a very basic dock and ship repair facility had been set up on the western shore of Sydney Cove, but it was far too small to fully rectify the problems of the two structurally unsound vessels, even if there had been enough skilled shipwrights to carry out the work to a satisfactory standard. Something had to be done so that there was at least one ship seaworthy enough to support and serve the colony, come what may. After due consideration and discussion, Governor Hunter decided that *Reliance* would be rebuilt to the best possible standard, using what skills and materials the colony and crew could provide. Only basic repairs would be made to *Supply*.

When it came to start the work, circumstances would arise that directly influenced what Flinders and Bass would do next. Flinders, the seafarer, was required to remain with the ship and work on the rebuild, but there was no reason for Bass, the ship's surgeon, to be present – so he occupied himself with more exploration. Understandably, this was a frustrating time for the equally ambitious explorer Flinders. 'The great repairs required by the Reliance would not allow of my absence,' he wrote.

> My friend Bass, less confined by his duty, made several
> excursions, principally into the interior parts behind Port
> Jackson; with a view to pass over the back mountains, and
> ascertain the nature of the country beyond them. His success
> was not commensurate to the perseverance and labour
> employed: the mountains were impassable; but the course of
> the river Grose resulted from one of these excursions.

Bass's 15-day excursion was one of many that failed to find a way across the craggy, often sheer mountain range, which had its foothills less than 40 miles to the west of the settlement. The ranges forming this impassable barrier, which would later become known as the Blue Mountains, remained unconquered for 25 years. It was not until 1813 that Gregory Blaxland, Lieutenant William Lawson and a young lad, William Charles Wentworth, finally scaled, hacked and trudged their way across the highlands and returned to Sydney Town with news of their discoveries.

When the ships were finally declared to be as fit for sea as could be achieved, plans were made for both to do the cattle run to Cape Town, and as Flinders and Bass were still very much part of

Reliance's crew, they were obliged to be aboard. This meant that their desire to continue with their exploration of the New South Wales coast would have to be delayed until their return ten months later. Regardless, there was one very beneficial side to making the trip: they would have ample time to consider what region they might explore next.

With the repairs complete, the two ships finally departed Sydney in September 1796. In planning the voyage, it was decided that they would sail to Cape Town on the downwind route, which meant the first stage would be a testing passage to the east, across the Southern Ocean and around the storm-haunted Cape Horn, before a run across the South Atlantic to an anchorage in Cape Town. Downwind it might have been, but this outward leg would almost certainly encounter barbaric, ice-laced gales and huge, storm-driven seas. In such conditions it was essential that the crews be ready to reduce sail at a moment's notice; if they weren't, precious canvas might be blown to tatters. Worse still, the ship might suffer a dismasting – and if there was one place you didn't want that to happen, it was in the Southern Ocean between the southern tip of New Zealand and Cape Horn. This region is more remote from civilisation and salvation than anywhere else on Earth.

While the ships were burdened by the weather, they were in relatively good shape when they reached Cape Town and dropped anchor. Once there, and after the desired cattle were procured, Captain Waterhouse and others opted to purchase for themselves numerous breeds of domestic animals for the benefit of the colony – and possibly their own pockets. The decision by Waterhouse and Lieutenant William Kent to privately purchase 26 merino sheep and introduce them to the colony was the foundation of what would become one of Australia's most important industries for centuries to come. Bass is known to have purchased a cow and

19 sheep, while Waterhouse's total purchase of animals was deemed enough to establish a small farm.

When the cargo had been loaded and secured for the long easterly voyage home, which began on 11 April 1797, the ship's manifest showed it to be a virtual Noah's Ark: it held 109 head of cattle, 107 sheep and three mares, plus other domestic animals and birds. A bemused Captain Waterhouse noted: 'I believe no ship ever went to sea so much lumbered.'

While Flinders did not purchase any animals for himself in South Africa, he arrived in Sydney Town with one – a black cat named Trim. It was born aboard *Reliance* while she lay at anchor in Cape Town, not long after Flinders had passed his examination to become a lieutenant. The kitten's mother had been with the ship as a resident rat catcher from the time it left England in 1794. Flinders was impressed by the entire litter, but there was one in particular that stood out, showing exceptional 'energy, agility and daring'. Flinders would later express his feelings in a short biographical novel he wrote about his feline friend, which was simply titled *Trim*.

The signs of superior intelligence which marked his infancy procured for him an education beyond what is usually bestowed upon the individuals of his tribe; and being brought up amongst sailors, his manner acquired a peculiarity of cast which rendered them as different from those of other cats as the actions of a fearless seaman are from those of a lounging, shame-faced ploughboy. It was, however, from his gentleness and the innate goodness of his heart that I gave him the name of ... Uncle Toby's honest, kind-hearted, humble companion ...

In playing with his little brothers and sisters upon deck by moonlight, when the ship was lying tranquilly in harbour, the

energy and elasticity of his movements sometimes carried him
so far beyond his mark that he fell overboard; but this was far
from being a misfortune; he learned to swim and to have no
dread of the water: and when a rope was thrown over to him
he took hold of it like a man, and ran up it like a cat.

Flinders decided on the name Trim having read Laurence Sterne's
novel *Tristram Shandy*. In that book, Uncle Toby's manservant,
James Butler, who went by the name of Trim, showed 'great
fidelity and affection' towards his master.

If crews of *Reliance* and the *Supply* thought the weather was
rough on the outward passage from Port Jackson, then there was a
lot worse to come on the voyage back. Trim, his master and many
other members of *Reliance*'s crew got their first taste of the meanest
mood the Southern Ocean could muster. Waterhouse described
the journey as 'one of the longest and most disagreeable passages I
ever made'; it was 'the most terrible [storm] I ever saw or heard of'.
He added that conditions were so extreme that he 'expected to go
to the bottom every moment'.

Not surprisingly, the ships were soon being pounded back into
a most unseaworthy state: the roaring and foaming seas were
enormous, the rigs were being tested to the limit by violent squalls,
and the decks were continually awash under several feet of water.
Reliance and *Supply* were at the mercy of the unforgiving elements
and literally falling apart at the seams: the gaps between the hull
and deck planks were becoming ever wider, and the ingress of
water to below decks was at times like being under a cascade
coming over a cliff. The pumps had to be manned continuously.
Conditions were so rough that some of the stock on board could
not cope and died. For the crews, it was an extreme ordeal; their
utmost skills of seamanship had to be applied in the face of some of

the worst weather imaginable. Their greatest challenge was to not overburden their respective ships and bring about a calamity.

Supply, in particular, was in grave danger of going down. It was as if just one more monstrous wave was all that was needed for her to disappear without trace in the desolate wilds of the Southern Ocean. Miraculously, that tragedy did not eventuate, thanks in no small way to the superb leadership of Lieutenant Kent.

Aboard *Reliance*, there was some form of light relief, even in the worst of the weather. Flinders explained this in his biographical tribute to the memory of Trim:

Trim was admitted upon the table of almost every officer and man in the ship: in the gunroom he was always the first ready for dinner, but though he was commonly seated a quarter of an hour before any other person, his modest reserve was such that his voice was not heard until everybody else was served. He then put in his request, not for a full allowance – he was too modest – nor did he desire there should be laid for him a plate, knife, fork or spoon, with all which he could very well dispense, but by a gentle caressing mew he petitioned for a little, little bit, a kind of tythe from the plate of each; and it was to no purpose to refuse it, for Trim was enterprising in time of need, as he was gentle and well-bred in ordinary times. Without the greatest attention to each morsel, in the person whom he had petitioned in vain, he would whip it off the fork with his paw, on its passage to the mouth, with such dexterity and an air so graceful that it rather excited admiration than anger. He did not, however, leap off the table with his prize, as if he had done wrong; but putting the morsel into his mouth and eating it quietly, would go to the next person and repeat his little mew; if refused his wonted tythe, he stood ready to take all advantages. There are some men so inconsiderate as to be talking when they should be eating, who keep their meat suspended in mid-air till a semi-colon in the discourse gives an opportunity of taking their mouthful without interrupting their story. Guests of this description were a dead mark for Trim: when a short pause left them time to take the prepared mouthful, they were often surprised to find their meat gone, they could not tell how.

While Kent was keen to sail hard so that he could round Van Diemen's Land, turn north and get a reprieve from the malevolence of the Southern Ocean, Waterhouse sailed *Reliance* more conservatively. As a result, the badly battered and still leaking *Supply* limped into Port Jackson 41 days ahead of *Reliance*.

When Waterhouse eventually anchored his ship in Sydney Cove on 26 June and went aboard *Supply*, he quickly realised she was 'in a most distressed and dangerous condition'; he believed she would never again be fit for sea. Needless to say, everyone was most impressed by the great seamanship exhibited by Kent in getting such a derelict vessel home safely. Such was his achievement that Flinders would later name a group of islands in the eastern part of what would become Bass Strait as 'the Kent Group', in his honour.

Inevitably, *Reliance*, too, underwent a thorough inspection from bowsprit to taffrail, masthead to heel and deck beams to keelson, and it became obvious she was also in a bad way: she would again need major repairs before she could put to sea once more. Indeed, Waterhouse was far from convinced that any reconstruction would be successful. 'We have taken everything out of her in hopes of repairing her,' he wrote. To no one's surprise, the rebuild, which commenced in late 1797, was a major project. It took many months to complete, and again Flinders was part of it.

The cargo delivered by *Supply* and *Reliance* brought some relief to the drought-stricken colony, but the two ships were not the talk of the town. Instead, Sydney Town was buzzing with news of a shipwreck and an almost inconceivable story of survival that had unfolded over recent weeks. A 250-ton merchant ship, *Sydney Cove*, had been deliberately grounded in the Furneaux Islands, off the north-east corner of Van Diemen's Land, to prevent her from sinking, and three of her crew had survived an incredible nine-week ordeal, mostly over land, to reach Sydney Town and raise the alarm. Inevitably, Flinders and Bass met the leader of the group, the ship's supercargo, William Clark, and learned more of his amazing story.

Clark's colourful account of events brought a frightening new resonance to their own recent adventures aboard *Tom Thumb II*. Clark revealed that two of the 16 men who had left the ship with him to try to reach Port Jackson – the chief mate and the ship's carpenter – 'were killed by Dilba, and other savages near Hat Hill'. Flinders and Bass realised immediately that Dilba was a member of the tribe of natives who had tried to lure them inland to the lagoon when they were searching for water near Hat Hill; it was clear that the apprehension they had felt at the time was well justified, and they and young Martin were lucky not to have been murdered.

The voyage of *Sydney Cove* from Calcutta was historic in many ways, but most significant was that she was the first privately owned merchant trading ship that had set sail with the sole intent of selling its cargo – which comprised foodstuffs, textiles of Indian, Chinese and European origin, livestock and a considerable amount of alcohol, including nearly 7000 gallons of spirits – to the colony. There was even a carriage and an organ in the hold. This was a purely speculative exercise for the ship's owners, one founded on news that the new British colony in Port Jackson could provide solid, long-term trading opportunities.

Little is known today of the ship, which is believed to have been originally named *Begum Shaw*. It was probably built in India, and indications are that she was more than likely a twin-decked, three-masted ship with an overall length of around 100 feet. It is also likely that she was designed as a light and fast coastal trading vessel, to be used primarily for short voyages. She was operated by Campbell & Clark, a small and relatively new trading company owned by two Scotsmen based in Calcutta. Since this was their first venture to New South Wales, they had decided to change the name of their ship to *Sydney Cove* in the hope that it would give them a better commercial entrée to the colony. If the mission had been successful, it was highly probable that they would then have established a regular trade route with the settlement.

The ship's commander was another Scotsman, 37-year-old Gavin 'Guy' Hamilton, who had been in India for more than a decade, while Clark, the man in charge of cargo operations on board, was the nephew of one of the company's principals.

On 10 November 1796, *Sydney Cove*, with a complement of 56 men aboard, left port on a fast and favourable tide and cruised the 60 nautical miles down the Hooghly River, before entering the Bay of Bengal and sailing south towards the equator. This was the start of a 7000-nautical-mile passage that would go horribly wrong, mainly because the ship was too light. She was simply not strong enough to cope with the arduous trans-oceanic voyage.

The first evidence of this came on 13 December, when *Sydney Cove* was hammered by a savage gale some 950 nautical miles south of the equator. The heavily laden ship began to labour in the rapidly rising seas, and within 24 hours a serious leak had developed in the hull planks of the starboard bow. The ship's carpenter set about trying to find and fix the problem, but after crawling through the dank and dark forward section of the hull he declared that the ingress of water through the bilge – which was at eight inches per hour – could not be stemmed from the inside, as the source of the leak was located behind heavy structural timbers. Captain Hamilton knew the only thing he could do was have his ship ride out the gale under storm sails while his men manned the pumps around the clock.

It was more than a week before conditions were calm enough for the crew to attempt to slow the leak by 'fothering' the starboard bow. This process involved lowering a sail – which had been folded to form a pad, and then filled with material such as wool and chopped oakum – over the side of the ship; using ropes, the men would draw it in against the damaged area of the hull. While it was not watertight, the patch would slow the flow of water into the bilge. It was a tedious and time-consuming task. This time, because of the rolling motion of the ship in the heavy Southern Ocean swell, the fothering failed and the patch was torn to pieces.

Consequently, it was back to manning the pumps and hoping there would be no more storms. By then there was no turning back. With the wind dictating his course, Hamilton could only continue south to a point in the Roaring Forties from which he could then steer to the east and run a safe course towards Van Diemen's Land.

In the last week of January, *Sydney Cove* was struck suddenly by an atrocious storm. Crewmen rushed aloft and began furling and reefing the sails; while they did, a blood-curdling scream punctuated the air, above the shriek of the wind through the rigging. It came as the ship rolled heavily in an extraordinarily large sea, causing the masts to go through a rapid and wild gyration. This motion was so violent that the second mate lost his grip on the yardarm and was pitched into the ocean. All those who watched in horror knew there was no chance of his being recovered.

Sails were by then being flogged to shreds by the wind, and the stress being placed on the hull by wind and wave was prising open the seams between an increasing number of the hull planks. This was a fight to the death between the sea and the sailors.

Remarkably, and with water continuing to flood into her hull, the still labouring *Sydney Cove* reached the southern tip of Van Diemen's Land and began heading north towards her destination, but all aboard knew there was no chance their ship could cover the remaining 600 nautical miles. Some of the crew were reported to be so 'frightened and benumbed' that they refused to man the pumps.

They sailed slowly up the eastern shoreline of Van Diemen's Land. As they neared the north-east corner of the coast, Hamilton had to make a decision. He knew from his charts that there was no known safe haven between there and Port Jackson, so after conferring with his senior crew he decided to run the ship onto a sandy shore on a nearby island, hoping to save the crew and as much cargo as possible.

With five feet of water sloshing through the hull, *Sydney Cove* was steered to the north-west, through what is now Banks Strait and towards a small island off the south-west corner of the Furneaux Group. There, Hamilton cautiously guided his ship into the smooth water off the island's eastern shore until the keel nudged the sandy bottom in less than 20 feet of water. It was 9 February.

Over the next few weeks the bulk of the cargo – except the alcohol – was unloaded onto what would become known as Preservation Island, where the men set up a camp. Hamilton insisted that, in order to protect the alcohol from the wants of the crew, it would be transferred to another, considerably smaller island just 200 yards away across a shallow channel. Most appropriately, it was named Rum Island.

An inspection of *Sydney Cove*'s hull confirmed everything Hamilton and his officers had feared: the ship was beyond repair. They also knew there was no chance of them being seen in the unlikely event of another vessel sailing along the coast of Van Diemen's Land, to or from Port Jackson, so they had to formulate their own rescue plan. They made the only logical choice available to them: to sail the ship's longboat 450 nautical miles to Port Jackson and alert the governor to their plight.

Given the load the longboat would be carrying across an open stretch of sea, a quick modification was made to make it more seaworthy: the freeboard was raised by the addition of an extra strake at the gunwale. That done, a crew of 17 of *Sydney Cove*'s 'best men' was chosen to man it. Hamilton decided that his ship's second mate, Hugh Thompson, would captain the longboat, and that he would be joined by supercargo William Clark, three additional Europeans, plus 12 'lascars' – deckhands from India and Asia.

On the morning of 26 February the longboat was loaded with provisions: rice, water, firearms and ammunition. Captain Hamilton gave Thompson a letter to carry to Governor Hunter, which advised him of their situation and requested that a ship be sent to recover them and their cargo. All was in readiness for a departure. The 17 men clambered aboard the longboat and rowed away from the beach. Once they had rounded the nearby headland of Cape Barren Island, they disappeared from the sight of those who remained onshore.

After sailing for three days, the men sighted land. As they closed in on it, thought was given to going ashore near what is now Cape Everard, but the weather was deteriorating rapidly and a strong south-westerly gale struck. As night was approaching, it was decided to set both the longboat's anchors and ride out the bad weather until morning.

Fortunately, the anchors held, but at sunrise it was obvious that the conditions were continuing to deteriorate. As a result, the small crew faced an increasingly dangerous predicament. Because they were anchored in shallow water relatively close to the shore, the seas were becoming steeper and more threatening. All too soon the waves were breaking over the boat and beginning to fill the bilge, so while some of the crew began bailing it out, Thompson and his senior men conferred. They agreed they could no longer remain at anchor, but it would be equally foolhardy to try to continue their voyage in such extreme conditions. They could only try to surf the longboat to the shore.

A small sail was set, the anchors abandoned, the tiller pushed across and the longboat's bow directed at the nearby beach. It was a death-defying manoeuvre in appalling conditions. Within minutes, the boat was in the grasp of the surf and charging towards the beach. Incredibly, the crew got through with everyone accounted for, even though the boat was almost full of water. Because it was so waterlogged they were unable to beach it, despite their best efforts, so they could only watch in helpless horror as their one means of survival was pummelled to pieces by the powerful surf.

After retrieving what they could from the water's edge – food, clothing, arms and ammunition – the men set up a primitive campsite on the beach. They remained there for two weeks, and in that time it was decided there was only one option available to them: to undertake a physically demanding and supremely dangerous trek of more than 300 miles along the often rugged, unknown and unforgiving eastern coastline of New South Wales until they reached Sydney Town. It was 15 March when that journey began.

Wherever possible, they remained on beaches, but often they were forced to hack their way through dense bushland, to scale escarpments and rugged hills, and to find ways around or across rivers so they could continue on their way north.

Three days after they set out, the group experienced their first encounter with a tribe of Aboriginals. Clark, who kept a diary written in pencil, wrote:

We this day fell in with a party of natives, about fourteen, all of them entirely naked. They were struck with astonishment at our appearance and were very anxious to examine every part of our clothes and body, in which we readily indulged them. They viewed us most attentively. They opened our clothes, examined our feet, hands, nails, etc., frequently expressing their surprise by laughing and loud shoutings.

On most days they averaged between ten and 14 miles, but as they progressed men began surrendering to fatigue and hunger and had to be left behind.

Some of the Aboriginal groups they met were friendly and offered the dwindling group fresh fish and guided them for some distance, but others were quite hostile and threatening. One such tribe – more than 100 men armed with spears and other weapons – attacked six of the group, wounding Thompson, Clark and one of the lascars, but all survived. The men soon realised that the closer they got to Port Jackson, the more aggressive the natives became – hence the attack on them near Hat Hill.

After that incident, only three, including Clark, remained alive, and they determinedly pressed on, trudging their way along the beaches and clifftops, conscious that with every step they were getting closer to salvation.

Ironically, it was when they reached the beautiful little inlet at Wattamolla – the same one that had provided life-saving shelter for Flinders, Bass and Martin aboard *Tom Thumb II* – that they savoured a sight seemingly heaven-sent. There in the bay was a small fishing boat, which had ventured south from Port Jackson. The men shouted and were seen by the fishermen. Less than a day later, on the evening of 16 May, they stepped ashore at Sydney Cove. By unfortunate default, they could lay claim to being the first land explorers of the south-east coast of New Holland.

While Clark initiated plans for the rescue of the men who had remained with the wreck of *Sydney Cove*, he also detailed the extraordinary 63-day slog that he and his shipmates had undertaken – one in which 14 had perished. While doing this he happened to mention that he had seen something intriguing embedded in an oceanfront cliff face just 20 miles south of Botany Bay, the area that Flinders, Bass and Martin had earlier explored. Both Flinders and Bass were excited by this revelation: it appeared that Clark had stumbled across a large exposed seam of coal.

This news was all Bass needed to inspire his next endeavour. Again, he had time on his hands, so with the support of Governor Hunter he decided to investigate the discovery. In August he set out in a small boat to search for what might be an exceptionally valuable asset for the colony. Sure enough, when he reached the location nominated by Clark – now known as Coalcliff – there it was, standing out like a beacon for all to see: a beautiful black layer of coal up to seven feet thick, sweeping across the cliff at a height of about 20 feet above sea level, before dipping into the ocean to the south. As Bass recorded, 'the lowest rock you can see when the surf retires is all coal'.

In fact, this was not the first time coal had been found in New South Wales. In 1791, little more than three years after the establishment of the colony, three convicts trying to escape Port Jackson uncovered an outcrop of the valuable black mineral on the coast about 60 miles to the north of Sydney Town. Bass's find was thought to be of far greater significance – but a month after he confirmed to Governor Hunter that it was coal that Clark had seen, an even greater find of the prized black ore was made to the north. Flinders detailed this when writing *A Voyage to Terra Australis*:

> In September, a small colonial vessel having been carried off by convicts, Lieutenant John Shortland, first of the *Reliance*, went after them to the northward, in an armed boat. The expedition was fruitless, as to the proposed object; but in returning along the shore from Port Stephens, Mr Shortland discovered a port in latitude 33°, capable of receiving small ships; and what materially added to the importance of the discovery, was a stratum of coal, found to run through the south head of the port, and also pervaded a cliffy island in the entrance. These coals were not only accessible to shipping, but of a superior quality to those in the cliffs near Hat Hill. The port was named after His Excellency governor Hunter; and a settlement, called New Castle, has lately been there established.

The fact that Flinders was again committed to being part of the team charged with rebuilding *Reliance*'s tired timbers didn't deter Bass from pursuing his own aspirations. He had one major project brewing in his mind, but in the meantime he would briefly turn his attention to the inland to the south-west, between Sydney Town and the foothills of the mountains, which was yet to be fully explored.

He set out in September, leaving the settlement on foot with Governor Hunter's acting commissary, James Williamson. Their first objective was to cross the area known as the Cow Pastures, then they would continue onto the flood plains skirting the Nepean River, which wended its way over 150 miles to the north. The two explorers crossed the river on numerous occasions before heading east; they eventually reached the coast near a place Bass already knew well, Wattamolla.

The trek had covered some 100 miles, yet while Bass documented his many observations regarding the nature of the land, his mind had been elsewhere. He was back at sea: he wanted to know once and for all if a strait existed between the southern coast of New Holland and Van Diemen's Land, or if it was all part of the same landmass. For Bass, this mystery was in need of a solution sooner rather than later, especially in light of *Sydney Cove*'s unfortunate demise off the coast of Van Diemen's Land.

Once back in Sydney, Bass had no trouble convincing Governor Hunter to support his proposed expedition. Hunter was equally intrigued by the conundrum: he had published an opinion piece following his voyage on *Sirius* from Cape Town to Port Jackson in 1789, his premise being based on observations he made when the ship was sailing 'between the islands of Schooten and Furneaux and Point Hicks':

> ... from our having felt an easterly set of current and when
> the wind was from that quarter (north-west), we had an
> uncommon large sea, there is reason to believe that there is
> in that space either a very deep gulf or a strait, which may
> separate Van Diemen's Land from New Holland.

Should it be proven that a strait existed, then the passage from England to Port Jackson would be shortened by some 300 nautical miles, and the ships would, more often than not, be sailing in more favourable weather conditions. Hunter had a high regard for Bass, which was evident in a letter he sent to the Duke of Portland in which he described the surgeon as 'a young man of a well-informed mind and an active disposition'. Hunter added that he was impressed by the fact that Bass had offered himself for the benefit of the public service while *Reliance* was laid up. He also noted that 'nothing would gratify him more effectually than my allowing him the use of a good boat and permitting him to man her with volunteers from the King's ships'.

The governor arranged for Bass to be provided with a well-found, double-ended whaleboat measuring 28 feet seven inches overall and built using banksia and cedar, both native timbers. Sufficient provisions for a six-week voyage were put aboard, and the required six volunteers were drawn from the ships in port at the time. Sadly, while the efforts of these few men were superbly heroic, only John Thistle became known to history as a crewmember.

It took Bass little more than a month to prepare for the voyage. On the evening of 3 December 1797, with everything in readiness, he stepped into the stern sheets of the whaleboat and took the helm. The crew positioned their oars between the thole pins on the gunwale and began to row the boat away from the shore and out of Sydney Cove. In a scene that would likely have included an envious Matthew Flinders, cheers from well-wishers filled the air as the small boat departed.

Bass's hopes for a smooth start to this testing ordeal were quickly dashed that night as the men got their first taste of the frequent southerly busters. This gale was so strong that it forced Bass to change course and take shelter in Port Hacking. A day or so later, when conditions had improved, they pressed on south, Bass's first point of interest being 'a hole of twenty-five or thirty feet in diameter; into which the sea washed up by a subterraneous passage'.

This would later become known as the Blowhole, and the region as Kiama.

Three days after departing Sydney, and while sailing in close proximity to the coast, Bass observed a pristine strip of white sand that formed a gentle arc; at its southern end was a delta-like shallow entrance to a river system. It was sufficiently appealing for him to stop there for three days so they could explore the area. When they eventually departed, Bass's impressions were such that he decided to name it Shoals Haven.

After rowing and sailing for 12 more miles, the men saw high cliffs standing as the entrance to a bay which Bass described, according to Flinders, as being 'a large open place of very unpromising appearance'. The expanse of water had been named Jervis Bay by Lieutenant Richard Bowen, a commander of the Third Fleet, which had passed the entrance in 1791. It appears that Bass didn't explore the bay to any great extent; in later years, the beautiful beaches that line the shores of Jervis Bay were declared to have the whitest sand in the world.

As well as taking the opportunity to explore the coastline as he progressed south, Bass made every effort to keep the boat's supply of fresh water at maximum capacity. When they reached the sheltered waters of what was known as Bateman Bay, however, a 12-mile excursion inland on the river failed to find a drop. Equally surprising was the absence of natives anywhere along the river, even though numerous humpies were sighted.

On 17 December, much to Bass's delight, the wind turned favourable, coming from the north-west, so he had no hesitation in launching the boat and pushing on. It was a superb run under sail that day, until another classic southerly change burst forth and again forced them to run for cover. They took shelter under a headland, where they beached the boat. The following day, when the seas abated to the degree where the whaleboat could enter a nearby shallow creek, Bass took the opportunity to explore inland. In a very short time he was captivated by the scenery that came with what he described as 'one of the prettiest of harbours ... Every small bight has its little sandy beach ... I have named this place Barmouth Creek.' It was later renamed Pambula.

After enjoying a night of restful sleep on the beach, the promise of another day of following winds saw the crew awake at first light. It was 19 December, and about two hours after the dipping lug sail was hoisted and trimmed to best catch the breeze, they had covered another 20 nautical miles towards their ultimate goal – the wide expanse of water they most wanted to explore. Their course kept them close to shore, and at this time a large and interesting bay began to become visible off the starboard bow. Bass noted that it comprised two large bights, so he named it Twofold Bay but decided to leave any exploration until the return voyage. With ominous clouds forming on the southern horizon, it was more important to press on and cover as many miles as possible before the southerly change arrived and stymied their progress.

Fortunately, when the front did arrive it was not as strong as expected, so with no accommodating shore or bay in sight, the group anchored close to the coast and slept on board. The following day the sea breeze returned and they enjoyed a rollicking and rapid downwind ride on a stiff north-easterly wind, until they reached the south-east corner of New Holland – Cape Howe – at midday. From here, a westerly component came into their course, and less than an hour later the seven seafarers were experiencing more exhilarating sailing as the whaleboat scudded down sparkling and blue-hued ocean swells just a short distance off the southern tip of Gabo Island – which, like Cape Howe, had been named by Captain Cook in 1770. They changed course again, this time to close on the coastline, and much to their delight they soon found a river and lagoon where they could refill their water casks.

Yet another gale began lashing the coast while the men were ashore, and it would literally stop them in their tracks for nine days. This meant spending Christmas Day exploring the lowlands and hills adjacent to the shore; it was not until New Year's Eve that the weather had calmed enough for them to resume their coastal probe to the west. That night, as if to welcome the coming year, the explorers were treated to one of nature's spectacles. Around midnight on what was a still, cloudless and clear evening, the brilliance of a full moon transformed the beach into a stripe of silver as far as they could see. While they could hear the dull, thunder-like sound of the surf rolling onto the beach, they were almost mesmerised by reflected moonbeams dancing in time with the gentle motion of the waves on a black and shiny sea, with a seabird occasionally sweeping silently across the scene. It was one of those surreal and special nights that cause men to love the sea: there was an almost overwhelming feeling of isolation and insignificance at being on the surface of the vast planet, yet it was at the same time an experience few others would know.

More remarkable still was that the land beyond the beach was full of mystery and beauty known only to its native population. With so little wind, the whaleboat made slow progress under sail, but the calm conditions allowed the men to get some sleep. In the morning, when first light began to flood the sky, there was still no end to the arc of sandy beach; accordingly, Bass named it Long Beach. In 1841 it became commonly known as Ninety Mile Beach.

Conditions remained perfect for sailing over the next few days. With the whaleboat averaging five knots and more, it was covering between 100 and 120 nautical miles every 24 hours. On 2 January Bass sighted what he believed to be some of the Furneaux group of islands; as this was where the crew of *Sydney Cove* was marooned, he decided to try to find the site and restock his dwindling food supplies.

Initially, the wind was favourable for a course to the south-south-east, but later in the day a change in wind direction brought rapidly rising seas – and, consequently, damage to the boat. Initially, Bass decided to press on in the vain hope that land might be sighted ahead, but as the waves built so their progress was slowed.

It took just one large and very steep wave for Bass to abandon his dogged determination and run for cover. As the whaleboat's bow burst through the crest of the wave and sent spray flying, there was nothing but air behind – no gently sloping back – so a crash-landing inevitably followed. The impact was too much for the cedar planking, and instantly a significant leak opened up in the starboard bow.

Bass knew immediately that there was only one thing to do to save the situation: tack the boat so that the damaged section would be above water, then turn the boat on a course back to the north, where they knew they would find land. They sailed on through what proved to be a drama-filled night, with Bass never quite sure whether his boat would remain seaworthy. Later, he modestly noted, 'We had a bad night of it, but the excellent qualities of the boat brought us through.' Really, it was his skill as a sailor that saved those aboard.

Early the next day, 3 January, land was sighted off the bow. As they rowed towards the shore, the crew saw seven men standing on the beach, whom they presumed to be natives. But much to their utter amazement, these men were convicts who had stolen a boat at Port Jackson and escaped.

It was a miracle that Bass had found them, and their story about how they came to be there was similarly incredible. The predicament faced by these men had started three months earlier, in October 1797, when they were part of a 14-man gang transporting stone by boat from Port Jackson to the recently established settlement on the Hawkesbury River, about 30 miles to the north. One day, while preparing to undertake their task, the men overpowered their guards, took command of the boat, loaded it with what provisions they could and headed for the high seas. A subsequent search by boat to the north and south had failed to find them; the men had set sail southwards in a perfect breeze and were well ahead of their pursuers.

The news that *Sydney Cove* had been beached on Preservation Island had led the convicts to concoct a far-fetched plan that would see them sail to the island, overpower anyone who was still there, repair and refloat the ship and sail it to China or another destination where they could find freedom. Yet a lack of seafaring and navigational skills led to the men becoming hopelessly lost off the inhospitable coastline, and with their rations running low and starvation looming, they decided to stop at an island they had found. Once there, key members of the gang decided that the easiest way to take the pressure off the meagre provisions they had remaining was to lure seven of their company to shore and then sail away without them.

When Bass arrived, these seven men had been on the island for five weeks, surviving on birds, seals and wildlife. Bass could do little to help them: he had neither sufficient rations nor space on the whaleboat to accommodate them over any distance, so he could only promise to return to the island on his return voyage to Sydney Town and do what he could then to assist.

Once Bass's crew had patched the boat as best they could, they continued to cruise along the coast to the west until they reached a large bay, which he named Western Port – because at that stage it was the westernmost bay that had been discovered. It was essential that they survey this waterway and also look for water, but not long after they sailed through the entrance yet another gale howled in from the south-west and made life extremely miserable.

The combination of these adverse elements, and the necessity to repair the boat properly, saw them stay within the bay for 13 days. During that time, Bass landed on Phillip Island, at the bay's entrance; he recorded in his diary that it was 'mostly barren, but is covered with shrubs and some diminutive trees'. The party saw clear evidence that natives had been in the region in considerable number, but they sighted only four. Bass hoped to make direct contact with them but was left to note that 'their shyness prevented communication'. The absence of natives caused him to deduce that they had more than likely moved into the hills, because the all too evident drought had brought about a lack of drinking water. Even so, food in the form of kangaroos, ducks and wild fowl was plentiful.

Bass had been away from Port Jackson for seven weeks, one week longer than planned, yet he still had no positive evidence that the coastal waters they were traversing were part of a strait or gulf. And the return voyage was still ahead of them. He was concerned about their diminishing provisions, even though they were successfully hunting wild birds and salting them down for food, so, reluctantly, he elected not to continue sailing to the west and instead to retrace their course home. Had he continued west for little more than 20 nautical miles, he would have discovered a huge bay covering 745 square miles – 35 times larger than Port Jackson. This bay would remain unknown for another four years, until John Murray sailed *Lady Nelson* through the entrance and made the discovery. It is now Port Phillip Bay and has the city of Melbourne on its northern shore.

True to his word, Bass returned to the island where he had found the seven convicts. Since leaving them a few weeks earlier, and knowing they could not survive on the island much longer, he had struggled to find a means to save their lives. Matthew Flinders related what Bass had subsequently explained to him:

> Mr Bass was able to execute the project he had formed for the seven convicts. It was impossible to take them all into the boat; therefore to five, whom he set upon the main land, he gave a musket, half his ammunition, some hooks and lines, a light cooking kettle, and directions how to proceed in their course toward Port Jackson. The remaining two, one of whom was old and the other diseased, he took into the boat with the consent of the crew, who readily agreed to divide the daily bannock [bread] into nine with them. He then bore away, with a fresh wind at west.

Their parting was a distressing ordeal for Bass and his volunteers, as they knew it would be near impossible for the five men to reach Port Jackson – a distance of more than 500 miles along a trackless, inhospitable and unexplored coast, where it was almost certain they would meet hostile natives – but there was nothing more that could be done.

Having given the convicts a chance to survive, Bass continued with his exploration. While doing so, he regularly wrote about being amid the islands of 'Furneaux's Land', but Flinders would later explain that, according to his own calculations, it appeared that Bass had been mistaken. Flinders wrote in *A Voyage to Terra Australis*:

> I have continued to make use of the term Furneaux's Land conformably to Mr Bass' journal; but the position of this land

is so different from that supposed to have been seen by captain Furneaux, that it cannot be the same, as Mr Bass was afterwards convinced. At our recommendation governor Hunter called it Wilson's Promontory, in compliment to my friend Thomas Wilson, Esq of London.

Foul weather yet again interrupted the return voyage, so Bass spent some days investigating the land and waters around the promontory. During this time, he became convinced that they were sailing on the waters of a massive strait. This, too, was detailed by Flinders:

> ... the rise of tide found to be ten or eleven feet, ten hours
> and a quarter after the moon passed over the meridian. The
> flood, after sweeping south-westward along the great eastern
> beach, strikes off for the Seal Islands and the promontory,
> and then runs westward, past it, at the rate of two or
> three miles an hour: the ebb tide sets to the eastward.
> 'Whenever it shall be decided,' says Mr Bass in his journal,
> 'that the opening between this and Van Diemen's Land is a
> strait, this rapidity of tide, and the long south-west swell that
> seems to be continually rolling in upon the coast to the
> westward, will then be accounted for.'

When writing about the promontory, Bass noted that it was 'well worthy of being the boundary point of a large strait, and a corner stone of this great island New Holland'.

On 2 February, the whaleboat sailed along the eastern side of the promontory and reached Corner Inlet, where the men were forced to take shelter. Much to Bass's surprise, when they went ashore they found the five convicts on the beach. They had covered 20 miles since Bass left them but were now stranded, being unable to find a way to cross a wide and deep channel at the entrance to a nearby inlet. Bass used the whaleboat to transport them to the next beach so they could continue on their way. Flinders later noted that 'nothing more had been heard of these five men, so late as 1803'. Their disappearance is a mystery to this day.

Unbeknown to Bass, while they were at Corner Inlet, Flinders was aboard the schooner *Francis* and 24 hours into a voyage south from Port Jackson to the wreck of *Sydney Cove*. In fact, the two great friends would pass each other at sea a few days later while travelling in opposite directions off the southern coast of New South Wales, but they did not make visual contact. The schooner was on its second mission to the wreck on Preservation Island to retrieve the cargo and men who were waiting to be rescued. While this voyage was being planned, Flinders had seen that there was an opportunity to explore the Furneaux Group while *Francis* remained at anchor there, and Governor Hunter had agreed.

It was not until 9 February that the wind was coming from a quarter that allowed Bass to set sail from Corner Inlet and continue to head home. However, the following morning the wind changed direction to the east and strengthened to near gale force. This caused the waves to dramatically increase in height, to the point where the whaleboat was in danger of being swamped. Bass had no desire to backtrack all the way to Corner Inlet, so he decided to brave the surf and take refuge on a nearby beach. It was a gutsy effort, and fortunately it was successful: all the men and the boat survived.

Once on the beach, the crew encountered a group of natives, which they had seldom done since leaving their home port. The men and women approached the strange-looking and oddly clad Englishmen with little hesitation and demonstrated a previously unseen level of friendliness, leading Bass to believe that this was the first time they had met white men.

On the morning of 11 February, Bass woke early to check the weather. When the dawn brought sufficient light he realised that the clouds building in the south-western sky were threatening yet another gale, so he decided to take the risk and run for it. The whaleboat was launched before sun-up, and the crew rowed as hard and fast as possible out through the surf until they were clear of any threat from the white water. Bass steered them onto a course that would take them around Gabo Island and then Cape Howe, which was 100 nautical miles away.

Challenging winds and rough seas would dog them almost all the way north. It was 15 February when the whaleboat finally reached Two Fold Bay, but Bass decided it would not be prudent to explore the region thoroughly. Instead, he elected to press on through the night while the conditions remained favourable. Nine days later, and after 1200 nautical miles of sailing, the fatigued and weather-worn seafarers, along with their two passengers, rounded the southern headland of Port Jackson and enjoyed the security that came with being on home waters.

Flinders would later reflect on the achievement of his friend:

It should be remembered, that Mr Bass sailed with only six weeks' provisions; but with the assistance of occasional supplies of petrels, fish, seal's flesh, and a few geese and black swans, and by abstinence, he had been enabled to prolong his voyage beyond eleven weeks. His ardour and perseverance were crowned, in despite of the foul winds which so much opposed him, with a degree of success not to have been anticipated from such feeble means. In three hundred miles of coast, from Port Jackson to the Ram Head, he added a number of particulars which had escaped Captain Cook; and will always escape any navigator in a first discovery, unless he have the time and means of joining a close examination by boats, to what may be seen from the ship.

Our previous knowledge of the coast scarcely extended beyond the Ram Head; and there began the harvest in which Mr Bass was ambitious to place the first reaping hook. The new coast was traced three hundred miles; and instead of trending southward to join itself to Van Diemen's Land, as Captain Furneaux had supposed, he found it, beyond a certain point, to take a direction nearly opposite, and to assume the appearance of being exposed to the buffetings of an open sea. Mr Bass, himself, entertained no doubt of the existence of a wide strait, separating Van Diemen's Land from New South Wales; and he yielded with the greatest reluctance to the necessity of returning, before it was so fully ascertained as to admit of no doubt in the minds of others. But he had the satisfaction of placing at the end of his new coast, an extensive and useful harbour, surrounded with a country superior to any other known in the southern parts of New South Wales.

It is most interesting to note that Flinders declared without hesitation that he considered Bass's endeavours to be unequalled in the annals of maritime history. Perhaps he had forgotten the incredible achievement of his captain aboard *Providence*, William Bligh, who had guided his 23-foot open launch across 3600 nautical miles of open ocean with virtually no food or navigational equipment.

In recognition of Bass's voyage, Governor Hunter sent a despatch to the Secretary of State in London. He advised that while it did appear there was a strait between New South Wales and Van Diemen's Land, it was still to be confirmed: 'He found an open ocean westward, and by the mountainous sea which rolled from that quarter, and no land discoverable in that direction, we have much reason to conclude that there is an open strait through.'

While Bass's expedition had not resolved the question that had been its prime motivation, it was without doubt a great success and had explored much new coastline of New Holland. Even so, Bass returned to Port Jackson frustrated by the knowledge that, had there been a larger vessel available to him, he would almost certainly have achieved his goal.

CHAPTER EIGHT

A Strait and Island Found

The first effort to recover the men and cargo from *Sydney Cove* in mid-1797 was stained with tragedy. On learning that the ship and the bulk of its crew were stranded more than 400 nautical miles to the south, Governor Hunter immediately ordered that the colony's 41-ton schooner, *Francis*, and the privately-owned 30-foot *Eliza* be deployed on a rescue mission as soon as possible. *Francis*, launched in 1793, was a robust little vessel that had been assembled using frames shipped from England as well as local timbers. The considerably smaller *Eliza*, which displaced around ten tons, was best described as a sloop-rigged, fully-decked longboat. Her experienced captain was Archibald Armstrong, previously the master of *Supply*.

It was the depth of winter when the two vessels reached Preservation Island and took aboard as many men and as much cargo as they could carry. Once fully loaded, they departed in company for the return voyage to Port Jackson on 21 June. Conditions were initially favourable, but within 24 hours a brutal storm that had brewed deep in the Southern Ocean hammered the tiny *Eliza* and sent her to a watery grave, along with the ten men believed to be aboard her. No trace of the vessel was ever found. This tragedy meant that the stranding of *Sydney Cove* had directly contributed to the loss of 24 lives in a matter of months.

The greatly saddened master of *Sydney Cove*, Captain Hamilton, met with Governor Hunter as soon as he arrived in Sydney Town aboard *Francis*. He briefed Hunter on the circumstances around the loss of his ship and what had to be done to complete the salvage effort. Hunter's decision was to send *Francis* back to the wreck to collect the remaining men and cargo, with Captain Reed in charge once again. Hamilton would accompany him to supervise the task.

Flinders' close allegiance to the governor meant that he was aware of this plan in the early stages of its preparation, and with his involvement in the rebuilding of *Reliance* essentially completed, he suggested to Hunter that he should sail aboard *Francis* and carry out some exploration of the Furneaux Group, where the wreck was located:

> On this occasion I was happy enough to obtain Governor
> Hunter's permission to embark in the schooner; in order to
> make such observations serviceable to geography and
> navigation, as circumstances might afford; and Mr Reed, the
> master, was directed to forward these views as far as was
> consistent with the main objects of his voyage.

Governor Hunter explained in a despatch back to England why he had decided that Flinders should make the voyage: 'I sent in the schooner Lieutenant Flinders of the *Reliance*, a young man well-qualified, in order to give him an opportunity of making what observations he could among those islands.'

Francis exited Port Jackson on 1 February, and as she progressed down the coast Flinders successfully impressed upon the captain the need to sail as near to the shoreline as safe navigation would allow. This gave him the opportunity to confirm the location of known land features on his chart, and to add new ones. One such discovery came two days out of port, when Flinders sighted Montague Island, south of Batemans Bay.

> Soon after noon, land was in sight to the S. S. E., supposed to
> be the Point Dromedary of Captain Cook's chart; but, to my
> surprise, it proved to be an island not laid down, though lying
> near two leagues from the coast. The whole length of this
> island is about one mile and a quarter, north and south; the two
> ends are a little elevated, and produce small trees …. This little
> island, I was afterwards informed, had been seen in the ship
> *Surprise*, and honoured with the name of Montague. When
> Captain Cook passed this part of the coast his distance from it
> was five leagues, and too great for its form to be accurately
> distinguished. There is little doubt that Montague Island was
> then seen, and mistaken for a point running out from under
> Mount Dromedary.

Francis sailed around the clock, and the eager Flinders remained on deck for as much of each night as possible, to ensure he missed nothing of interest. The morning after the position of Montague Island was confirmed on his chart, Flinders sighted and named another prominent feature of the south-east corner of New Holland.

> At nine we came abreast of a smooth, sloping point which,
> from its appearance, and being unnoticed in Captain Cook's

chart, I named Green Cape. On the south side, the coast trends
west, three or four miles, into a sandy bight, and then
southward to Cape Howe ... There were several fires upon the
shore; and near one of them, upon an eminence, stood seven
natives, silently contemplating the schooner as she passed.

As they sailed further south, they came across a previously
unknown cluster of islands, which Flinders placed on his chart as
the Kent Group: a tribute to his brave and heroic friend William
Kent, the man whose exceptional seafaring skills had saved *Supply*
on her return voyage from Cape Town the previous year.

On approach to the Furneaux Islands, Flinders became
intrigued by an inexplicable anomaly in the ship's compass bearings
when she changed course. His sightings showed a variation of up
to three degrees at times; an inaccurate compass reading could
easily bring a ship to grief. The cause of these anomalies would
challenge Flinders for many years to come.

On the evening of 12 February, *Francis* came to anchor in a
well-protected stretch of water on the eastern side of Preservation
Island. Flinders noted that:

The ship *Sydney Cove* had been run on shore between
Preservation and Rum Islands, and part of her hull was still
lying there; but the sea thrown in by western gales had, in
great measure, broken her up, and scattered the beams,
timbers, and parts of the cargo, upon all the neighbouring
shores.

On 16 February Flinders was provided with a small boat so he
could undertake a five-day excursion around and onto the adjacent
islands. The initial stage was through Armstrong's Channel, which

separated two of the larger islands in the Furneaux Group. It had been given this name as a mark of respect for Captain Archibald Armstrong, following the loss of *Eliza* some months earlier.

Flinders' survey also presented the opportunity to observe and identify birds, animals and sea life, including the 'womat' (wombat), which was prevalent on the islands. So too were hair seals, as Flinders recorded:

These rocks were also frequented by hair seals, and some of them (the old males) were of an enormous size, and of extraordinary power. I levelled my gun at one, which was sitting on the top of a rock with his nose extended up towards the sun, and struck him with three musket balls. He rolled over, and plunged into the water; but in less than half an hour had taken his former station and attitude. On firing again, a stream of blood spouted forth from his breast to some yards distance, and he fell back, senseless. On examination, the six balls were found lodged in his breast; and one, which occasioned his death, had pierced the heart: his weight was equal to that of a common ox.

During his stay, Flinders noted that not all the water available on the island was potable: 'Well tasted fresh water is collected, at certain seasons, in small pools near the east end of Preservation Island; but that which drains from the rocks was first used by the *Sydney-Cove*'s crew, until several of them died.'

It became apparent that thousands of shearwaters – also known as sooty petrels – had been killed by the crew of *Sydney Cove* – some for food, but some by trampling on their burrows, which covered almost every square foot of Preservation Island. Flinders also made some interesting notes regarding the penguins on the islands:

The penguin of these islands is of the kind denominated little. They were generally found sitting on the rocks, in the day time, or in caverns near the water side. They burrow in the same manner as the sooty petrel; but, except in the time of rearing their young, do not seem, like it, to return to their holes every night. Their flesh is so strong and fishy, that had not the skins served to make caps, rather handsome, and impenetrable to rain, the penguins would have escaped molestation.

With the remnants of the crew and cargo from *Sydney Cove* aboard *Francis*, she set sail on 25 February for Port Jackson, but the as yet unanswered question about the existence of a strait to the north of Van Diemen's Land led Flinders to request Captain Reed to sail to the south-south-west so he could better gauge the land formations in that area. Before turning north towards home, and having observed the smoke from fires on the land, he made some important notes:

The smokes which had constantly been seen rising from it showed that there were inhabitants; and this, combined with the circumstance of there being none upon the islands, seemed to argue a junction of Van Diemen's Land with New South Wales ... On the other hand, the great strength of the tides setting westward, past the islands, could only be caused by some exceedingly deep inlet, or by a passage through to the southern Indian Ocean. These contradictory circumstances were very embarrassing; and the schooner not being placed at my disposal, I was obliged, to my great regret, to leave this important geographical question undecided.

When *Francis* arrived back in Port Jackson, Bass had been home for two weeks. He and Flinders met almost immediately and compared their notes on the coastlines they had just explored – one to the south, near Van Diemen's Land, and the other to the north, on the coast of New Holland. All this had done was to deepen the mystery that had confounded them for some time. '[T]here seemed to want no other proof of the existence of a passage between New South Wales and Van Diemen's Land,' wrote Flinders, 'than that of sailing positively through it; but however anxious I was to obtain this proof, the gratification of my desire was required to be suspended by a voyage to Norfolk Island in the *Reliance*.'

Flinders' commitment to duty saw him aboard *Reliance* for a two-month return voyage to the island between May and July 1798. Its primary purpose was to transfer to the island a surgeon, D'Arcy Wentworth (whose son William – then seven years old – would later be one of the three men to first cross the Blue Mountains).

When he returned to Port Jackson, Flinders was eager to start sailing south with Bass so they could gather conclusive proof of the existence of a gulf or strait to the north of Van Diemen's Land, but again he had to curb his enthusiasm. He was first ordered to sit as a member of the Vice-Admiralty Court of New South Wales and hear a case relating to an attempted mutiny on the high seas aboard the convict ship *Barwell* between Cape Town and Sydney by some members of the New South Wales Corps. Ensign George Bond was one of the supposed ringleaders plotting the overthrow, but he and others were quickly clamped into irons after they were seen drinking a toast and shouting 'Damnation to the King and country!'. The court sat for six days before reaching a verdict of 'not guilty', due to insufficient evidence.

Governor Hunter, like Bass and Flinders, was almost certain that a passage existed between Van Diemen's Land and the southern coast of New Holland, linking the Indian Ocean and the Furneaux Islands, so he had no hesitation in preparing a mission that would prove their theory. A suitable vessel – the recently built *Norfolk*, a 25-ton burthen sloop measuring 35 feet overall and with a beam of 11 feet – came their way by chance. She had a bowsprit not much shorter than her length on deck, and her hull was well-rounded in shape. She had been built on Norfolk Island as part of plans to establish a more frequent link with Port Jackson for supplies and despatches, but as soon as she arrived at Sydney Cove, in June 1798, she was commandeered by the governor, named *Norfolk* and placed under the command of Flinders, who in turn had 'the happiness to associate my friend Bass in this new expedition, and to form an excellent crew of eight volunteers from the king's ships'. However, Flinders faced one frustration: 'a time keeper, that essential instrument to accuracy in nautical surveys ... was still impossible to obtain'.

Norfolk was not the ideal boat for such an undertaking: she was chosen only because she was the best available at the time. To the expert eye, her hull shape suggested she was robust but in fact she was not. The biggest problem was that she was 'soft', simply because her builders had used the only available timber, Norfolk pine, for her hull planks. On her maiden voyage from the island to Port Jackson, it was quickly realised that this material flexed in rough seas, causing the seams to open up and the vessel to take on water. It was only because she had two pumps installed that the crew was able to stay ahead of the leaks in the worst weather.

Some modifications were carried out in a bid to make the claustrophobic and dark quarters below deck more habitable for the ten men on board. With that work complete, she cleared Port Jackson on 7 October and began nosing her way south on what was planned to be a 12-week endeavour. Governor Hunter's commission gave Flinders the 'authority to penetrate behind Furneaux's Islands;

and should a strait be found, to pass through it and return by the south end of Van Diemen's Land; making such examinations and surveys on the way as circumstances might permit.'

With the wind being fair and with the assistance of the south-flowing current, *Norfolk* was making around six knots, and by the following morning Mount Dromedary was abeam. They reached Cape Howe at ten p.m. and Flinders decided to lower the sails and lay a-hull until daylight, in order to get the best possible navigational reference from the cape before venturing onto the broad expanse of open water to the south. His plan to drift with the whim of the weather was quickly put to rest at first light, when conditions turned against them: 'The wind had veered to south-west, and the weather having a bad appearance, we bore up for Two-fold Bay.'

Once at anchor inside the well-protected bay, they put their time to good use. Bass explored the shoreline and its surrounds, while Flinders did an extensive survey of the bay by small boat. Flinders and the men accompanying him experienced more than they expected, however.

Our attention was suddenly called by the screams of three women, who took up their children and ran off in great consternation. Soon afterward a man made his appearance. He was of a middle age, unarmed, except with a whaddie, or wooden scimitar, and came up to us seemingly with careless confidence. We made much of him, and gave him some biscuit; and he in return presented us with a piece of gristly fat, probably of whale. This I tasted; but watching an opportunity to spit it out when he should not be looking, I perceived him doing precisely the same thing with our biscuit, whose taste was probably no more agreeable to him, than his whale was to me. Walking onward with us to the

long beach, our new acquaintance picked up from the grass a
long wooden spear, pointed with bone; but this he hid a
little further on, making signs that he should take it on his
return. The commencement of our trigonometrical
operations was seen by him with indifference, if not
contempt; and he quitted us, apparently satisfied that, from
people who could thus occupy themselves seriously, there
was nothing to be apprehended.

Two days later they were still holed up due to the inclement
weather, so Flinders began surveying the western shore of the bay.
Once again, he had an interesting encounter with the local
inhabitants:

> I was preparing the artificial horizon for observing the
> latitude, when a party of seven or eight natives broke out in
> exclamation upon the bank above us, holding up their open
> hands to show they were unarmed. We were three in
> number, and, besides a pocket pistol, had two muskets.
> These they made no objection to our bringing, and we sat
> down in the midst of the party. It consisted entirely of young
> men, who were better made, and cleaner in their persons
> than the natives of Port Jackson usually are; and their
> countenances bespoke both good will and curiosity, though
> mixed with some degree of apprehension. Their curiosity
> was mostly directed to our persons and dress, and constantly
> drew off their attention from our little presents, which
> seemed to give but a momentary pleasure. The approach of
> the sun to the meridian calling me down to the beach, our
> visitors returned into the woods, seemingly well satisfied
> with what they had seen.

Bad weather forced Flinders to abandon an attempt to leave the bay on 12 October, but they finally got underway in a freshening north-easterly sea breeze two days later. On reaching Cape Howe, the two explorers agreed that a course of south-west-by-west would bring them in sight of the Furneaux Islands, which their chart had at 39 degrees south latitude.

Throughout the daylight hours all eyes scanned the horizon in search of land, which was sighted on 17 October and identified by Flinders: it was 'the largest of the two clusters which I had discovered when in the Francis, and named Kent's Group'. Soon after, however, they had a significant setback when, while taking soundings at around 30 fathoms, their only deep-sea lead line parted and they lost the lead. Because of this they would be unable to record the fathoms in the deeper waters for the remainder of the voyage and would have to make any approach to land more cautiously. The remaining lead line was only suitable for shallow-water readings.

Twenty-four hours later, islands in the Furneaux Group were sighted, but threatening weather caused Flinders to stay at sea under storm sails that night. There was nothing safer than sea room in the conditions.

Finally, before noon on 19 October, they were able to close on the shore and find a safe anchorage at the eastern end of Preservation Island. It was apparent that the basic structure that Captain Hamilton had built and called home before he abandoned it nine months earlier was still standing, so Bass and Flinders went ashore to see whether the chickens and pigeons he had left there remained. 'The house remained in nearly the same state,' wrote Flinders in his journal, 'but its tenants were not to be found, having probably fallen a prey to the hawks.'

For the next 11 days *Norfolk* remained at anchor while a howling gale and driving rain lashed the islands almost incessantly.

Once they were able to weigh anchor, they continued to sail among the islands, noting latitudes and longitudes for as many as possible, sketching their profiles and describing the topography, flora and fauna. They could have stayed and explored considerably longer, but the real challenge lay to the west – that point where they would either exit a strait or be contained by a landmass that extended north to New Holland.

The logical course from where they were at this time was to reach the northern coast of Van Diemen's Land, which they could see less than 15 miles away, then cruise to the west along that hitherto unknown coastline, until they found their answer.

They made their first landfall at a point they named Cape Portland, and from there they began making cautious progress to the west – but it was almost not cautious enough. They were quite close to the shore when the wind faded to a whisper. Suddenly, they realised *Norfolk* was being swept along by a fast-flowing tidal current towards a shallow reef – and there was nothing they could do about it. The little ship was trapped in a wildly swirling eddy, and all the crew could do was hang on and hope it would not strike the bottom.

There was not even time to release the anchor, which could well have made matters worse, in any case. A shout went up when the lead line showed two fathoms – just twelve feet – which meant there were only inches to spare under the keel. The reef was clearly visible to those men peering anxiously over the side. They knew that if they hit the bottom, *Norfolk*'s pine hull planking was unlikely to withstand the impact.

Much to everyone's relief, this drama ended as quickly as it had begun. The next heave of the lead showed they had cleared the rocky ledge and were back in deep water. With still virtually no wind, *Norfolk* was only sailed one mile to the west, where she was anchored in 11 fathoms, just to the east of Waterhouse Island, named in recognition of the master of *Reliance*.

On 2 November a gentle breeze wafted in from the east, so the explorers decided to seize the opportunity and cover more miles westward. After hoisting the sails and weighing anchor, they first guided *Norfolk* through the two-mile-wide passage between Waterhouse Island and the mainland. At the time, Flinders deduced that, with the island being home to an incredible number of seabirds and seals, 'the natives of Van Diemen's Land were not able to get across here, and that, consequently, they had no canoes upon this part of the coast'. The ten men aboard *Norfolk* were constantly in awe of the crystal-clear waters they were crossing, and the magnificent bays, 'pleasant hills' and golden beaches that lay off to leeward. Mother Nature was excelling herself.

About 45 nautical miles west-south-west of Waterhouse Island, they sighted and named Low Head. Beyond here, an important discovery lay in waiting.

There was some appearance of an opening, and at two o'clock, this excited so much hope that I ventured to bear away before the wind. We advanced rapidly with the flood, and at four, had passed Low Head and were steering S E by S, up an inlet of more than a mile wide. After advancing three miles, we approached a low, green island; and being uncertain which was the deepest side, I took the most direct ... From 8 fathoms, the next cast of the lead was 3½, and immediately the sloop was aground. Fortunately, the bottom was soft, and the strong flood dragged her over the bank without injury.

We could not but remark the contrast between the shores of this inlet, covered with grass and wood down to the water's edge, and the rocky sterile banks observed in sailing up Port Jackson: it spoke favourably for the country, and added to the satisfaction we felt in having made the discovery.

The 'inlet' they discovered on 4 November would be named the Tamar River, and in 1804 the colony's third settlement – after Sydney Town and Hobart Town – was established on its banks. It was named Patersonia, after its founding commandant, Lieutenant Colonel Paterson, but he later changed it to Launceston in honour of the colony's third governor, Philip Gidley King, who was born in Launceston, Cornwall.

The deeper the explorers moved upstream, the more intriguing this river became, so much so that they would spend the next 16 days exploring the waterways and the surrounding land. With their progress being virtually unimpeded by shallows, Flinders and Bass made sure they surveyed as much of the region as possible in the time available. They did not reach the point where Launceston is sited today, however, adjacent to the impressive Cataract Gorge. As was the case throughout this entire expedition, they sounded the depths, took sun sights to position the principal features on their chart, sketched the lie of the land, put names to many points of interest and documented their observations in considerable detail.

Flinders was surprised to see further evidence that the local Aboriginals did not have the means to cross expanses of water. He wrote that:

Green Island is covered with long, coarse grass and bushes, with a few small trees intermixed. The large, noisy gulls frequent it for the purpose of breeding, as do the swans, several of whose deserted nests were found with the broken

egg-shells in them. These were corroborating proofs, that the
natives of this part of Van Diemen's Land have not the
means of transporting themselves across the water; for Green
Island is scarcely two cables length from the shore.

There was a proliferation of wildlife on the banks of the river, so
the men returned from almost every excursion to the shore with
fresh supplies for their larder. These same excursions allowed
Flinders and Bass to seek contact with the natives but, unlike the
hunters, they had little success.

In returning to the sloop, I took off Mr Bass and his party,
together with a kangaroo weighing between eighty and
ninety pounds, which he had shot out of a considerable
flock. Our fresh provisions were still further increased by an
addition of six swans, caught this evening with the boat.

There were many recent traces of natives on the shore;
and after returning to the sloop, we saw, on the opposite side
of the arm a man who employed or amused himself by
setting fire to the grass in different places. He did not stay to
receive us, and we rowed down to Middle Island where a
smoke was rising. The natives shunned us there also; for soon
after landing, I saw three of them walk up from the shoal
which joins Middle Island to the opposite low, sandy point.
The party appeared to consist of a man, a woman, and a boy;
and the two first had something wrapped round them which
resembled cloaks of skins.

The strength of the tidal flows experienced each day left no doubt
that this was a major river system that had its origins well inland,
and that was enough to convince the explorers they should stay and

investigate everything they could before they had to return to sea and continue sailing along the coast to the west. *Norfolk* was small enough to be rowed using long oars mounted on the gunwale, and the men often used that form of propulsion when the tide was slack or running with them. Most days, though, they would work the strong flood tides to move *Norfolk* further upstream, and then, when it came time to depart, ride the ebb back to the coast.

The time to turn back came on 10 November, and it was another ten days before they cleared Low Head and returned to their westerly track. An unholy gale from the west-north-west quickly burst onto the scene. It was accompanied by rapidly rising seas, immediately making the northern coast of Van Diemen's Land a threatening lee shore for *Norfolk*, which was already struggling to make headway.

With only a heavily reefed mainsail and small jib set, Flinders, Bass and the crew did everything within their power to hold their ground against the might of the elements for more than 24 hours. Flinders noted that 'we were not without apprehensions of the shore for the following night, so much did the sloop drive to leeward'. The little *Norfolk* was rearing like a wild steer off the crest of every wave, all the time tossing cloudbursts of heavy spray through the air. Occasionally she would stagger and shudder under the burden of water on deck, which, as she rolled in response to the savage seas, would pour through the scuppers and down the topsides in long cascades. Pity the poor man on the tiller, struggling to peer through the spray and pelting rain while bracing himself against the violent motion of his charge.

Some hours later, the wind changed direction towards the west and brought a glimmer of respite. The change allowed *Norfolk* to alter course to the north; soon after, the crew sailed towards a safe anchorage in the lee of the Chappelle Isles, on the western side of the Furneaux Group. The explorers had been forced to retrace their tracks but they were now safe. Interestingly, it was Flinders who named this group – for reasons that would later become apparent. He also noticed a high peak on one of the islands that had the profile of a pyramid; he named it Mount Chappelle.

Resting at anchor presented Flinders with the opportunity to observe from the shore a lunar eclipse on 24 November; he logged all details of the transit of the Earth's shadow across the moon's face. The following day, when the gale eased, Flinders and Bass decided that, even though the wind was against them, they should depart the anchorage and beat to windward.

It wasn't a wise decision. Before long, they realised it was the sea state and not the wind that was impeding their progress, so they opted to bear away and seek shelter in Armstrong's Channel. Once there, they caught up with *Nautilus*, a sealer that had departed Sydney at the same time as *Norfolk*. *Nautilus* was under the command of Captain Charles Bishop, who had sailed to the region with the intention of hunting the herds of seals that inhabited the islands. It had been a very successful exercise: Bishop had on board 9000 sealskins and several tons of seal oil. This encounter, and Bass's subsequent meetings with Bishop, would have a major influence on the explorer's life, possibly even contributing to his mysterious disappearance some years later.

Nautilus was about to return to Sydney Town, so Flinders and Bass asked Bishop to inform Governor Hunter of the discoveries they had made so far, and to advise him that their schedule had been impeded considerably by the constant presence of contrary winds. The explorers then bade Bishop farewell.

That night, when the wind was calm, they decided to row *Norfolk* away from the anchorage and search for a favourable breeze offshore, one that would allow them to return to the coast of Van

Diemen's Land. Yet again, though, another harrowing gale appeared from beyond the horizon and forced them to run for shelter, this time inside the entrance of the river they had discovered near Low Head. It turned out to be very fortunate that they were able to reach this anchorage as the tempest which had forced them there '... was more violent and of longer continuance than any of the preceding'. It kept them holed up for almost a week, and inevitably despair and frustration descended upon all on board: nearly eight weeks of their planned twelve-week voyage had elapsed, and every day lost decreased their chance of completing their mission.

Finally, on 3 December, they were able to weigh anchor and guide *Norfolk* out of the river mouth, a wide waterway that was later named Port Dalrymple by Governor Hunter as a tribute to Alexander Dalrymple, the naval hydrographer. Once clear of Low Head, Bass and Flinders picked up a light breeze that favoured their course. It lasted for 48 hours, enabling them to reach the jagged cliffs of what they would name Rocky Cape, some 60 nautical miles west of Low Head. From there they sighted an interesting topographical feature about ten nautical miles to the north-west, a pot-shaped hill more than 400 feet high, which they named Circular Head. Flinders noted:

> Circular Head is a cliffy, round lump, in form much
> resembling a Christmas cake; and is joined to the main by
> a low, sandy isthmus. The land at the back is somewhat
> lower than the head, and is formed into very gentle slopes.
> A slight covering of withered grass gave it a smooth
> appearance; and some green bushes scattered over it
> much resembled, at a distance, a herd of seals basking
> upon a rock.

As they cruised past this headland at around ten a.m., 'three hummocks of land then came in sight to the north-westward, the southernmost and highest having something of a sugar-loaf form'.

It was then that the first signs indicating they might be about to unravel the mystery of the strait began to appear, but even so, Flinders was still not convinced that it existed.

> From the time of leaving Port Dalrymple no tide had been observed, until this morning. It ran with us, and continued until three o'clock; at which time low land was seen beyond the three hummocks. This trending of the coast so far to the north made me apprehend, that it might be found to join the land near Western Port, and thus disappoint our hopes of discovering an open passage to the westward; the water was also discoloured, as if we were approaching the head of a bay, rather than the issue of a strait; and on sounding, we had 17, and afterwards 15 fathoms on a sandy bottom.

During the afternoon of 7 December, 'a breeze sprung up from the south-westward, and threatened a gale from that boisterous quarter'. While sailing to windward was not *Norfolk*'s strong point, the crew managed to get her upwind to a position where, at six p.m., they achieved a good anchorage in the lee of the northernmost of the three 'hummocks' they had seen during the day. It was here that Flinders and Bass became increasingly confident that they were on the verge of a history-making discovery.

> Mr Bass and myself landed immediately to examine the country and the coast, and to see what food could be procured; for the long detention by foul winds had obliged me to make a reduction in the provisions, lest the object of

our voyage and return to Port Jackson should not be accomplished in the twelve weeks for which we were victualled. At dusk, we returned on board, having had little success as to any of the objects proposed; but with the knowledge of a fact, from which an interesting deduction was drawn: the tide had been running from the eastward all the afternoon, and contrary to expectation, we found it to be near low water by the shore; the flood, therefore, came from the west, and not from the eastward, as at Furneaux's Isles. This we considered to be a strong proof, not only of the real existence of a passage betwixt this land and New South Wales, but also that the entrance into the Southern Indian Ocean could not be far distant.

Still unaware that they were in the lee of an island, the explorers called on the crew to weigh anchor at six a.m. on 9 December. Using the light south-easterly wind to good effect, they soon rounded the north-east corner of the 'three-hummock land' and pursued a course along its northern shore. Although they did not know it, they were only five nautical miles from the point where they could change course to the south and sail down the western coast of Van Diemen's Land, thus revealing the existence of what would be named Bass Strait. Incredibly, though, it was a phenomenon of nature that held their greatest interest at that time – one that would, however, add to the evidence that there was a large island to their south.

A large flock of gannets was observed at daylight, to issue out of the great bight to the southward; and they were followed by such a number of the sooty petrels as we had never seen equalled. There was a stream of from fifty to eighty yards in depth, and of three hundred yards, or more, in breadth; the birds were not scattered, but flying as compactly as a free movement of their wings seemed to allow; and during a full hour and a half, this stream of petrels continued to pass without interruption, at a rate little inferior to the swiftness of the pigeon. On the lowest computation, I think the number could not have been less than a hundred millions; and we were thence led to believe, that there must be, in the large bight, one or more uninhabited islands of considerable size.

Calculations later published in Flinders' book, *A Voyage to Terra Australis*, revealed the magnitude of what he, Bass and the crew had observed.

Taking the stream to have been fifty yards deep by three hundred in width, and that it moved at the rate of thirty miles an hour, and allowing nine cubic yards of space to each bird, the number would amount to 151,500,000. The burrows required to lodge this quantity of birds would be 75,750,000; and allowing a square yard to each burrow, they would cover something more than 181 geographic square miles of ground.

Only a matter of hours later, *Norfolk* rounded the northernmost tip of an island, which Flinders named Hunter Island in honour of the governor of the colony. It was there that the men were left in no doubt that they had every reason to celebrate.

The coast on the west side of the channel lies nearly south, and rises in height as it advances towards the cliffy head ...

Beyond this there was nothing like main land to be seen; indeed, this western land itself had very little the appearance of being such, either in its form, or in its poor, starved vegetation. So soon as we had passed the north sloping point, a long swell was perceived to come from the south-west, such as we had not been accustomed to for some time. It broke heavily upon a small reef, lying a mile and a half from the point, and upon all the western shores; but, although it was likely to prove troublesome, and perhaps dangerous, Mr Bass and myself hailed it with joy and mutual congratulation, as announcing the completion of our long-wished-for discovery of a passage into the Southern Indian Ocean.

To the north-west, they could see a small, rocky island about six miles away, barely protruding above the surface of the ocean; it was one of more than 50 that would eventually be discovered in Bass Strait. It resembled a snow-capped peak, having a collar of white water surging onto its rocks and being blanketed by thousands of white birds. Needing to replenish their food stocks before heading south, Flinders and Bass decided to head to this conveniently located craggy little outcrop.

Once there, it became apparent that the water was too deep for anchoring, so while Bass took his musket and went ashore in the tender, Flinders stood off and cruised *Norfolk* slowly around the islet under considerably reduced sail. He observed that there was no evidence of land to the north, but 'clearly distinguishable in the opposite direction was a steep island at the distance of four leagues'. He was, in fact, looking at the north-western corner of Van Diemen's Land.

At 2.30 p.m. Bass returned 'with a boat load of seals and albatrosses' and reported that both species showed no fear of humans. The albatross, which were nesting, covered almost all the ground above high water on the island and did not 'derange themselves for the new visitors, other than to peck at their legs as they passed by'. The island's position was noted as 40 degrees and 25 minutes latitude and 2 degrees and 7 minutes longitude west of Port Dalrymple, and Flinders decided on a name for it: Albatross Island. *Norfolk* was then turned head-to-wind so that the fore-and-aft sails could be hoisted, and the helmsman bore away on a course that would leave Hunter Island on the larboard (port) side. Before long, another four small islands were sighted. Flinders named the largest of them Trefoil Island because it was shaped like a clover leaf; he noted on his chart that the entire group would be known as Hunter's Isles.

By now Flinders and Bass were convinced that the extended coastline they were seeing to the south was the western shore of Van Diemen's Land. It was a thought that excited them immensely, as they then knew they were about to position a very large landmass on the world map.

Their first point of interest was a cape with high black cliffs. It appeared treacherous and most uninviting, so, fittingly, they named it Cape Grim. Thirty years later, this name would assume an even more sinister air when four sheep farmers armed with muskets massacred 30 Aboriginals, before hurling many of the bodies from the top of the 60-metre-high cliffs surrounding Suicide Bay into the sea below.

By 11 December, two days after they turned south at Hunter Island, *Norfolk* was 50 miles down the coast when the crew saw a remarkable feature: a 750-foot-high, pyramid-shaped peak, which they estimated was about eight miles inland from the coast. Having positioned it on the chart, Flinders decided on a name: Mount Norfolk – 'after my little vessel', he wrote, which, despite its

FLINDERS

shortcomings, was serving the explorers well. Flinders' bond with *Norfolk* led him to note, with some affection, that 'upon the whole she performed wonderfully; seas that were apparently determined to swallow her up she rode over with all the ease and majesty of an old experienced petrel'.

The same day, they recorded the appearance of a small inlet – what is now known as Macquarie Harbour – but after steering towards the opening for a short while, they abandoned plans to explore further after 'seeing rocks in it'; a wind change also made the coast far less inviting. Flinders recorded sighting two small mountains, which he believed were those seen by Abel Tasman when he had discovered this coast on 24 January 1642. 'I have therefore named the first Mount Heemskerk, and the latter Mount Meehan,' he wrote, 'after his two ships'. (Their names were actually *Heemskerck* and *Zeehaen*.)

History has revealed that there are few more perilous coastlines in the world than the one Flinders and Bass were paralleling at this time. The entire shore lies within the bounds of the Roaring Forties, a region where storm fronts charge around the world almost unimpeded by any landmass. It is not unusual for these weather systems to pack winds of 80 knots, and because each one has a westerly component to it, this high-cliffed coast becomes a lee shore and, therefore, a potential death-trap. There are almost no bays, harbours or inlets where shelter can be secured – as Flinders and Bass were about to find out.

> The heavy south-west swell, which had met us at the
> entrance of the Indian Ocean, still continued to roll in, and
> set dead upon this coast; and the wind blew fresh at WNW.
> Under these circumstances, we looked out for some little
> beach where, in case of necessity, the sloop might be run on

shore with a prospect of safety to our lives; for should the
wind come three or four points further forward, there was
no probability of clearing the land on either tack. No such
beach could, however, be discovered; and we therefore
carried all possible sail to get past this dreary coast.

Norfolk was extremely fortunate to escape. Had the weather turned
ever so slightly against them, it would have almost certainly been
driven onto the rocks and pulverised into driftwood. Those on board
would have had no chance of survival, and their voyage would have
been added to the annals of unsolved maritime mysteries.

Today, charts are dotted with the location of hundreds of
wrecks on these west-facing shorelines, which have forever snared
the unwary and the unfortunate. This was evident 47 years later,
when Australia's worst civil maritime disaster occurred on the
western side of King Island, just 35 miles north of where *Norfolk*
had stopped at Albatross Island. In the early hours of 20 April 1845,
the emigrant sailing ship *Cataraqui*, which was en route to Sydney
with 410 passengers and crew on board, was driven ashore by a
raging westerly gale with the loss of 401 lives.

By now, Flinders, Bass and crew were becoming frustrated by
the drawn-out monotony of the coastline they were skirting, which
was desolate, dangerous and far from fascinating for these intrepid
explorers. Flinders' lack of enthusiasm for the coastal scenery is
apparent in the notes he made upon sighting the rugged De Witt
Range, north of what is now Port Davey:

The mountains which presented themselves to our view in
this situation, both close to the shore and inland, were
amongst the most stupendous works of nature I ever beheld,
and it seemed to me are the most dismal and barren that can

be imagined. The eye ranges over these peaks, and curiously formed lumps of adamantine rock, with astonishment and horror.

Relief – in the form of more familiar and interesting territory – was not far away. Within 24 hours, *Norfolk* had passed Port Davey and was closing on a major turning point, South West Cape, a steep and jagged sliver of land that jutted out into the ocean for nearly two miles. Once she rounded the cape, there were fewer than 40 nautical miles to be sailed before the helm was put across and the course altered towards the north. This would put Adventure Bay, which Flinders recalled well from his voyage to Tahiti with Captain Bligh aboard *Providence*, just a few miles away. Most importantly, from this point they would, in broad terms, be heading for Port Jackson.

In the early afternoon, having covered 15 nautical miles since clearing South West Cape, the fickle and precarious nature of their existence in this hostile part of the world was once again driven home. At any time an unseen reef, a sudden change in the weather or a problem with their ship could bring an end to *Norfolk*, their expedition and themselves. Their lives really were in the lap of the gods.

At this time we were one mile within, or north of the largest of the islands [De Witt Island]; and saw with some surprise, for it is three miles from the main, that its grassy vegetation had been burnt. From hence we steered for the easternmost isle, lying off a wide open bight in the coast, and afterwards hauled up for the South Cape. The wind died away at six o'clock, when the Cape was one mile distant; but thick clouds were gathering in the south and west, and strong gusts

with heavy rain presently succeeded. Fortunately, the squalls
came from the westward, so that we were enabled to get
further from those stupendous cliffs; had they come from the
south, the consequences might have been fatal to the *Norfolk*.

At four a.m. on 14 December, *Norfolk*'s course was still being
influenced by adverse weather. After rounding The Friars – so
named by Furneaux in 1773 because some of the islands resembled
the heads of bald friars – they entered Storm Bay, intending to stop
in Adventure Bay. However, a strong northerly wind caused them
to abandon this plan. They continued north in the hope they could
enter the Derwent River, but this too proved impossible due to
the same weather system. Eventually, they took shelter in the
northern end of D'Entrecasteaux Channel, immediately west of the
river mouth.

With the wind continuing to blow strongly from the north-
west, any desire Flinders still held to explore the Derwent River
left him, and he decided to continue moving to the east, where
they could investigate Frederick Henry Bay and what lay beyond.

There had been confusion over the identity of this bay for more
than 150 years. In 1642 Abel Tasman named as Frederick Henry
Bay what is today known as Blackmans Bay, just inside the entrance
to the Derwent, but in 1773, Furneaux, exploring further to the
east, believed he had arrived at Frederick Henry Bay, and the name
remained where Furneaux placed it on his chart. *Norfolk* entered the
bay on 15 December and over the next few days sailed as far as
possible into the waterway to the east, discovering yet another large
bay. The crew spent three days there before returning to Storm Bay.

The great eastern bay now quitted had never been entered
till this time; and as it is proved not to be Frederik Hendrik's,

I have named it Norfolk Bay. It is about eight miles long, north and south, and three to five miles broad from east to west. The largest fleet may find shelter here, with anchorage on a good bottom of 4 to 9 fathoms deep.

Like Frederick Henry Bay, Storm Bay was also a misnomer. Tasman's expedition had been struck by a storm when it was in the region, so the following day he named what we know as Adventure Bay (where his two ships were sheltering) as Storm Bay. Over the centuries, however, mapmakers had confused his name for the nine-mile-long, four-mile-wide bay with that for the entire gulf, which measures 16 miles by 25 miles. It was a case of boundary creep.

Flinders was still keen to make an excursion into the Derwent River, and finally, when on 21 December the wind turned in *Norfolk*'s favour, he achieved his goal. Over the next nine days the men sailed, rowed and drifted around 18 miles up the river to a point where they could go no further – Herdsman's Cove. They went ashore on numerous occasions, and when they reached Sullivan's Cove – where Hobart is now situated – Bass landed on the river bank and climbed the 4170 feet to the top of 'Mount Table' (today Mount Wellington).

At Herdsman's Cove they decided to go ashore to eat, and when they returned to the ship later that evening they had bagged 14 swans for their food store. The next day they returned to Risdon Cove so they could top up their kegs with fresh water and prepare *Norfolk* for sea.

With everything in readiness, the crew manned the windlass and cranked the anchor up to the end of the cat head so the cat tackle could be attached and the anchor securely stowed. The last day of 1798 and first day of 1799 were consumed by the passage to the entrance of the river and on to Storm Bay, where 24 hours later they were forced to run for cover when a south-easterly gale proved impenetrable for the little ship. By 4 January they had cleared Storm Bay and, much to their delight, taken a hard turn to port, their bow then on the rhumb line for Port Jackson.

Wherever possible, Flinders and Bass closed on the coastline so they could add to their ever-expanding chart, which was now peppered with points of interest that had not previously been known to any European. It was an exciting time, but they were soon to realise that they were far from safely home.

[W]e steered to pass between Cape Barren and the great northern island, intending to explore the west side of the latter in our way. At five o'clock breakers were seen two miles to the north ... [and] hoping to find a sufficient depth for the sloop round the island which lies in the opening, [we] stood on till the soundings diminished to nine feet, and breakers were seen all round ahead, from beam to beam. It was then near sun-set, and the breeze right aft; but whilst I was considering what could be done for our safety, the wind shifted suddenly, as if by an act of Providence, to the opposite quarter, and enabled us to steer back, out of this dangerous place, with all sail. At nine o'clock the wind returned to the south-eastward, having just lasted long enough to take us out of danger.

On 9 January *Norfolk* cleared the north-east corner of Van Diemen's Land, and little more than 24 hours later they were rounding Cape Howe. This was a moment for celebration: they had completed their loop and charted Van Diemen's Land, proving the existence of the strait. But there was a howling south-easterly gale blowing at the time, so they hung on to all the sail they could, to ensure that they rode the favourable system as far north as possible.

> On the 11th, and the gale still continuing, we anchored within the heads of Port Jackson at ten o'clock the same evening, having exceeded, by no more than eleven days, the time which had been fixed for our return.
>
> To the strait which had been the great object of research, and whose discovery was now completed, Governor Hunter gave, at my recommendation, the name of Bass' Strait. This was no more than a just tribute to my worthy friend and companion, for the extreme dangers and fatigues he had undergone in first entering it in the whale boat, and to the correct judgment he had formed from various indications, of the existence of a wide opening between Van Diemen's Land and New South Wales.

CHAPTER NINE

Commander Flinders Takes the Helm

Flinders, Bass and Governor Hunter could justifiably have expected a wave of tributes to flow from London once news of the discovery of Bass Strait, and their charting of the coast of Van Diemen's Land, reached England. In fact, it barely raised a ripple of excitement.

The English were, at the time, totally absorbed by the actions of a man whose war machine was running rampant across Europe. His name was Napoleon Bonaparte, and his homeland, France, was a mere 20 miles to the east of England's white cliffs of Dover – just a few hours under sail. What alarmed the English most was that high on Napoleon's list of priorities was to attack, cripple and conquer Great Britain – something the French had wanted to achieve for centuries.

The deep-seated concern held by the English government, the military and the public was apparent in a letter written by Sir Joseph Banks to Governor Hunter, which reached Sydney Town before the successful completion of the circumnavigation of Van Diemen's Land by Flinders and Bass. Banks wrote that:

The political situation is so difficult, and His Majesty's
Ministers so fully employed in business of the deepest
importance, that it is scarce possible to gain a moment's
audience on any subject but those which stand foremost in
their minds; and colonies of all kinds, you may be assured,
are now put into the background.

While the explorers were preparing their search for Bass Strait half
a world away, Napoleon was finalising his plans to make a major
naval assault on England, as the forerunner to a land-based attack.
The deeper he got into those plans, however, the more he realised
that the French fleet was nowhere near strong enough to
overwhelm the ships of the Royal Navy. Instead, then, he
developed another long-term strategy, turning his attention to
conquering Egypt so that his army could take up a position from
which it could put a stranglehold on Britain's interests in India.

As it turned out, this strategy was destined for disaster. Napoleon
did not expect the Royal Navy to pursue his fleet across the
Mediterranean to Egypt. More importantly, he had underestimated
the tactical brilliance and fighting skills of Rear-Admiral Horatio
Nelson. In August 1798 the Battle of the Nile saw Nelson and his
fleet annihilate the French. All but four of Napoleon's 17 ships were
blasted into submission in what was an horrific battle. The British
lost 213 men and had 677 wounded, while the French are estimated
to have lost as many as 5000, either killed or wounded. One British
seaman described the horrendous scene: 'An awful sight it was, the
whole bay was covered with dead bodies, mangled, wounded, and
scorched, not a bit of clothes on them but their trousers.'

Nelson's crushing victory came little more than 50 days after
Flinders and Bass had boarded *Norfolk* in Sydney Town and steered
the little ship down harbour to the open sea. What these young

explorers achieved was, in the world of exploration and geography, of great importance to England and the world. Proving both the existence of Bass Strait and that Van Diemen's Land was an island were considered to be the most significant discoveries since the exploits of Captain Cook in the 1770s. Understandably, the turmoil in Europe diluted the accolades that Flinders and Bass received, but Flinders did win one highly valued and unexpected 'reward' – the recognition and friendship of none other than Sir Joseph Banks, the great supporter of Captain Cook, Captain Bligh and all the major maritime expeditions undertaken by British explorers in that era.

Back in New Holland, the rugged and impenetrable mountain range not far to the west of Sydney Town continued to frustrate all attempts to explore the vast inland. This natural blockade led Hunter, Flinders and Bass to realise that a major river system somewhere along the coast of New South Wales might provide an alternative means of reaching the interior.

So, with Flinders having successfully completed the Bass Strait expedition, and with there being no need for him aboard *Reliance* for the immediate future, the governor supported his request to try to find that river system on the coastline to the north of Port Jackson. Flinders anticipated that a six-week survey might take him as far as 500 nautical miles from the settlement, to the large bays sighted and named by Captain Cook in 1770. One of these was to the east of the Glass-house Mountains, while the other, Hervey's Bay, was adjacent to the middle of what is known today as Fraser Island. 'I had some hope of finding a considerable river discharging itself at one of these openings,' wrote Flinders, 'and of being able by its means to penetrate further into the interior of the country than had hitherto been effected.'

Flinders was pleased to learn from Governor Hunter that the sloop *Norfolk* would be provided for the mission, and equally satisfying for him was that his brother, Samuel, who was still a midshipman aboard *Reliance*, would be released so he could be a member of the expedition team. Unfortunately, Bass would not be joining them, as Flinders noted with disappointment: 'Of the assistance of my able friend Bass I was, however, deprived, he having quitted the station soon after our last voyage, to return to England.'

There was, however, one more interesting and important inclusion among the men who would crew *Norfolk*: Bungaree, whom Flinders described as 'a native, whose good disposition and manly conduct had attracted my esteem', would travel with them, in the hope that he could communicate with any Aboriginals they might meet during the voyage, and quell any threats of aggression, should the need arise.

While *Norfolk* was being prepared for this expedition, a circumstance arose that gave a powerful insight into Flinders' character and the level of respect he had gained from Governor Hunter: a controversial and hotly debated court case that took place in March 1799. The governor had appointed Flinders, Waterhouse and Lieutenant Kent as three of the seven men who would decide the fate of a former convict, Isaac Nichols, who had been charged with receiving a quantity of tobacco which he was alleged to have known had been stolen.

The case revealed once again the considerable animosity that existed between the New South Wales Corps and the governor and his naval associates. Along with the three men Hunter had appointed to the case, there were three corps members, as well as a judge advocate who was similarly antagonistic towards the colony's leader. The consensus across Sydney Town was that the accused was being framed by the corps because its men resented the fact that he had corrected his ways to the point where he had become a popular and prosperous member of the community, and a friend of the governor.

Hunter believed that this attempted ruination of Nichols was based on false and malicious evidence, but, not surprisingly, when the verdict was handed down on 12 March 1800, the three corps members and the judge advocate saw Nichols found guilty of the crime and sentenced to 14 years in prison on Norfolk Island.

Governor Hunter was convinced that this was a complete injustice: he remained firm in his belief that the tobacco had been planted in Nichols' house with the intention of implicating him in the crime. He declared that the finding and the sentence were a travesty, so on 1 April he suspended the sentence and commenced an appeal process to the Secretary of State in London. He asked Flinders to provide part of the submission, which he did, drafting a detailed and carefully reasoned analysis of the case and the evidence presented. It was an impressive document.

Unfortunately, because of the length of time taken for mail to be transported to and from London, it took three years for a reply to arrive. But it was worth the wait: Nichols was pardoned and went on to gain an even higher standing within the community. In 1809 he was appointed the first postmaster of New South Wales, and over the years he became known for the dinners he hosted to celebrate the anniversary of First Landing Day, or Foundation Day.

It was 8 July, midwinter, when *Norfolk* departed Port Jackson and turned north. The following day, Flinders recognised Port Stephens, which Captain Cook had noted on his chart as he sailed the coast. Had he or Cook turned to port and cruised through the entrance to this waterway, they would have discovered a beautiful expanse of deep water two and a half times the size of Sydney Harbour – around 50 square miles – which was surrounded by low rolling hills. Almost a century later, in 1899, a New South Wales

Royal Commission was so impressed by Port Stephens that the area around North Arm Cove was considered as a site for Australia's national capital. Unfortunately, however, time was of the essence for both Cook and Flinders on their journeys: they couldn't stop at every point of interest they observed along the way. Flinders sailed north for another 25 nautical miles, and there he made the first of many topographical discoveries: Sugarloaf Point.

Norfolk's progress was often frustrated by adverse currents and contrary winds, so it was not until 11 July that she was sailing among the Solitary Islands, 240 nautical miles north of Port Jackson. Much to Flinders' delight, he was able to identify and position five previously unseen rocky islands, and while he was impressed by the heavily timbered coastline, there was no way he could have envisaged that, fewer than 50 years later, a bustling lumber-gathering settlement – Korff's Harbour – would be established there. In the years that followed, as many as 450 vessels would call there annually to load the high-quality timber.

Flinders had constantly been scanning the coast for any indication of a river entrance that might allow *Norfolk* or the tender to sail inland and explore, but there was also another, more pressing reason to find a place to land. *Norfolk* had developed a serious leak, which had started just two days after setting sail from Port Jackson but had worsened as time went by. Thirty nautical miles to the north of North Solitary Island, Flinders spotted a cove and named it Shoal Bay. It was protected enough for him to go ashore, but not a suitable site for repairing the vessel.

Once on the beach, Flinders walked to the top of an adjacent hill to get a panoramic view of the region and maybe sight a river. He declared there was nothing of interest to be seen – yet he was actually standing right above the mouth of one of the coast's mightiest waterways, a river system that, apart from the Murray-

Darling, was the largest river on the continent south of the Tropic of Capricorn. It had its origins some 250 miles upstream and encompassed a catchment area of more than 8500 square miles. It would be another 26 years before the existence of what was initially called 'the Big River' became known. In 1839 it was named the Clarence River.

The search for a suitable spot to beach *Norfolk* for repairs was proving fruitless, so the expedition continued north, to the most easterly point on the coast of New South Wales, Cape Byron, while the pumps were constantly manned.

When *Norfolk* had cleared that promontory, Flinders decided to skirt the coast for another 75 nautical miles until they reached a very picturesque headland that had been named Point Look-out by Captain Cook. Flinders knew from Cook's chart that some form of bay existed to the west of this point, and eventually he saw it through the narrow gap between Point Look-out and the island to its north. However, the passage towards the bay was far too shallow for *Norfolk* to negotiate, so he continued to sail towards what Cook had designated as Glass-house Bay – in reality, the entrance to Moreton Bay.

On rounding Cape Moreton, a vast expanse of water was visible to the south and west, but every effort Flinders made to find a safe course into the bay was frustrated by a seemingly endless maze of sandbanks and shallow channels. Eventually, suitably deep water was found to the west, and this allowed *Norfolk* to be sailed south to an anchorage off a low spit of land that, for unfortunate reasons, would become known as Point Skirmish.

It was 16 July, and Flinders noticed some natives on the shore. The tender was launched, and he, Bungaree, and some of his men went ashore in the hope they could meet with them. Flinders later gave a simplistic assessment of what ensued: 'There was a party of natives on the point, and our communication was at first friendly; but after receiving presents they made an attack, and one of them was wounded by our fire.'

Initially, the Aboriginals had been fascinated by the hat Flinders was wearing and tried to snatch it from his head. The Englishmen had decided it was time to retreat to the ship, but as they went to board the tender a native hurled a spear at them. It missed its mark, but suddenly the visitors faced a 'them or us' situation. Aware of 'the great influence which the use of superior power has in savages to create respect and render their communications friendly', Flinders grabbed his musket and took aim at the offender. The gun misfired twice, then on the third attempt it fired, wounding the man who had thrown the spear. It was an act Flinders regretted, but it was the only option under the circumstances, as he saw it. He and his men then retreated hurriedly to *Norfolk*.

(Flinders believed that the beach they had just left was part of the mainland, but on today's maps it is recognised as Bribie Island. Also, the location of Skirmish Point on modern maps is not the actual site of this confrontation, which is now known as South Point.)

Those aboard *Norfolk* were convinced that the waterway they were exploring would have at least one major river flowing into it, and they believed they had found it when they entered what appeared to be an estuary just to the west of Point Skirmish. Flinders named it Pumice-stone River because of the large volume of pumice stone on its shores. Time would reveal, however, that this was not a river, but merely a long and very shallow bay extending to the north; it led 'towards the remarkable peaks called the Glass Houses, which were now suspected to be volcanic, and excited my curiosity', Flinders noted. Unfortunately, his desire to explore these striking features would have to be held over for some days.

Most importantly for the seafarers, the source of *Norfolk*'s leak had finally been located. It was in a plank close to the keel, and, as a temporary watertight repair, oakum was wedged into the gap from inside the hull. Four days later they landed on a beach on the western side of the spit, five miles north of Point Skirmish, where proper repairs could be made. After three days of heavy toil the offending hull strake was finally made good.

Flinders hoped to investigate and scale at least one of the Glass Houses' peaks, and on the day the repair was completed he set out with Bungaree and two sailors. They took the tender as far into Pumice-stone River as possible, then trudged for nine miles through swamps and over rugged and rocky terrain towards the conical formations, the highest of which was more than 1800 feet in altitude.

> We reached the top of a stony mount, from whence the
> highest peak was four miles distant to the north-west. Three or
> four leagues beyond it was a ridge of mountain, from which
> various small streams descend into Pumice-stone River ...
> Early on the 27th, we reached the foot of the nearest Glass
> House, a flat-topped peak, one mile and a half north of the
> stony mount. It was impossible to ascend this almost
> perpendicular rock; and finding no marks of volcanic eruption,
> we returned to the boat, and to the sloop the same evening.

In the ensuing days, they had a far more amiable contact with the Aboriginals than that at Point Skirmish, but there was one somewhat embarrassing scare. On 18 July, while exploring the bay to the south, the Englishmen feared they were about to be attacked by some 20 natives who were paddling their canoes towards *Norfolk*. Flinders called for the decks to be cleared and the men to be armed in preparation for a possible confrontation, only to realise that their 'attackers' were fishermen who were actually standing on a shallow sandbank and beating the water with sticks to drive fish into their nets.

Flinders subsequently made an appraisal of the local inhabitants:

> These people were evidently of the same race as those at Port Jackson, though speaking a language which Bongaree could not understand. They fish almost wholly with cast and setting nets, live more in society than the natives to the southward, and are much better lodged. Their spears are of solid wood, and used without the throwing stick. Two or three bark canoes were seen; but from the number of black swans in the river, of which eighteen were caught in our little boat, it should seem that these people are not dextrous in the management either of the canoe or spear.

As the general exploration continued, Captain Cook's voyage was often in Flinders' thoughts: 'The long slip on the east side, which I have called Moreton Island, as supposing it would have received that name from Captain Cook, had he known of its insularity, is little else than a ridge of rocky hills, with a sandy surface.'

During the 15 days that *Norfolk* spent in the bay, Flinders sailed well into its southern sector, to a point about 10 nautical miles down the western shore of North Stradbroke Island. Prudent navigation was always important: the depth of a channel in this region could go from 12 fathoms to three fathoms in little more than a boat length. It was probably this cautious approach, the low sun angles and the constant need to work the tides that led to Flinders not seeing the entrance to a major river on the western shore of the bay – what is now the Brisbane River.

On the afternoon of 31 July, with all sails set to capture the fresh south-east sea breeze, *Norfolk* cleared the bay and steered on a course to the north that paralleled the long, gently curving sandy coastline. Flinders' notes on the bay they were leaving were blunt and to the point: 'It was so full of sandbanks and shallows it was not possible to define any passage that a ship could take into it without being confronted by danger.'

Soon after midday on 2 August, *Norfolk* was abeam of Sandy Cape, the northernmost point of Fraser Island, which subsequent exploration would confirm as the world's largest sand island. From there, careful navigation was again necessary as they sailed close to the edge of the treacherous Break-sea Spit for ten nautical miles. When *Norfolk* reached the northern extremity of the spit, she had a depth of only three-and-a-half fathoms under her keel; minutes later she was in 17 fathoms. Once clear of the spit, the crew wore ship, went onto port tack and headed back towards Sandy Cape, where they anchored in the lee of its western shore for the evening.

The next morning the crew weighed anchor and sailed *Norfolk* 40 nautical miles to the south-west, into the confines of Hervey's Bay. As was the case at Moreton Bay, they spent 48 frustrating hours trying to navigate their way around a myriad of shallows. At this point Flinders decided he'd had enough and 'the examination of Hervey's Bay concluded' – it was time to return to the safety of deep water and commence the homeward voyage.

Norfolk headed back to Break-sea Spit, and once they were there, a pleasant northerly wind prevailed – perfect for a delightful run down the coast. There was also a strong southerly current assisting her speed; it was so strong, in fact, that she had gained an advantage of more than 200 nautical miles by the time she was anchored snugly in Port Jackson on the evening of 20 August.

Flinders' concluding comments on this chapter of his exploration of the coast of New South Wales were somewhat downcast in tone:

> I must acknowledge myself to have been disappointed in not
> being able to penetrate into the interior of New South
> Wales, by either of the openings examined in this expedition;
> but, however mortifying the conviction might be, it was
> then an ascertained fact, that no river of importance
> intersected the East Coast between the 24th and 39th degrees
> of south latitude.

Flinders' claim of 'an ascertained fact' was possibly the only blemish in his incredible career. He might be forgiven for reaching such a conclusion, however, considering the pressure of time he faced on the voyage and the vastness of the area he covered. But the fact is that he missed finding two major rivers – the Clarence and the Brisbane. On each occasion, he was close, but not close enough to actually see them. Regardless, he was now captivated by a desire to explore more of the coastline of this amazing land. He also still wished to be the first person to penetrate the inland via a river system. As he noted, 'The vast interior of this new continent [is] wrapped in total obscurity.'

Reliance, which had continued to deteriorate, was now considered to be beyond repair, and Governor Hunter 'judged it proper to order her home while she may be capable of performing the voyage'. Waterhouse remained her captain, and many of the crew, including Flinders, who had sailed her out from England were also aboard for the passage home. There was one additional passenger not on the manifest – one who really could call the *Reliance* home – Flinders' faithful furry friend, Trim.

Hunter gave Waterhouse the responsibility of delivering import-ant despatches for government officials, at the same time directing him to throw them overboard should they find themselves in danger of being captured by an enemy ship. Aside from this threat, there were no guarantees that this barely seaworthy vessel would make her home port under normal circumstances. Her frames and planks were so frail that it was a distinct possibility she would surrender to a storm along the way and sink.

Indeed, it turned out to be a rough passage. The hull was taking on around ten inches of water every hour, which meant that the pumps had to be manned regularly. This task was given to the two convict stowaways who emerged from below deck two days after *Reliance*'s crew had farewelled Sydney Town on 3 March 1800.

After *Reliance* reached the rugged and remote island of Saint Helena, she sailed north through the Atlantic alongside four East India Company vessels as protection from the French. Then, off the coast of Ireland, HMS *Cerberus*, a 32-gun frigate, became her escort, leading her into the English Channel and on to Portsmouth, where *Reliance* anchored on 26 August. It was the end of a voyage of almost six months from Port Jackson – which meant that Trim had now completed a lap of the world, becoming probably the first feline to do so. Flinders and many of *Reliance*'s crew were home after an absence of more than five years.

Just four weeks earlier, *Woodford* had reached England with Bass on board. As fate would have it, Bass and Flinders would never meet again; both would again see Port Jackson but never at the same time. Following his return to England, Bass was granted 12 months' leave, and in that time he began working on a venture with the captain of the sealer *Nautilus*, Charles Bishop, which would see them transporting goods to New South Wales for sale. Within three months of reaching England, Bass had fallen in love with and married Captain Waterhouse's sister, Elizabeth. The ceremony took place in St James's Church, Piccadilly, on

8 October 1800. With Bass now a member of the Waterhouse family, the captain took it upon himself to help finance the trading ship that Bass and Bishop were proposing.

In that same month, *Reliance* finally reached the docks at Deptford, and Flinders was able to quit the ship. He stepped ashore as a man of far greater status within the navy and in society than he'd been as a 20-year-old midshipman when he had departed England in February 1795 aboard the same ship. He was now a naval lieutenant and an explorer of considerable distinction – a man who had literally made a mark on the world through his historic discoveries. Flinders sought no acclaim for himself as a result of his achievements, but it was forthcoming nevertheless – most notably from Sir Joseph Banks, the president of the world's oldest and most respected scientific institution, the Royal Society.

Banks would hold that post for a remarkably long time – from 1777 to 1820 – and his influence in British society extended to the very top, to King George III and the parliament. Flinders' admission to this illustrious circle affirmed his nation's recognition of his many achievements and virtually assured him of even greater opportunities in the future. Banks and Flinders also shared a common bond: they were both Lincolnshire men. No one knew better than Banks the value of Finders' accomplishments as an explorer in the antipodes.

Not long after he set foot on English soil, Flinders wrote to Sir Joseph and formally expressed his desire to extend his exploration of the coast of New Holland. He was:

> ... offering my services to explore minutely the whole of the coasts, as well those which were imperfectly known as those entirely unknown, provided the Government would provide me with a proper ship for the purpose. I did not address

myself in vain to this zealous promoter of science; and Earl Spencer, then First Lord of the Admiralty, entering warmly into the views of his friend, obtained the approbation of his Majesty, and immediately set out a ship that could be spared from the present demands of war, which Great Britain then waged with most of the Powers of Europe.

When he wrote *A Voyage to Terra Australis*, Flinders elaborated on his motivations:

The voyages which had been made, during the seventeenth and eighteenth centuries, by Dutch and by English navigators, had successively brought to light various extensive coasts in the southern hemisphere, which were thought to be united; and to comprise a land, which must be nearly equal in magnitude to the whole of Europe. To this land, though known to be separated from all other great portions of the globe, geographers were disposed to give the appellation of Continent: but doubts still existed, of the continuity of its widely extended shores; and it was urged, that, as our knowledge of some parts was not founded upon well authenticated information, and we were in total ignorance of some others, these coasts might, instead of forming one great land, be no other than parts of different large islands.

There was one other very important matter that had to be addressed:

It is necessary, however, to geographical precision, that so soon as New Holland and New South Wales were known to form one land, there should be a general name applicable to the whole; and this essential point having been ascertained in the present voyage, with a degree of certainty sufficient to authorise the measure, I have, with the concurrence of opinions entitled to deference, ventured upon the re-adoption of the original Terra Australis; and of this term I shall hereafter make use, when speaking of New Holland and New South Wales, in a collective sense; and when using it in the most extensive signification, the adjacent isles, including that of Van Diemen, must be understood to be comprehended.

There is no probability, that any other detached body of land, of nearly equal extent, will ever be found in a more southern latitude; the name Terra Australis will, therefore, remain descriptive of the geographical importance of this country, and of its situation on the globe: it has antiquity to recommend it; and, having no reference to either of the two claiming nations, appears to be less objectionable than any other which could have been selected.

When, in 1814, *A Voyage to Terra Australis* was published, Flinders added an important addendum to the preceding paragraphs: 'Had I permitted myself any innovation upon the original term, it would have been to convert it into Australia; as being more agreeable to the ear, and an assimilation to the names of the other great portions of the earth.' Little did he know what influence his suggestion would have.

Back in 1801, however, Banks quickly became interested in Flinders' proposal to undertake the ultimate challenge – a circum-navigation of New Holland so that its coastline and geography could be explored, charted and documented – and thus to reveal to the world the secrets of the largely undiscovered perimeter of this landmass (or landmasses), 'the fifth part of the world'. The pair scoured the charts and documents that Flinders had produced, discussing what strategy would be needed for the expedition to be successful. Before long, the project in its entirety sat well with Banks, and he decided to progress it through the official channels.

At this time, Flinders was also working diligently to prepare a relatively simple 35-page booklet that would be published for the benefit of the Admiralty and other navigators who might sail the waters he had traversed. It was published in 1801 with the wordy yet pertinent title 'Observations on the Coasts of Van Diemen's Land, on Bass's Strait and its Islands, and on Parts of the Coasts of New South Wales, Intended to Accompany the Charts of the Late Discoveries in those Countries, by Matthew Flinders, Second Lieutenant of His Majesty's Ship Reliance'. Not surprisingly, Flinders dedicated the booklet to his mentor, Sir Joseph: 'Your zealous exertions to promote geographical and nautical knowledge, your encouragement of men employed in the cultivation of the sciences that tend to this improvement, and the countenance you have been pleased to show me in particular, embolden me to lay the following observations before you.'

These were happy days for the 26-year-old on another front too. While away in New South Wales, Flinders had done his best to stay in contact with his family, but in particular with his sister, Susannah, his 'two Sisters of the half blood', Hannah and Henrietta, and the daughters of the Chappelle and Franklin families, all of whom lived in the same neighbourhood in Lincolnshire. He referred to them collectively as 'my charming sisters' and wrote whenever he could to tell them of his adventures. In one of those letters, written for all to enjoy, he masked a message for one of these 'sisters': 'never will there be a more happy soul than when I return. O, may the Almighty spare me all those dear friends without whom my joy would be turned into sorrow and mourning.'

It became clear that the hidden message was aimed at Ann Chappelle, because on 25 September 1800 he wrote to her and laid bare the feelings he had harboured for her during the previous five years.

> You are one of those friends ... whom I consider it
> indispensably necessary to see. I should be glad to have some
> little account of your movements, where you reside, and
> with whom, that my motions may be regulated
> accordingly ... You see that I make everything subservient to
> business. Indeed, my dearest friend, this time seems to be a
> very critical period of my life. I have long been absent ...
> have done services abroad that were not expected, but which
> seem to be thought a good deal of. I have more and greater
> friends than before, and this seems to be the moment that
> their exertions may be most serviceable to me. I may now
> perhaps make a bold dash forward, or may remain a poor
> lieutenant all my life. My dear friend Annette ... with the
> greatest sincerity, I am her most affectionate friend and
> brother, Matthew Flinders.

There had been no evidence of Flinders' romantic feelings for Ann while he was in Sydney Town, but Mount Chappelle and the Chappelle Isles, named during *Norfolk*'s expedition to Bass Strait and Van Diemen's Land, leave no doubt that she was his distant love. Flinders, who was younger than Ann, described her as a 'witty, generous, raven-haired beauty with rich red-brown eyes'. Much to his delight, she did not deter him from making further advances. It is highly likely that he would have taken time to see her when he returned home to visit his family, his friends and his 'charming sisters'.

Flinders' plan to circumnavigate New Holland was well received by those in authority, as he explained when he wrote *A Voyage to Terra Australis*.

> The plan was approved by that distinguished patron of
> science and useful enterprise [Sir Joseph Banks]; it was laid
> before Earl Spencer, then first Lord Commissioner of the
> Admiralty; and finally received the sanction of His Majesty,
> who was graciously pleased to direct that the voyage should
> be undertaken; and I had the honour of being appointed to
> the command.

Three factors had influenced the decision to appoint Flinders to this task. In June 1800 the French had advised the British that they intended to explore the South Pacific in the interests of science, but the British feared they were actually planning to claim unknown parts of New Holland. Secondly, the East India Company was concerned that the French would establish a rival operation through a settlement somewhere on the coast of New Holland, which would directly impact the company's lucrative business. Thirdly, Sir Joseph Banks recognised what the strategic and financial importance of Flinders' mission meant to the long-term interests of Great Britain.

For Flinders, the fact that Lord Spencer had endorsed the expedition and agreed to him as its leader was a proud moment in his career. Apart from holding the highest office within the Admiralty, it was Lord Spencer who had seen greatness in Horatio Nelson and chosen him to lead the Royal Navy into battles that had crippled the French as a naval power.

The vessel chosen for this project – which, most appropriately, was named HMS *Investigator* – was the best available at the time. Flinders didn't allude to its shortcomings when he later wrote of the ship:

> The *Investigator* was a north-country-built ship, of three-hundred and thirty-four tons; and, in form, nearly resembled the description of a vessel recommended by Captain Cook as best calculated for voyages of discovery. She had been purchased some years before into His Majesty's service; and having been newly coppered and repaired, was considered to be the best vessel which could, at that time, be spared for the projected voyage to Terra Australis.

The good news for Flinders was that his vessel was only five years old. The bad news was that she was being spared from war service by the Royal Navy because she was in such poor condition. A dockyard survey described the lower deck hull beams as being 'wainy and sappy', an indication that the ship had been built using green, and not properly dried, timber: she could well be 'soft' in her construction. However, that didn't greatly concern him: he needed only to think of his experiences with unsound vessels such as *Reliance* and *Norfolk*.

Investigator was a 22-gun sloop-of-war measuring 100 feet overall, with a beam of 29 feet and draft of 14 feet. She was originally built as a collier, a 'Geordie Brig' at Monkwearmouthshore, on the north bank of the River Wear in Sunderland, and named *Fram*. Her owner-builder sailed her primarily on coastal routes with cargos of coal and merchant goods, until in April 1798 she was bought by the government for £2530. She was assigned to the Royal Navy, renamed HMS *Xenophon*, armed and put into service as an escort vessel for merchant convoys in the English Channel.

Flinders was granted permission by the Navy Board to fit out *Investigator* 'in such a manner as I should judge necessary'. As she was a collier, her high-volume hull shape allowed for a simple refit. This included the addition of another deck to provide accommodation for the master and some of the crew, plus storage areas, all being planned around what was likely to be a three-year mission. As a precaution against the 'termites of the sea' – the ravenous teredo worm – the underwater part of her hull was re-coppered to a point 'two streaks higher than before'.

Lieutenant Flinders went aboard as *Investigator*'s commander on 25 January 1801, in Sheerness. There was nothing remarkably different about her since her refit. There was a hold in the deck amidships, and the ship's launch, measuring about 23 feet in length, was lashed to two athwartships beams immediately above it. The quarterdeck, which was two steps up from the waist of the ship, was enclosed by a solid timber rail with a taffrail across the stern. Flinders was pleased to see that the helm position, which was located immediately forward of the mizzen mast, was reasonably well protected, should the ship ever be pooped by following seas.

Investigator's general proportions reminded the new commander somewhat of *Providence*, on which he had sailed into the Pacific with Captain Bligh. This vessel was only seven feet shorter in overall length but quite a bit lighter in displacement – 334 tons against 406 tons – and was manned by a crew of 88, while *Providence* had carried 134. There were other distinct features that were familiar to Flinders: the steeply angled bowsprit, which aimed towards the sky at 45 degrees, the bold lines of the hull, and the sail plan, which was carried on three masts. *Investigator* was his first senior commission in naval ranks, and he was pleased by what he saw, even though her construction might be suspect.

The ship came to Flinders with a full complement of men, but not all were suitable or available for the expedition. He was offered crew from HMS *Zealand* as replacements; he later explained the procedure by which he chose the majority of the 87 men who would join him:

Such of the officers and crew as were aged, or did not volunteer for this particular service, were discharged; and able young men were received in lieu from His Majesty's ship *Zealand* ... Upon one occasion, where eleven volunteers were to be received from the *Zealand*, a strong instance was given of the spirit of enterprise prevalent amongst British seamen. About three hundred disposable men were called up, and placed on one side of the deck; and after the nature of the voyage, with the number of men wanted, had been explained to them, those who volunteered were desired to go over to the opposite side. The candidates were not less than two-hundred and fifty, most of whom sought with eagerness to be received; and the eleven who were chosen, proved, with one single exception, to be worthy of the preference they obtained.

On 16 February, the explorer was even more pleased with the way his life was evolving. This was the day that the Admiralty advised him he had been promoted to the rank of commander within the Royal Navy.

Simultaneously, Flinders' romance with Ann Chappelle was blossoming. His ultimate desire would have been to have her travel with him, as his wife, to Port Jackson, where they could set up a residence while he undertook his exploration activities. However, the responsibilities of overseeing the preparation of his ship meant

Flinders did not have a lot of free time for romantic interests: *Investigator* was scheduled to sail as soon as possible.

By April, marriage was being openly discussed. Early that month, Flinders replied to a series of questions from his love:

H.M.S. *Investigator*, at the Nore, April 6, 1801.

My dearest friend,

Thou hast asked me if there is a *possibility* of our living together. I think I see a *probability* of living with a moderate share of comfort. Till now I was not certain of being able to fit myself out clear of the world. I have now done it, and have accommodation on board the *Investigator*, in which as my wife a woman may, with love to assist her, make herself happy. This prospect has recalled all the tenderness which I have so sedulously endeavoured to banish. I am sent for to London, where I shall be from the 9th to the 19th, or perhaps longer. If thou wilt meet me there, this hand shall be thine for ever. If thou hast sufficient love and courage, say to Mr. and Mrs. Tyler [her mother and stepfather] that I require nothing more with thee than a sufficient stock of clothes and a small sum to answer the increased expenses that will necessarily and immediately come upon me; as well for living on board as providing for it at Port Jackson; for whilst I am employed in the most dangerous part of my duty, thou shalt be placed under some friendly roof there. I need not, nor at this time have I time to enter into a detail of my income and prospects. It will, I trust, be sufficient for me to say that I see a fortune growing under me to meet increasing expenses. I only want a fair start, and my life for it, we will do well and be happy. I will write further to-morrow, but shall most anxiously expect thy answer at 86 Fleet Street, London, on my visit on Friday; and, I trust, thy presence immediately afterwards. I have only time to add that most anxiously I am, Most sincerely thine,

Matthew Flinders.

There was an addendum to this letter, which was influenced by *Investigator*'s rapidly approaching departure date. Should the marriage proceed, Flinders realised, then news of his nuptials might not sit well at that time with his superiors, including Banks. 'It will be much better to keep this matter entirely secret,' Flinders wrote. 'There are many reasons for it yet, and I have also a powerful one: I do not know how my great friends might like it.'

Flinders' response to Ann's questions obviously achieved everything that he had wished for. Having travelled to London as planned, he then headed for Lincolnshire, where, on 17 April 1801, in a 600-year-old stone church in Partney, he married Ann. Her stepfather, Reverend William Tyler, conducted the ceremony. (Her mother, Anne, had remarried after her seafarer father, John Chappelle, died from an illness while at sea at the age of 40.) The marriage register read:

Matthew Flinders, Commander in His Majesty's Royal Navy and Ann Chappelle, of this parish, were Married in this Church by Licence this seventeenth Day of April in the Year One Thousand eight Hundred and one By me Wm. Tyler, Rector of Bratoft.

It appears that few, if any, of Flinders' immediate family or relatives were at the ceremony: certainly not his parents. On the day of the wedding, he explained in a letter to his cousin, Henrietta, how hurriedly things had come together:

> Everything was agreed to in a very handsome manner, and just at this time I was called up to town and found that I might be spared a few days from thence. I set off on Wednesday evening from town, arrived next evening at Spilsby, was married next morning, which was Friday; on Saturday we went to Donington, on Sunday reached Huntingdon, and on Monday were in town. Next morning I presented myself before Sir Joseph Banks with a grave face as if nothing had happened, and then went on with my business as usual. We stayed in town till the following Sunday, and came on board the *Investigator* next day, and here we have remained ever since, a few weeks on shore and a day spent on the Essex side of the Thames excepted.

The fact that the marriage was a rushed affair also meant many of Matthew and Ann's close mutual friends were not at the ceremony. This was evident in a letter written by the bride the following day to Elizabeth Franklin, Matthew's stepmother's niece:

> April 17th, 1801.

> My beloved Betsy,
>   Thou wilt be much surprised to hear of this sudden affair; indeed I scarce believe it myself, tho' I have this very morning given my hand at the altar to him I have ever highly esteemed, and it affords me no small pleasure that I am now a part, tho' a distant one, of thy family, my Betsy. It grieves me much thou art so distant from me. Thy society

would have greatly cheered me. Thou wilt to-day pardon
me if I say but little. I am scarce able to coin one sentence or
to write intelligibly. It pains me to agony when I indulge the
thought for a moment that I must leave all I value on earth,
save one, alas, perhaps for ever. Ah, my Betsy, but I dare not,
must not, think [that]. Therefore, farewell, farewell. May the
great God of Heaven preserve thee and those thou lovest,
oh, everlastingly. Adieu, dear darling girl; love as ever,
though absent and far removed from your poor
     Annette.

As this letter shows, both Ann and her new husband expected that
she would travel to Sydney Town with him aboard *Investigator*, and
they began planning their life accordingly.

In another letter written sometime later by Ann to a friend,
Fanny, she explained what attracted her to Matthew:

I don't admire want of firmness in a man. I love *courage* and
determination in the male character. Forgive me, dear Fanny,
but *insipids* I never did like, and having not long ago tasted
such delightful society I have now a greater contempt than in
former days for that cast of character.

With both her parents coming from seafaring backgrounds, Ann
knew all too well the stress that mothers, wives and loved ones had
to endure while their men were at sea, sometimes for years at a
time. So she was understandably excited by the prospect of sailing
to Sydney Town with her new husband and establishing a home
there while he undertook his explorations.

Flinders was equally enthusiastic about having his wife join
him in a distant land and share the excitement of a project that

would have otherwise seen them separated for several years. It was not unusual for a wife to accompany her husband on foreign missions: there were even occasions where the wife of a captain of a Royal Navy ship was aboard with him in battle.

It is not difficult to understand the shock that the newlyweds felt, therefore, when a communication arrived from Sir Joseph Banks on 21 May, while *Investigator* lay in Sheerness awaiting orders from the Admiralty to proceed to sea.

> I have but time to tell you that the news of your marriage, which was published in the Lincoln paper, has reached me. The Lords of the Admiralty have heard also that Mrs. Flinders is on board the *Investigator*, and that you have some thought of carrying her to sea with you. This I was very sorry to hear, and if that is the case I beg to give you my advice by no means to adventure to measures so contrary to the regulations and the discipline of the Navy; for I am convinced by language I have heard, that their Lordships will, if they hear of her being in New South Wales, immediately order you to be superseded, whatever may be the consequences, and in all likelihood order Mr. Grant to finish the survey.

Flinders was stunned by the news that his wife would not be permitted to sail with him to Port Jackson, and that he could be 'superseded' for the mission. He was certain there must have been a misunderstanding, so on 24 May he replied to Sir Joseph.

> I am much indebted to you, Sir Joseph, for the information contained in your letter of the 21st. It is true that I had an intention of taking Mrs Flinders to Port Jackson, to remain

there until I should have completed the voyage, and to have then brought her home again in the ship, and I trust that the service would not have suffered in the least by such a step. The Admiralty have most probably conceived that I intended to keep her on board during the voyage [the circumnavigation of New Holland], but this was far from my intentions ... If their Lordships' sentiments should continue the same, whatever may be my disappointment, I shall give up the wife for the voyage of discovery; and I would beg of you, Sir Joseph, to be assured that even this circumstance will not damp the ardour I feel to accomplish the important purpose of the present voyage, and in a way that shall preclude the necessity of any one following after me to explore.

It would be too much presumption in me to beg of Sir Joseph Banks to set this matter in its proper light, because by your letters I judge it meets with your disapprobation entirely; but I hope that this opinion has been formed upon the idea of Mrs Flinders continuing on board the ship when engaged in real service.

Banks decided to put Flinders' explanation before the Admiralty, but Flinders interceded before that was done. After a week spent considering the situation and what the success of the expedition meant to his wife and him as a family, on 3 June he wrote once more to Sir Joseph.

I feel much obliged by your offer to lay the substance of my letter before the Admiralty, but I foresee that, although I should in the case of Mrs Flinders going to Port Jackson have been more particularly cautious of my stay there, yet their

Lordships will conclude naturally enough that her presence would tend to increase the number of and to lengthen my visits. I am therefore afraid to risk their Lordships' ill opinion, and Mrs Flinders will return to her friends immediately that our sailing orders arrive.

Flinders was soon to learn the reason for his wife not being permitted to join him for the voyage and a new life in Port Jackson. While *Investigator* was lying at anchor in Sheerness, Earl St Vincent, who was about to become the First Lord of the Admiralty, happened to be passing in a boat so took the opportunity to pay a surprise visit to young Commander Flinders so he could learn more of the planned voyage. Unfortunately for Flinders, though, everything that could have gone wrong at the time did. There was no lookout on the ship to report the approach of the Earl's boat and as a consequence no berthing party was there to welcome him, and no officer was on the quarterdeck – three matters which could easily be seen as a lack of discipline aboard the ship. But worse was to come: Earl St Vincent was able to enter the captain's cabin unannounced and, as he would later report back to the Admiralty, Mrs Flinders, who was aboard at the time, was seen to be making 'too open a declaration of that being her home' as she was 'seated in the captain's cabin without her bonnet'.

CHAPTER TEN

Investigator on the Southern Coast

Flinders' heart was heavy following the Admiralty's resolute declaration that his wife of mere weeks was forbidden to sail with him aboard *Investigator* to Sydney Town. The plan they had committed to before they made their vows was now in ruins.

As if this decree from the Lords – and a not so subtle admonishment from his mentor, Sir Joseph Banks – weren't enough of an emotional burden for Flinders, there was more to come. He received a letter from his father prior to *Investigator* setting sail from England, and in it Flinders senior left his son in no doubt that he did not approve of his marriage.

It was a shattering blow for a man who held his father in such high esteem, but as disappointing as the news was, Flinders opted not to reply in haste. Instead, he took time to compose a warm but firm response.

I wish, my dear father, to say a little upon a former letter of yours ... in which you seem to think that my conduct has

I wish, my dear father, to say a little upon a former letter of yours ... in which you seem to think that my conduct has

225

not been altogether that of a dutiful or at least of an affectionate son. That you should think so, occasioned much uneasiness both to me and to my dear wife, for I find her so much superior in penetration and judgement to the generality of women, that there are but few occurrences upon which I do not consult her ...

I am sorry, that you feel dissatisfied with my marriage. Tis true I did not formally ask your consent to it, but when Miss Chappelle had been considered ... in a previous conversation you made not one objection to her.

From seeing your letters, she feels as under your displeasure, which adds to her present uneasiness. The time of my marriage, you say my dear father, is the worst part of it. It is certain I should not have married but with the idea of taking her with me. Others had been allowed this privilege, and I could not foresee that I should have been denied it. Yet I am by no means sorry for having married. If you knew her worth, you could not regret it. I am happy to add here, that her health is so far improved at this time ... Her letter today from Battersea says that she is able to run upstairs.

I leave her with a kind mother and family ...

Begging you, my dear father, and my mother and family to accept my love and duty I remain your affectionate son.

M. Flinders

Despite these frustrations, Flinders' focus remained firmly on the task ahead: to be the explorer who revealed to the world the outline of a landmass that was known to lie within an area covering a near inconceivable 5,500,000 square miles.

With *Investigator*'s refit in Sheerness completed and the ship ready for sea, her new commander, who had just turned 27, eased her away from the dock and out to The Nore, an anchorage at the mouth of the Thames Estuary, fewer than 10 miles away. Once there, he awaited his orders from the Admiralty so he could finally sail for the Southern Hemisphere:

> I was anxious to arrive upon the coasts of Terra Australis in time
> to have the whole of the southern summer before me ... I took
> advantage of this delay to remedy an inconvenience, under
> which we were otherwise likely to suffer. The quantity of
> provisions necessary to be carried out did not leave room in the
> holds for more water than fifty tons; but by removing ten of the
> long guns, and substituting a few light carronades which could
> be carried on the upper deck, ten tons more of water might be
> received, without reducing our efficient strength; for the ship
> was too deep to admit of the guns below being used in bad
> weather, whereas the carronades would be always serviceable.

The directors of the East India Company saw 'the voyage being within the limits of the Company's charter, from the expectation of our examinations and discoveries proving advantageous to their commerce and the eastern navigation', so the company directors committed £600 for food for 'the men of science, the officers of the ship' and Commander Flinders. They also advised they would match the £600 with an identical amount, should the circumnavigation be completed.

On 26 May Flinders was directed to move his ship to the anchorage at Spithead, at the eastern end of the Solent. His final orders would be delivered to him there; once they were received, *Investigator* was free to set sail, enter the Atlantic and turn south.

This passage to Spithead was only 150 miles, but it wasn't without incident, as Flinders later explained:

> In working up under Dungeness, on the evening of May 28, we made a trip in shore, towards the town of Hythe, as I supposed from the chart. A little after six, the officer of the watch had reported our distance from the land to be near two leagues; and there being from 10 to 14 fathoms marked within two or three miles of it, and no mention of any shoal lying in the way, I intended to stand on half an hour longer; but in ten minutes, felt the ship lifting upon a bank. The sails were immediately thrown aback; and the weather being fine and water smooth, the ship was got off without having received any apparent injury. This sand is laid down in the Admiralty charts, under the name of the Roar; and extends from Dungeness towards Folkstone, at the distance of from two and a half, to four miles from the land. The leadsman, having found no bottom with 15 fathoms at ten minutes before six, had very culpably quitted the chains when his watch was out, without taking another cast of the lead; and the ship, in going at the rate of two knots and three-quarters, was upon the bank at twenty minutes after six.

The incident was so minor that Flinders could have let it go unreported, but he was a meticulous navigator and felt it was his duty to advise the Admiralty so that its charts could be corrected. Unfortunately, the Lords appear to have remained prickly towards Flinders since the incident with his wife, so, as Sir Joseph Banks advised him a few days later, they saw the grounding as a sign of incompetence. In addition, there was another occurrence that held their displeasure, as Sir Joseph continued:

I yesterday went to the Admiralty to enquire about the *Investigator*, and was indeed much mortified to learn there that you had been on shore in Hythe Bay, and I was still more mortified to hear that several of your men had deserted, and that you had had a prisoner entrusted to your charge, who got away at a time when the quarter-deck was in charge of a midshipman. I heard with pain many severe remarks on these matters, and in defence I could only say that as Captain Flinders is a sensible man and a good seaman, such matters could only be attributed to the laxity of discipline which always takes place when the captain's wife is on board, and that such lax discipline could never again take place, because you had wisely resolved to leave Mrs Flinders with her relations.

It was a mild admonishment from the great man but Flinders felt he had to defend his honour. He responded accordingly:

Finding so material a thing as a sandbank three or four miles from the shore unlaid down in the chart, I thought it a duty incumbent upon me to endeavour to prevent the like accident from happening to others, by stating the circumstances to the Admiralty, and giving the most exact bearings from the shoal that our situation would enable me to take, with the supposed distance from the land. It would have been very easy for me to have suppressed every part of the circumstance, and thus to have escaped the blame which seems to attach to me, instead of some share of praise for my good intentions ...

Flinders also denied emphatically any responsibility for the alleged desertions:

My surprise is great that the Admiralty should attach any blame to me for the desertion of these men from the *Advice* brig, which is the next point in your letter, Sir Joseph. These men were lent, among others, to the brig, by order of Admiral Graeme. From her it was that they absented themselves, and I reported it to the Admiralty.

Once *Investigator* had reached Spithead, it was decided that, as a precaution, she should be put into a dry dock in nearby Portsmouth so the hull could be inspected for damage. She was given the all-clear and returned to the offshore anchorage. By now, Flinders was becoming increasingly exasperated at the time the Admiralty was taking to deliver his final orders to him. He vented this disappointment in a letter to his father on 10 July:

My dear father
In the letter of June 21 to my mother I gave you every reason to think that we should have been at sea long before this. I was deceived in my expectation of receiving my final orders before leaving town, nor indeed have I received them yet. I am much mortified at being thus delayed, nor am I fully acquainted with the cause. Great pressure of more important business than ours is the external one, but I think there must be something more; for I saw the passport, and my instructions which were signed; so that there appears to be little else to do than to send them down to me yet this is not done. We are completely ready for sea. Our men of science, our stock of live cattle, everything on board; and 12 hours after receiving orders should probably be out of sight of Spithead.

Flinders and his new bride communicated virtually on a daily basis, and their letters revealed a wealth of love. 'I am just as awkward without thee as half of a pair of scissors without its fellow,' Flinders wrote. 'I trust that a very short period indeed will now see me absent from England and each wasting day will then bring nearer the period of my return. Rest confident, my dear, of thy ardent and unalterable affection of thy own MF; he does love thee beyond everything.'

Eventually, on 17 July, the orders arrived. It was a 1650-word document, titled 'By the Commissioners for executing the office of Lord High Admiral of the United Kingdom of Great Britain and Ireland, etc.', and it spelled out everything that was expected of the expedition and its commander.

> You should proceed in [the sloop you command] to the coast of New Holland for the purpose of making a complete examination and survey of the said coast, on the eastern side of which His Majesty's colony of New South Wales is situated ...
>
> [W]hen you shall have completed the whole of the surveys and examinations as abovementioned, you are to lose no time in returning with the sloop under your command to England for farther orders, touching on your way, if necessary, at the Cape of Good Hope, and repairing with as little delay as possible to Spithead, and transmit to our secretary an account of your arrival.

Apart from having the comfort of his much-loved moggy, Trim, while on board *Investigator*, Flinders was pleased to see that things were finally falling into place as he had hoped. For example, there appeared to be one bonus – a consideration from the Admiralty, among the many directives for Flinders and his crew:

So soon as you shall have completed the whole of these surveys and examinations as above directed, you are to proceed to, and examine very carefully the east coast of New Holland, seen by captain Cook, from Cape Flattery to the Bay of Inlets; and in order to refresh your people, and give the advantage of variety to the painters, you are at liberty to touch at the Fejees [Fiji], or some other of the islands in the South Seas.

Flinders also received from the Admiralty a passport signed by the French government, with an addendum stating that he was 'to act in all respects towards French ships as if the two countries were not at war'.

Investigator was then free to sail. Flinders made some last-minute preparations, sending a longboat to shore with an order for some fresh provisions, and these were delivered the following morning. While awaiting the stores, the 87 men Flinders had in his crew readied the ship for sea. Everything on deck and below was secured so it could not break free in the event of rough weather. At the same time, final checks of halyards, sheets, lines and rigging were made.

Flinders held great confidence in the senior officers he had chosen to support him. This inner sanctum included close associates from *Reliance* who were equally enthusiastic about making the return voyage to Port Jackson and remaining with the ship for the circumnavigation. Flinders had appointed John Thistle to the position of master. He had been aboard *Norfolk* for the voyage through Bass Strait and around Van Diemen's Land, and was a man noted for his ability to climb a mast faster than anyone else. The Admiralty had appointed a number of 'men of science', to the project – an astronomer, a naturalist, a natural-history painter, a landscape painter, a gardener and a 'miner', as well as four servants to support them. To Flinders' pleasure, his brother Samuel would again join him, this time as one of the ship's two lieutenants.

Among the six master's mates and midshipmen was Flinders' young nephew by marriage, John Franklin. Later in his life, Franklin would claim that this voyage with Flinders had kindled his desire to explore unknown territories. So successful was he in this that he was eventually knighted for his achievements; he also became lieutenant-governor of Tasmania from 1837 to 1843. In 1845, at the age of 59, Franklin would lead an ill-fated two-ship expedition that set out to locate the Northwest Passage through the Canadian Arctic. Well into the voyage, when the two ships were near King William Island, they were trapped by ice. Eventually, after they failed to return home, an extensive search for them was conducted across the white and wild wilderness, but without success. Franklin died aboard his ship, HMS *Erebus*, about a year after the ship became icebound, and eventually all members of the expedition perished. If there was a positive side to this tragedy, however, it was that the wide search for the men did lead to the discovery of a possible passage through which ships could pass.

Flinders could not get to sea soon enough, so immediately the stores came aboard, the capstan clacked into action, the anchor was weighed and stowed, then the sails were progressively unfurled to catch the light easterly wind that was blowing.

Fewer than 50 miles into the voyage, Flinders made some interesting observations regarding *Investigator*'s compass – an extension of what he had seen during his previous expeditions in Australia. He found that there were considerable variations – up to four degrees – in the reading of the compass when it was removed from the binnacle and positioned elsewhere on the ship's deck.

These 'compass deviations', as they are now known, were caused by iron within the ship and by the Earth's magnetic field. Flinders would record these variations throughout the entire voyage, noting that they were different in the Northern and Southern Hemispheres and close to the equator. His research into this problem, and his subsequent findings over the years, continue to be important in compass installations to this day.

Within two weeks of departure, when *Investigator* was well into the Atlantic and being steered towards Madeira, the commander made another realisation. He and his crew were seeing firsthand why this ship had been spared from the Royal Navy's fleet and made available for the expedition.

It was calm on the 31st, and I had a boat lowered down and went round the ship with the carpenter, to inspect the seams near the water line, for we had the mortification to find the ship beginning to leak so soon as the channel was cleared, and in the three last days she had admitted three inches of water per hour. The seams appeared sufficiently bad, especially under the counter and at the butt ends, for the leak to be attributable to them; and as less water came in when the ship was upright than when heeling to a beam wind, I hoped the cause need not be sought lower down.

On reaching Madeira on 3 August and anchoring off the town of Funchal, on the island's southern shore, Flinders had his carpenters do what they could to stem the leaks. After four days, with the repairs complete, *Investigator* was prepared to sail again. Once clear of the lee of the island, the temporary repairs were immediately put to the test as *Investigator* was hammered by a howling east-north-easterly wind, which was so strong that the call from the master went out to clew up almost every sail so the chance of damage to the ship was minimised.

As well as safeguarding the seaworthiness of his vessel, Flinders had to care for the health of his crew. From this point in the voyage he ordered 'lime juice and sugar to be mixed with the grog'; this concoction was 'given daily to every person on board'.

As *Investigator* neared the equator, the leaks reappeared – now worse than ever – apparently because the ship was twisting to the degree that the caulking was being squeezed out of the seams between the planks.

The leakiness of the ship increased with the continuance of the south-west winds; and at the end of a week, amounted to five inches of water an hour. It seemed, however, that the leaks were mostly above the water's edge, for on tacking to the westward they were diminished to two inches. This working of the oakum out of the seams indicated a degree of weakness which, in a ship destined to encounter every hazard, could not be contemplated without uneasiness. The very large ports, formerly cut in the sides to receive thirty-two-pound carronades, joined to what I had been able to collect from the dock yard officers, had given me an unfavourable opinion of her strength; and this was now but too much confirmed. Should it be asked, why representations were not made, and a stronger vessel procured? I answer, that the exigencies of the navy were such at that time, that I was given to understand no better ship could be spared from the service; and my anxiety to complete the investigation of the coasts of Terra Australis did not admit of refusing the one offered.

At around seven a.m. on 8 September, *Investigator* 'crossed the line'. Flinders had no desire to curtail the crew's celebrations, especially since there was a large number of men who had not previously ventured into the Southern Hemisphere. Flinders' contingent of marines included a drummer and a fife player, and they were put to good use:

> It was a part of my plan for preserving the health of the people, to promote active amusements amongst them, so long as it did not interfere with the duties of the ship; and therefore the ancient ceremonies used on this occasion, were allowed to be performed this evening; and the ship being previously put under snug sail, the seamen were furnished with the means, and the permission, to conclude the day with merriment.

Once *Investigator* clawed her way out of the doldrums and entered the zone of the south-east trade winds, Flinders became even more concerned about the safety of his ship, which was then averaging just under four knots. 'The swell from the southward,' he wrote, 'with which these winds were for some days accompanied, caused the ship to work so much, that she soon let in as great a quantity of water on this tack, as she before had done on the other.' He had no option but to reconfigure the loading arrangement on board so that stresses on the ship's structure were reduced. Two 18-pound carronade-style cannons were moved from the main deck to the hold, and numerous other heavy items were shifted as well.

'After this was done,' Flinders was pleased to note, 'the tremulous motion caused by every blow of the sea, exciting a sensation as if the timbers of the ship were elastic, was considerably diminished; and the quantity of water admitted by the leaks was also somewhat reduced.' There is no doubt, however, that he continued to harbour concerns about whether *Investigator* would survive, should they encounter a fearsome storm in the Southern Ocean.

It was 17 October when *Investigator* hauled onto the wind, rounded the Cape of Good Hope and entered the safe anchorage of False Bay – a much better option in the prevailing conditions than lying at anchor in Cape Town's Table Bay, 30 nautical miles to the north, where the land formed an undesirable lee shore. Flinders proudly recorded that all officers and men had remained in fine health since departing Spithead. Apart from the compulsory taking of lime juice and sugar in the tropics, and sauerkraut and vinegar in the higher latitudes, Flinders strove to make the conditions aboard ship as healthy as possible.

I had begun very early to put in execution the beneficial plan, first practised and made known by the great captain Cook. It was in the standing orders of the ship, that on every fine day the deck below and the cockpits should be cleared, washed, aired with stoves, and sprinkled with vinegar. On wet and dull days they were cleaned and aired, without washing. Care was taken to prevent the people from sleeping upon deck, or lying down in their wet clothes; and once in every fortnight or three weeks, as circumstances permitted, their beds, and the contents of their chests and bags, were opened out and exposed to the sun and air. On the Sunday and Thursday mornings, the ship's company was mustered, and every man appeared clean shaved and dressed; and when the evenings were fine, the drum and fife announced the fore castle to be the scene of dancing; nor did I discourage other playful amusements which might occasionally be more to the taste of the sailors, and were not unseasonable.

By the end of October, *Investigator* was considered to be ready for sea once more: provisions and stores were aboard, sails had been examined, repaired and re-bent on the spars, and the re-caulking of the suspect sections of the hull had been completed. Unfortunately for Flinders, a valuable member of the expedition team, the astronomer John Crosley, who had been ill for much of the time since leaving England, had decided it was best to stay ashore in Cape Town and recover there. With no suitable replacement among the crew, Flinders' only option was to assume this role himself. This would place a considerably greater burden on his position as commander.

Flinders was on deck before sunrise on 4 November, and by the time the golden orb had blazed its way above the eastern horizon he had made a decision: the wind was suitably strong and from the right direction for them to set sail and head for New Holland. The crew busied themselves across the deck and through the rig, making the necessary preparations before weighing anchor and leaving port.

As always, any significant activity on deck saw Trim in the middle of the action: 'When the nature of the bustle upon deck was not understood by him,' wrote Flinders, 'he would mew and rub his back up against the legs of one and the other, frequently at risk of being trampled underfoot, until he obtained the attention of someone to satisfy him. He knew what good discipline required, and on taking in a reef, never presumed to go aloft until the order was issued; but so soon as the officer had given the words "Away up aloft!", up he jumped along with the seamen; and so active and zealous was he that none could reach the top before or so soon as he did.'

Once clear of the bay, *Investigator* was turned to the east and began a 4600-nautical-mile haul towards Leeuwin's Land, the south-western corner of the large but little-known part of the globe that would hold Flinders' attention for much of the next 18 months. His mind was filled with anticipation; on reaching Leeuwin's Land, his latest voyage of discovery would begin in earnest.

Flinders' first challenge was to explore, survey and sketch the yet to be detailed land to the east, always sailing as close as possible to the coast. His primary task was to confirm, one way or the other, whether this coastline was part of one enormous continent or whether it was made up of a number of islands with waterways extending from the Southern Ocean through to Torres Strait. Should it prove to be one continuous coastline, Flinders realised, then it would stretch for more than 2000 nautical miles, from Leeuwin's Land right across to Bass Strait and Cape Howe.

In planning his course across this vast and often volatile sector of the world's oceans, Flinders kept prudent seamanship at the forefront of his mind. He knew he was sailing a leaky ship that could easily surrender to the worst of storms, should they venture into the Roaring Forties and even higher latitudes, so he had to be conservative. Having sailed through this region on three previous occasions, he knew all too well how bad things could get, so he opted for a course that would never see the ship sail south of the thirty-seventh parallel. He considered such a course 'to be sufficiently distant from the verge of the south-east trade to insure a continuance of western winds; and to be far enough to the north, to avoid the gales incident to high latitudes'.

This would prove to be a wise decision on the commander's part. As it turned out, the winds were never at any stage so strong that the call had to go out to close-reef the topsails; most of the time, *Investigator* was running with the yards squared to the following wind or sailing full-and-by, with a perfect wind from the western sector filling every sail that could be set. Over one 12-day stretch she averaged a most impressive 6.5 knots, which meant she covered around 160 nautical miles a day.

On the rare occasion when the ship was beset by a calm, Flinders continued with his research. The deviations in the compass, and the effect that being in the Southern Hemisphere had on the compass needle, still intrigued him. Again he experimented, moving the helmsman's compass from the binnacle to other locations on the ship and logging the differences in readings. In another experiment, Flinders lowered a bucket that had been specially modified with valves to a depth of 150 fathoms so he could bring a sample of water from that level back to the ship and compare its temperature with that of the water on the sea surface.

When he was certain that his ship was finally closing on land, Flinders adopted an especially cautious approach to his navigation. There were two reasons. Firstly, he was uncertain about the accuracy of a traced copy of a 'general' chart of the coast by the French Rear-Admiral Bruni d'Entrecasteaux, 'which had been furnished to me from the hydrographical office at the Admiralty' before leaving England. Secondly, 'notwithstanding the nearness of the land there were no signs of such proximity: no discolouring in the water, no sea weed, no new birds, and but few of the species before seen'.

Considerable relief came on Sunday, 6 December 1801, when the shallow hills of the promontory on Leeuwin's Land were sighted low on the horizon off the port bow. A brisk north-westerly wind was blowing, so *Investigator* was hauled up – the port side braces were eased and the sheets to starboard trimmed accordingly, while back aft the men at the mizzen mast sheeted home the spanker. The ship could then sail a course that would see her close on the coast but remain a comfortable distance from the rocky islets and reefs that extend five nautical miles south-east of the cape. From that point,

Flinders' survey of the coastline would begin, even though 'the examination ... was not prescribed in my instructions to be made at this time; but the difference of sailing along the coast at a distance, or in keeping near it and making a running survey, was likely to be so little that I judged it advisable to do all that circumstances would allow whilst the opportunity offered'.

It was Flinders who named the 'most projecting part' of Leeuwin's Land: 'This supposed isle is, therefore, what I denominate Cape Leeuwin, as being the south-western and most projecting part of Leeuwin's Land.' It was the first topographical feature he named during the voyages of *Investigator*, but by the time he had completed the expedition he would be credited with putting the names of some 240 points of interest across the southern half of the continent and around Van Diemen's Land on his charts. Captain Cook, by comparison, had 103 features between Point Hicks and Cape York attributed to him.

Europeans had been aware of this southern coastline for nearly two centuries, yet the finer detail was unknown; Flinders would correct that anomaly. The name 'Leeuwin's Land' had appeared on Dutch charts after a Dutch East Indiaman, *Leeuwin*, sailed past the 'low-lying sandy dunes' in March 1622. In 1627 the Dutch ship *Gulden Zeepard* ('golden seahorse') had become the first recorded European vessel to actually sail the southern coast.

It was a 1000-nautical-mile venture from Cape Leeuwin to what Flinders would name Fowler's Bay (after one of his two lieutenants aboard *Investigator*), just west of Ceduna in South Australia. Considering the era and the equipment available to them, the coastline had been surprisingly well mapped by the *Gulden Zeepard*'s captain, François Thijssen, and the Dutch explorer Pieter Nuyts, who was on board. Thijssen referred to a significant stretch of the coast as 'Land van Pieter Nuyts', after the highest-ranking officer on the ship.

In 1791, a decade before the arrival of *Investigator*, the British vessel *Cape Chatham*, with George Vancouver as captain, reached Cape Leeuwin then sailed 175 nautical miles to the east and anchored in a large sound – the site of today's Albany. After spending a week in this inlet, Vancouver named it King George's Sound – in honour of the monarch at the time – then decided to continue east. *Cape Chatham* had covered some 220 nautical miles and was approaching an island about 25 nautical miles offshore when adverse conditions began to prevail. Vancouver could see no sense in trying to push on, so he decided to abandon the coastal exploration and return to his planned voyage to north-west America across the Pacific. Appropriately, he named the island he could see Termination Island.

A year later, d'Entrecasteaux also sailed this coast during his search for the missing explorer Lapérouse, but, running short of water and unable to find a suitable source on the barren and inhospitable shoreline, he too abandoned his survey. The only other European explorer known to have been in these southern waters was another Frenchman, Louis Aleno de Saint Aloüarn. He anchored his ship off Leeuwin's Land in 1772 in the hope he might rendezvous with his countryman Yves-Joseph de Kerguelen-Trémarec, after their two ships lost visual contact during a Southern Ocean fog. He soon gave up and sailed north along what was a partly known coast, until he reached Dirk Hartog Island on 17 March 1772. He went ashore there and formally claimed possession of Western Australia on behalf of King Louis XV.

King George's Sound promised the sheltered water that Flinders was seeking after the long haul from False Bay, and *Investigator* anchored there on 8 December. Flinders wrote that the bay was 'the proper place in which to prepare ourselves for the examination of the south coast of Terra Australis ... where the

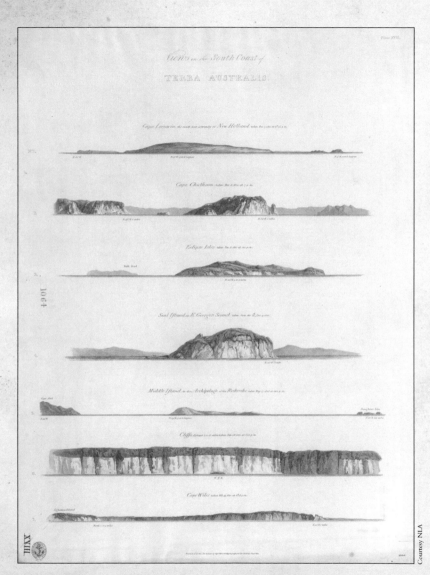

A newly discovered land: Flinders' superbly detailed drawings of the south coast of Terra Australis.

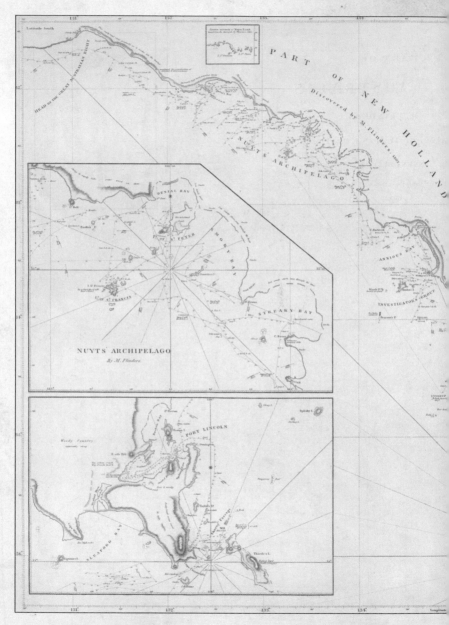

Fine detail: Chart of Terra Australis by Matthew Flinders, Commander of HM Sloop
Investigator, South Coast Sheet III (1802).

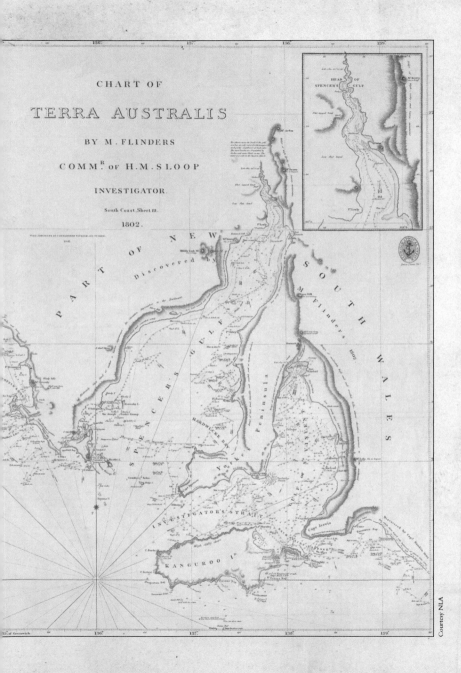

CHART OF

TERRA AUSTRALIS

BY M. FLINDERS

COMM.ᴿ OF H.M. SLOOP

INVESTIGATOR.

South Coast, Sheet III.

1802.

PART OF NEW

SOUTH WALES

Discovered by

SPENCER'S GULF

York's Peninsula

INVESTIGATOR'S STRAIT

KANGUROO Iˢ.

HEAD OF
SPENCER'S GULF

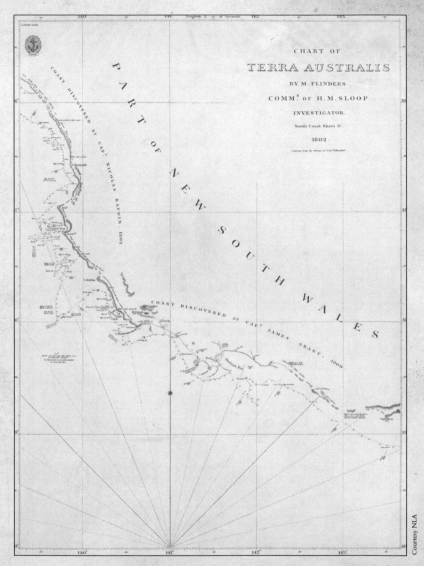

Bearings from his boat: Chart of Terra Australis by Matthew Flinders, Commander of HM Sloop *Investigator*, South Coast Sheet IV (1802).

Salvation for sailors on a sand cay: The loss of *Porpoise* and *Cato* more than 200 nautical miles from land.

Living in hope: View of Wreck Reef Bank at low water following the loss of *Porpoise* and *Cato*.

(Continue the pagination, and leave no more space between N.º 1 and 2
than between two chapters)

~~Appendix~~

X

N.º 2 (Type one size smaller)

On the errors of the ~~magnetic needle on ship-board, and in the immensity of~~ compass arising from attractions within the ship; and others from the magnetism of land; with precautions for obviating their effects in marine surveying.

~~Differences of variation from changing the direction of the Investigator's head, or the place of the compass.~~ A ~~standard established~~ mean performed for the difference at the binnacle, in each hemisphere. ~~Mode in which the observed~~ ~~have been corrected to the true variation, in this voyage; and the proper variation found for the bearings in the survey. Similar errors have existed in other ships. Analogy between the attraction of iron in the ship, and of the land; with exceptions. Precautions necessary in the use of the compass in marine surveying.~~

Several ~~suspected~~ instances ~~have been mentioned~~ in the course of this voyage, where the compass showed ~~different~~ variation ~~on being removed~~ in the direction of the ship's ~~head being~~ ~~changed~~ and some ~~which differ~~ ~~each time on removing the com~~ pass from one part of the ship to another; ~~In the english Channel, off the Start,~~ ~~third off the Start, off the Start;~~ where the true variation was about 25.º west, observations on the binnacle gave 29.½º, whilst others taken (sixty-eight miles lower down Channel) upon the booms before the main mast, gave only 24.º; and in the experiment made with five compasses, Vol. I. p. 18, the mean ~~difference between the~~ variation at the binnacle ~~and on the booms~~ was ~~1.~~ 37.º greater than on the booms. Finding that the situation of the compass was ~~thus~~ an object of importance, I determined very early in the voyage ~~in the survey of~~ ~~the coasts of Terra Australis~~ to ~~keep~~ place it always upon the binnacle, both when taking bearings for the survey, and when observing azimuths or amplitudes; nor, in any observations taken by myself, was it ever displaced except by way of experiment; but the officers occasionally ~~took variations~~ observed from different parts of the ship, when the sun could not be seen from the binnacle, until they were at length convinced that such observations were of no utility, either to the survey or for ascertaining the true variation.

It soon became evident, however, that ~~fixing~~ keeping the compass ~~in one~~ ~~upon one~~ ~~practical enough that the compass should always~~ ~~stand~~ ~~on~~ one spot was not sufficient alone to insure accuracy; ~~a change in~~ ~~when in use; for ~~ever~~ changing the direction of the ship's head ~~would point to~~ a difference ~~in the needle~~ and it was ~~became~~ necessary to ascertain ~~what the quantity was~~ the nature and proportional quantity of this difference, ~~before~~ a remedy ~~could be applied.~~ † ~~which way, that a proper correction might be made.~~ This could not be done in a satisfactory manner, until towards the conclusion of the voyage, when a great variety of observations were collected, but it ~~very soon appeared~~ that the iron in the ship had an attraction on the needle, and drew it forward from the binnacle ~~toward~~ ~~the main mast.~~ There was ~~however~~ this remarkable distinction taken at different dips of the needle in the Southern magnetic Hemisphere,

Observations from which are deduced the errors of varication at the Investigator's be made when changing the direction of the ship's head from the magnetic meridian was at East or West, at different dips of the needle on the Southern magnetic Hemisphere

Time 1802	Lat. S.	Lon E.	Az or Amp.	Comp.s	Observer *	Ships H.d	Var. obs.	Variat. supp.d true	Err.r of true obser.n	Err.r at 3 points	Dip S.°	Remarks
April												
a.m. 10	35.48	139.3	Amp.	N.°3	C	W by S	5.11 E	1.41 E	3.30 +			
p.m. ..	35.49	139.12	Az	..	..	S.E	0.50 W		2.31	3.34	66	Encounter B.
p.m. 12	36.42	139.50	..	..	..	S.SE½E	1.25 E	3.0	1.35			
a.m. 15	37.30	139.40	Amp.	..	..	South	4.8					
a.m. 16	37.50	139.41	..	..	..	S E by S	2.39	4.8		3.23	67	Off C. Buffon
.. ..	37.56	139.41	Az	..	..	S.S.E	2.2		1.54			
p.m. ..	37.55	139.48	..	..	..	N.E.⅛	2.2					
a.m. 22	39.38	144.40	..	..	..	W.S.W	11.52	8.30	3.22			
a.m. 24	39.38	144.1	..	..	..	South	7.59			3.26	68	Bass Strait
p.m. 25	38.36	144.20	..	..	..	N.E by E½E	3.41	7.30				
a.m. 26	38.38	144.30	Amp.			N.N.E⅛E	6.48		2.16			
								Means		3.28	67	
1802 Jan.												
a.m. 16	34.5	123.9	Az	N.°3	C	W.S.W	0.54 W	3.30 W	2.36 +			
1803 May												
p.m. 20	34.4	123.10	..	N.°1	..	East	6.10	..	2.40	2.45	64	J. Green I. Bay
1802 Feb.												
p.m. 15	34.5	135.9	..	..	..	S E by E	1.33	1.11 E	2.44			
..	34.6	135.9	Amp.	..	..	S W by W	3.56 E		2.44	3.10	..	Off P.t Drummond
Mar.												
p.m. 16	34.7	137.19	..	..	..	S W by S	4.38	2.50 E	1.48 +			
a.m. 17	34.16	137.16	Az	..	F	E by N	0.10 W		3.0			Off P.t Pearce
p.m. 17	34.22	137.21	..	..	C	S E	0.35	2.0	2.35	3.10	..	Spencer's Gulph
p.m. 18	34.42	137.14	Amp.	..	..	S.S.W	3.15 E		1.15 +			
p.m. 20	34.36	138.18	..	..	..	S by W	5.22			3.15	..	I. G. of S.t Vincent
a.m. 29			Az	..	..	S E⅛	2.27	4.45	2.10			
								Means		3.9	64	
1802 Jan.												
p.m. 19	32.40	125.25	Az	N.°1	C	E by N	7.15 W	4.30 W	2.45			
p.m. 20	32.30	125.40	..	N.°1,2,3	C&F	South	4.26			2.48	62	Off South East
p.m. 21	32.32	125.54	..	N.°1	C	N.E	6.13	4.15	1.58			
p.m. 22	32.24	126.23	Amp.	..	..	S by E	4.10					
a.m. 24	32.7	128.1	Az	..	..	E by N	6.4	3.0	3.4	3.8	..	
p.m. 25	32.17	128.2	..	N.°1,2,3	F	S by E	3.0					
a.m. 31	32.15	132.39	..	N.°1	..	E by N	2.49	0.0	2.49	2.52	..	Nuyt's Archip.
Feb.												
a.m. 2	32.23	132.56	..	..	C	S½W	0.19 E					
								Means		2.56	62	
1802 Jul.												
a.m. 28	25.0	153.23	Amp.	N.°3	C	N W by N	9.39 E	0.12 E	1.27 +			
a.m. 29	24.43	153.27	..	..	F	S E⅛ S	6.33	..	1.39	2.36	53½	Off Indian Head
Sept.												
a.m. 3	22.23	150.16	Az	N.°1	..	S E by E	6.31	8.45	2.14			I. Sheat-water B.
.. ..			..	N.°2,3	..	W N W	11.15		2.30 +	2.41	50½	D.o ships swung
								Means		2.39	52	

* In the column of observers

C means Commander, F lieutenant Flinders, and T M.r Thistle the master.

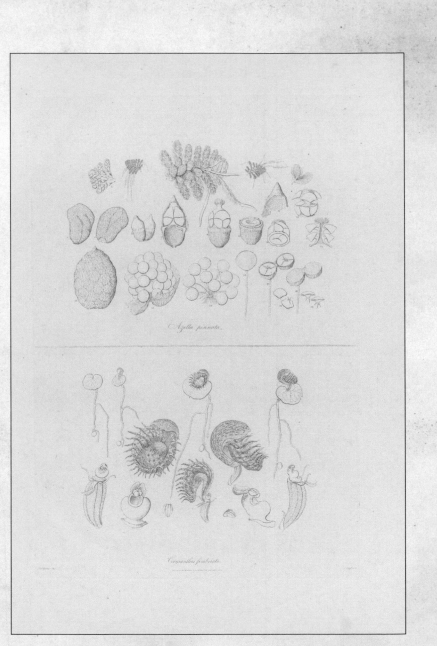

From land and sea: Botanical drawings from *A Voyage to Terra Australis*.

masts could be stripped, the rigging and sails put into order, and communication had with the shore without interruption from the elements'. After a few days, *Investigator* was moved into the even more protected Princess Royal Harbour, in the north-west corner of the sound, and while the crew carried out maintenance on their ship, Flinders and the botanists regularly went to shore in the cutter to survey the land and collect samples of the local flora.

Investigator lay at anchor for more than four weeks and a shore base of tents was established on a nearby beach. Inevitably, contact was established with the local natives, and as time passed, the relationship between the two sides became increasingly amicable. Flinders wrote about one of the more humorous and enjoyable moments:

Our friends the natives continued to visit us; and the old
man with several others being at the tents this morning,
I ordered the party of marines on shore to be exercised in
their presence. The red coats and white crossed belts were
greatly admired, having some resemblance to their own
manner of ornamenting themselves; and the drum, but
particularly the fife, excited their astonishment; but when
they saw these beautiful red-and-white men, with their
bright muskets, drawn up in a line, they absolutely screamed
with delight; nor were their wild gestures and vociferation to
be silenced but by commencing the exercise, to which they
paid the most earnest and silent attention. Several of them
moved their hands involuntarily, according to the motions;
and the old man placed himself at the end of the rank, with a
short staff in his hand, which he shouldered, presented,
grounded as did the marines their muskets, without,
I believe, knowing what he did. Before firing, the Indians

were made acquainted with what was going to take place; so
that the vollies did not excite much terror.

A seaman named Smith noted with great interest that these
Aboriginals 'rubbed their skin against ours, expecting some mark of
white upon theirs, but finding their mistake they appeared surprised'.

After spending both Christmas and New Year's Eve in the
harbour – apparently without much celebration – the crew headed
Investigator back to sea on 4 January, but not before Flinders had
sailed her back and forth across the sound with a net set from the
stern, trawling the bottom for samples of shells, fish and other items
that might be of interest to 'the men of science' on board. Once
offshore, the commander took it upon himself to carry out the
majority of the survey of the coastline.

> I ... endeavoured to keep so close in with the land that the
> breaking water on the shore should be visible from the ship's
> deck; by which means our supposed distance would be little
> subject to error, and no river or opening could escape being
> seen. This close proximity could not, however, be obtained
> in every part, especially where the coast retreated far back;
> but it was always attempted where practicable and unattended
> with much danger or loss of time; and when it could not be
> done, I was commonly at the mast head with a [spy]glass. All
> the bearings were laid down so soon as taken whilst the land
> was in sight, and before retiring to rest I made it a practice to
> finish up the rough chart for the day, as also my journals of
> astronomical observations, of bearings, and of remarks.

While Flinders was busy mapping the coast, the man swinging the
lead from the chains was equally active, constantly plumbing the

depths and noting them for his commander. Other crew were aloft as lookouts, all the time watching for anything that might indicate a navigational hazard for *Investigator*: white water, a change in the colour of the water, or a swirling eddy.

Flinders was leading by example: he was relentless in his efforts to present to the Admiralty the most detailed depiction of the vast and remarkable coastline he was observing. At numerous points along the coast, he called for the sea bed to be trawled so samples of marine life could be collected for analysis. Wherever possible – and when time permitted – he would land the botanists ashore so they could add to their collection of specimens, and the artist was given the opportunity to sketch the landform or any other salient feature that caught his eye. More often than not, Flinders too went ashore, usually with a theodolite so he could map the coastline more accurately. He also took considerable time studying the indigenous people of the region, comparing their stature and dialect with those who lived around Port Jackson. He wrote an extensive list of all Aboriginal words relating to features of the human body, and had the surgeon, Mr Hugh Bell, take measurements of their bodies.

As they pushed on to the east, all on board *Investigator* were increasingly amazed by the seemingly endless wall of vertical cliffs they were observing – all between 160 and 320 feet in height, and some unbroken by any form of beach for up to 200 miles. In fact, the men were observing the southern rim of the largest block of limestone on Earth, a 100,000-square-mile plain that was nearly treeless and riddled with caves and natural underground drainage systems. They could not have dreamt that the land that lay beyond those cliffs was so flat and featureless that, 90 years later, when steam locomotives were part of everyday life, the world's longest dead-straight (and virtually dead-flat) section of railway line – a tad under 300 miles – would stretch across that plain.

A circumstance on 9 January reminded everyone of the fickle nature of his own mortality – how a voyage like this into unknown territory could easily come to grief: the ship wrecked and all hands lost. These brave sailors took it all in their stride: danger was, in today's parlance, simply an occupational hazard. At the time, *Investigator* was near Termination Island – off the modern-day town of Esperance – and was confronted by yet another labyrinth of treacherous reefs and low-profile rocky islets, any one of which could claim the vessel.

> ... the view from the mast head was almost as crowded as before; but with this difference, that the islands were smaller, and the low rocks and patches of breakers more numerous. Seeing no probability of reaching a space of clear water in which to stand off and on during the night, and no prospect of shelter under any of the islands, I found myself under the necessity of adopting a hazardous measure; and with the concurrence of the master's opinion, we steered directly before the wind for the main coast, where the appearance of some beaches, behind other islands, gave a hope of finding anchorage. At seven in the evening we entered a small sandy bay; and finding it sheltered everywhere except to the south-westward ... the anchor was dropped in 7 fathoms, sandy bottom. The critical circumstance under which this place was discovered induced me to give it the name of Lucky Bay.

Flinders and every one of his 87 crew knew how rare it was to find such a sheltered cove on this coastline of never-ending cliffs. Had they not been so fortunate, they would have been forced to probe their way through the darkness, hoping not to plough onto any one of the countless reefs or islands that were scattered across the sea surface. The odds would have been stacked greatly against them.

After sailing another 750 nautical miles, naming many places along the way, Flinders began to realise that he was at the northernmost point of this coastline; it began to dip south-east quite rapidly. It was 28 January 1802, and as he sat at his table in his cabin that evening, working under the dim light of a flickering lantern, he took the time to appreciate the form of the coastline he had charted. It had the shape of the top of a large loop of rope – a bight. This would eventually lead Flinders to name it the Great Australian Bight.

Interestingly, the explorer Edward John Eyre is widely credited with naming the Great Australian Bight after he led the first land-based expedition to traverse 1000 miles along the coastline between Ceduna, South Australia, and Albany, Western Australia, in 1840–41. In fact, the first appearance of the name was in volume one of Flinders' *A Voyage to Terra Australis*, published in 1814 – the year before Eyre was born – but based on notes written on 28 January 1802: 'At the termination of the bank and of the second range of cliffs the coast became sandy, and trended north-eastward about three leagues; after which it turned south-east-by-east, and formed the head of the Great Australian Bight ...' Flinders then noted that the chart of the region created by d'Entrecasteaux was incorrect by a considerable margin in its positioning of 'the head of the Great Bight'.

From the time he had reached Cape Leeuwin, Flinders had been able to use the charts provided by the Admiralty for reference purposes only; they were quite inaccurate. This meant that, for the safety of his ship and his men, he had to use every navigational skill he possessed. After progressing to Fowler's Bay, however, Flinders was 'sailing blind': whatever lay between there and Western Port Bay, which Bass had discovered, was unknown. For all he knew, they might find they were dealing with two or more vast islands, or one large continent. Every man on board realised they were getting close to resolving one of the world's great geographical questions.

The wind mostly remained favourable as *Investigator* meandered her way along the coastline. At one stage Flinders came across a number of islands, which he named the Investigator Group; he named the largest of them Flinders Island, in honour of his brother, Samuel. Nothing out of the ordinary was observed until 20 February, when *Investigator* reached Linguanea Island, named after a British naval station in Jamaica, which Flinders had apparently visited when sailing with Bligh. When they were abeam of the island, the mystery of this coast, and of the land that lay ahead, only deepened: after rounding a nearby coastal headland, it was discovered that the land 'took the uncommon direction of N. 15° W', and that no land could then be seen to the north-east. No one knew whether this was a gulf or the strait they'd thought they might find.

Night was approaching, so Flinders decided to anchor half a mile off the shore in seven fathoms. As they approached the anchorage, he noticed that the surface of the water was surging with ripples – this was something he believed could only be created by a tidal flow. The intrigue heightened, as Flinders recorded:

A tide from the north-eastward, apparently the ebb, ran
more than one mile an hour; which was the more
remarkable from no set of tide, worthy to be noticed, having
hitherto been observed upon this coast. No land could be
seen in the direction from whence it came; and these
circumstances, with the trending of the coast to the north,
did not fail to excite many conjectures. Large rivers, deep
inlets, inland seas, and passages into the Gulph of
Carpentaria, were terms frequently used in our conversations

of this evening; and the prospect of making an interesting discovery seemed to have infused new life and vigour into every man in the ship.

The entire crew sensed they were on the brink of a breakthrough on this voyage of discovery. Sadly, however, tragedy would strike before they even got started.

Early on the morning of 21 February, the cutter was launched and Flinders was rowed to the land to the east of their anchorage, as he was 'anxious to ascertain its connexion with or separation from the main'. On confirming it was an island, he 'gave to it the name of Thistle's Island from the master who accompanied me'. The surveying and scientific activities continued through the day. During the afternoon, Thistle and Midshipman William Taylor took the cutter and a party of six men to a nearby beach on the mainland to collect water for the ship.

At dusk in the evening the cutter was seen under sail, returning from the main land; but not arriving in half an hour, and the sight of it having been lost rather suddenly, a light was shown and lieutenant Fowler went in a boat, with a lanthorn, to see what might have happened. Two hours passed without receiving any tidings. A gun was then fired, and Mr Fowler returned soon afterward, but alone. Near the situation where the cutter had been last seen he met with so strong a rippling of tide that he himself narrowly escaped being upset; and there was reason to fear that it had actually happened to Mr Thistle. Had there been daylight, it is probable that some or all of the people might have been picked up; but it was too dark to see anything, and no answer could be heard to the hallooing or to the firing of muskets.

The tide was setting to the southward and ran an hour and a half after the missing boat had been last seen, so that it would be carried to seaward in the first instance; and no more than two out of the eight people being at all expert in swimming, it was much to be feared that most of them would be lost.

Almost certainly, the cutter was swamped and capsized in the turbulent tidal race that Fowler experienced while searching for the missing men. The search resumed early the next day.

At daybreak I got the ship under way and steered over to the main land, in the direction where the cutter had been seen; keeping an officer at the masthead, with a glass, to look out for her. There were many strong ripplings, and some uncommonly smooth places ... and seeing a small cove with a sandy beach, steered in and anchored in 10 fathoms. A boat was despatched in search of the lost cutter, and presently returned towing in the wreck, bottom upward; it was stove in every part, having to all appearance been dashed against the rocks. One of the oars was afterwards found, but nothing could be seen of our unfortunate shipmates. The boat was again sent away in search; and a midshipman was stationed upon a headland, without-side of the cove, to observe everything which might drift past with the tide. From the heights near the extremity ... I examined with a glass the islands lying off, and all the neighbouring shores, for any appearance of our people, but in vain.

The crew was in mourning, none more so than Flinders, who had lost a highly valued shipmate and a close friend in Mr Thistle. He penned a heartfelt eulogy of the man:

Mr Thistle was truly a valuable man, as a seaman, an officer,
and a good member of society. I had known him, and we
had mostly served together, from the year 1794. He had
been with Mr Bass in his perilous expedition in the
whaleboat, and with me in the voyage round Van Diemen's
Land, and in the succeeding expedition to Glass House and
Hervey's Bays ... His zeal for discovery had induced him to
join the *Investigator* when at Spithead and ready to sail,
although he had returned to England only three weeks
before, after an absence of six years ... His loss was severely
felt by me, and he was lamented by all on board, more
especially by his messmates, who knew more intimately the
goodness and stability of his disposition.

Immediately after this incident, Flinders related a remarkable story
concerning the loss of the master:

This evening, Mr Fowler told me a circumstance which I
thought extraordinary; and it afterwards proved to be more
so. Whilst we were lying at Spithead, Mr Thistle was one
day waiting on shore, and having nothing else to do he went
to a certain old man, named Pine, to have his fortune told.
The cunning man informed him that he was going out on a
long voyage, and that the ship, on arriving at her destination,
would be joined by another vessel. That such was intended,
he might have learned privately; but he added, that
Mr Thistle would be lost before the other vessel joined. As
to the manner of his loss the magician refused to give any
information. My boat's crew, hearing what Mr Thistle said,
went also to consult the wise man; and after the prefatory
information of a long voyage, were told that they would be

shipwrecked, but not in the ship they were going out in: whether they would escape and return to England, he was not permitted to reveal.

This tale Mr Thistle had often told at the mess table; and I remarked with some pain in a future part of the voyage, that every time my boat's crew went to embark with me in the *Lady Nelson*, there was some degree of apprehension amongst them that the time of the predicted shipwreck was arrived. I make no comment upon this story, but recommend a commander, if possible, to prevent any of his crew from consulting fortune tellers.

Later, Flinders went to the beach where the missing men had gone in search of water – which he had named Memory Cove – and erected a memorial, comprising a copper plate mounted atop a stone cairn. The promontory where the cove is located he named Cape Catastrophe, and the seven nearby islands each took the name of one of the men who had been lost with Thistle.

The crew continued searching for any trace of the men for three days. Flinders went out in a small boat and scoured every cove and shoreline to the north. He did find a small keg that had belonged to Thistle, along with some splintered timber from the cutter, but nothing else. With the north having been covered, Lieutenant Fowler was then sent to the south.

This morning lieutenant Fowler had been sent to search the southern islands … for any remains of our people; but he was not able to land, nor in rowing round them to see any indication of the objects of his pursuit. The recovery of their bodies was now the furthest to which our hopes extended; but the number of sharks seen in the cove and at the last

anchorage rendered even this prospect of melancholy
satisfaction extremely doubtful.

Investigator's pressing lack of water dictated that they should sail
north. After 15 nautical miles they entered a harbour that had
been sighted by crew from the top of some hills on the mainland.
The anchor was weighed on the morning of Thursday,
25 February, and *Investigator* glided through the narrow channel
separating Thistle Island from the mainland, then sailing north
until the course was changed hard to port around a headland,
which was given the name of Flinders' home town, Cape
Donington. The adjacent harbour became Boston Bay, after the
village in which he had lived for many years, and the entire
region was recognised as Port Lincoln, 'in honour of my native
province'.

After a frustrating search for suitable water – much of it was
too salty – a site was found where holes could be dug in the white
clay and water extracted from them. It was a slow and arduous
process, and it took several days to collect the desired 60 tons of
water, but this gave the scientists ample time to study the
surroundings. In the years to come, it was suggested that only the
lack of a suitable natural water supply had prevented Port Lincoln
from becoming the capital of the state of South Australia.

Having deployed his crew on numerous tasks, Flinders himself
surveyed and sounded the surrounding waters, charting as accurately
as possible the position of the nearby islands. He employed an
interesting technique. Knowing *Investigator*'s exact location at
anchor, he went to the south-east end of Boston Island, having 'left
orders on board the ship to fire three guns at given times'. When he
saw the smoke belch from the cannons, he timed how long it was
before the sound reached him; on the supposition that sound travels

at 1142 feet per second and that 6060 feet make up a geographic mile, he was able to pinpoint the position where he stood.

Investigator lay at anchor in Boston Bay until 6 March, but before the northward exploration of the unknown coast started, Flinders directed Lieutenant Fowler to take one of the ship's boats to Memory Cove so that one final search could be made for the bodies of the missing men. Fowler returned two days later and reported that he had walked the shores of Memory Cove, revisited Thistle Island and also sailed along the shores of the passage 'but could find neither any traces of our lost people nor fragments of the wreck'.

As the ship sailed north from Boston Bay, all the men were excited by the prospect that they might be at the entrance to a wide and long strait. Within forty-eight hours of departure, however, their hopes were fading fast: the water was becoming shallower, and evidence of land was emerging ever so faintly in the east. 'Our prospects of a channel or strait cutting off some considerable portion of Terra Australis grew less,' Flinders noted, 'for now it appeared that the ship was entering a gulph.'

Within three days, the leadsman brought progress to a halt, calling from the chains that he had just registered a depth of two and a half fathoms. 'The ship was instantly veered to the eastward, and on the water deepening to 7, we let go the anchor,' Flinders wrote.

The following day, the botanists and others were sent ashore to carry out their studies, while Flinders and the surgeon, Mr Bell, set off to investigate the waters to the north. The further they travelled, the more apparent it became that the coastlines to east and west of them were closing towards a common point. On returning to the ship, Flinders ordered the crew to sail as far north as possible, then take to the tender once more, but it was a short-lived exercise. On 10 March they ran out of water and were surrounded by mudflats.

Flinders estimated that the gulf they had discovered was 185 miles long and 48 miles wide. After placing its outline on the chart, he gave it the name Spencer's Gulf, in honour of Lord Spencer (an ancestor of the late Diana, Princess of Wales).

With nothing more to be learned, it was time to continue the expedition's search of the waters to the east. The departure took place on 13 March, but was not without incident.

> ... we got under way ... having a light breeze from the
> north-westward. The western shore had been followed in
> going up, and for that reason I proposed to keep close to the
> east side in returning; but before eight o'clock the water
> shoaled suddenly from 4 to 2 fathoms, and the ship hung
> upon a mud bank covered with grass, two or three miles
> from the shore. A kedge anchor was carried out astern; and
> in half an hour we again made sail downward.

On exiting Spencer's Gulf, Flinders named the southernmost headland on the eastern side Cape Spencer, and from there he set a course to the south-east, to the nearest point of land that could be seen. *Investigator* arrived there on 24 March. A safe anchorage was located in a large bay open to the north-west, and even before the anchor was set, all on board were surprised by the number of kangaroos that could be seen on shore. It was a prime opportunity to replenish their supply of meat.

> The whole ship's company was employed this afternoon in
> skinning and cleaning the kangaroos; and a delightful regale
> they afforded, after four months' privation from almost any
> fresh provisions. Half a hundred weight of heads, forequarters
> and tails were stewed down into soup for dinner on this and

the succeeding days; and as much steaks given, moreover, to both officers and men as they could consume by day and by night. In gratitude for so seasonable a supply I named this southern land Kangaroo Island.

After two days at the island – which, much to Flinders' surprise, had no Aboriginal inhabitants – he called for the exploration of what appeared to be yet another gulf to the north to begin. Within hours, the ship was crossing what is now known as Investigator Strait. Their course was towards Cape Spencer, at which point Flinders planned to turn north and examine as much of the coastline as possible.

Before long, it was confirmed that this was another gulf, although this one covered about half the area of Spencer Gulf. After sailing as far as possible into the gulf, Flinders landed on the western shore on 30 March and climbed the foothills of a nearby ridge of land so he could get a better appreciation of his surroundings. Before the day was complete, he had made some notes on his observations:

> In honour of the noble admiral who presided at the Board
> of Admiralty when I sailed from England, and had
> continued to the voyage that [support] which Earl Spencer
> had set the example, I named this new inlet the Gulph of
> St Vincent. To the peninsula which separates it from
> Spencer's Gulph I have affixed the name of Yorke's
> Peninsula, in honour of the Right Honourable Charles
> Philip Yorke, who followed the steps of his above-
> mentioned predecessors at the Admiralty.

As Flinders wrote, 'our examination of the gulph of St Vincent was now finished', but before leaving the area he noted that 'Yorke's

Peninsula ... is singular in its form, bearing some resemblance to a very ill-shaped leg and foot'. He was pleased with the detail he had managed to obtain in both gulfs, so he decided to return to Kangaroo Island, from where he could check the accuracy of his timepiece through sun sights and also add to the ship's meat larder by hunting more kangaroos.

After a five-day stay, at sunrise on the morning of 7 April the launch was hauled aboard *Investigator* and her anchor weighed so she could continue to sail east into uncharted territory. In his notes on what he had observed during the explorations of the gulfs, Flinders had referred to how few Aboriginals they had seen, and how those who were spotted seemed to be very timid. Most interestingly, in referring to their shyness, he wrote, 'Such seemed to have been the conduct of these Australians ...' This appears to be the only time he referred to the natives as 'Australians'; usually he described them as 'Indians'.

Flinders would have liked to stay longer at Kangaroo Island, but he was feeling the pressure of time. 'The approach of the winter season,' he wrote, 'and an apprehension that the discovery of the remaining unknown part of the South Coast might not be completed before a want of provisions would make it necessary to run for Port Jackson.' An unexpected and initially dramatic delay to his progress came just 24 hours later.

... at four a white rock was reported from aloft to be seen
ahead. On approaching nearer it proved to be a ship standing
towards us, and we cleared for action, in case of being
attacked. The stranger was a heavy-looking ship, without any
top-gallant masts up; and our colours being hoisted, she
showed a French ensign, and afterwards an English jack
forward, as we did a white flag. At half-past five, the land

being then five miles distant to the north-eastward, I hove
to, and learned, as the stranger passed to leeward with a free
wind, that it was the French national ship *Le Géographe*,
under the command of captain Nicolas Baudin. We veered
round as *Le Géographe* was passing, so as to keep our
broadside to her, lest the flag of truce should be a deception;
and having come to the wind on the other tack, a boat was
hoisted out, and I went on board the French ship, which had
also hove to.

Flinders was aware that there was a French expedition somewhere
in the waters surrounding New Holland; indeed, the British
government had issued the French with passports so they would be
granted safe passage in the event of England and France being at
war. The convoy comprised two ships, *Le Géographe* and *Le
Naturaliste*, which had originally been built as part of Napoleon's
ill-conceived fleet, with which he had hoped to attack England.
They had departed from Le Havre nine months before *Investigator*
finally hoisted sail at Spithead. He also knew that there was some
concern within the British government that the French might be
intending to claim some part of New Holland – this was, of course,
one of the reasons for *Investigator*'s expedition. Now, the two sides
were meeting bow-to-bow at a place which, until that moment,
no one had known existed.

There was no provocative behaviour by either side as the two
ships came within hailing distance in a shallow bay on the mainland
coast 30 nautical miles north-west of Kangaroo Island. Flinders
subsequently noted that, 'in consequence of our meeting here,
I distinguished it by the name of Encounter Bay'. One wonders
whether, at this time, Flinders' mind returned to the loss of John
Thistle, and to what Fowler had told him about the fortune teller

who had predicted that Thistle would be lost before his ship encountered another vessel.

Being unable to speak French, Flinders had *Investigator*'s naturalist, Robert Brown, join him aboard *Le Géographe* to act as an interpreter. They were ushered into Baudin's cabin, and through the Frenchman's fractured English and Brown's translation of his French, the two commanders learned much about each other's endeavours.

Baudin explained that, on sighting a sail on the horizon, he and his crew had initially believed it to be *Le Naturaliste*; the two French ships had lost contact during a savage gale on the eastern side of Bass Strait on 7 March. Unbeknown to Baudin, *Le Naturaliste*'s captain, Jacques Hamelin, had subsequently sailed into Bass Strait and reached Western Port, where he was surveying some of the region, but with his crew rapidly taking ill with scurvy, he quit his exploration work and headed for Port Jackson to seek medical help from the British governor.

Baudin and Flinders compared notes and charts and discussed their respective voyages and discoveries. The French captain stated that he, too, had lost crewmen in an unfortunate accident with one of the ship's boats off the coast of Van Diemen's Land. Baudin also said that, despite his close examination of the coastline, he had 'found no ports, harbours or inlets, or anything of interest' between Wilson's Promontory and their current position. Somehow, Flinders would later realise, Baudin had missed the entrance to Port Phillip Bay.

Flinders felt that Baudin had taken a somewhat lethargic approach to his expedition. His background was the merchant service, not the French Navy, but he did have an interest in natural history and research; indeed, that was why the noted French botanist Antoine Laurent de Jussieu had recommended him for the task with the words, 'No choice could be happier than that of

Captain Baudin'. But Jussieu had backed a procrastinator, as Ernest Scott, professor of history at the University of Melbourne, explained in *The Life of Captain Matthew Flinders R.N.* in 1914:

> If Baudin had been the keen and capable commander that those who secured his appointment believed him to be, he should have discovered and charted the whole of the unknown southern coast of Australia, before Flinders was many days' sail from England. The fact that this important work was actually done by the English navigator was in no measure due to the sagacity of the Admiralty – whose officials procrastinated in an inexplicable fashion even after the *Investigator* had been commissioned and equipped – but to his own promptness, competence and zeal, and the peculiar dilatoriness of his rivals. Baudin's vessels reached Île-de-France [Mauritius] in March, 1801, and lay there for the leisurely space of forty days. Two-thirds of a year had elapsed before they came upon the Australian coast. But Baudin did not even then set to work where there was discovery to be achieved. Winter was approaching, and sailing in these southern seas would be uncomfortable in the months of storm and cold; so he dawdled up the west coast of Australia, in warm, pleasant waters, and made for Timor, where he arrived in August. He remained in the Dutch port of Kupang till the middle of November – three whole months wasted, nearly eleven months consumed since he had sailed from France. In the meantime, the alert and vigorous captain of the *Investigator* was speeding south as fast as the winds would take him, too eager to lose a day, flying straight to his work like an arrow to its mark, and doing it with the thoroughness and accuracy that were part of his nature.

Less than 24 hours after *Investigator* and *Le Géographe* crossed tacks, they went their separate ways. The French headed towards Kangaroo Island, as Flinders had advised Baudin that he would find water and be able to hunt fresh meat there, and *Investigator* continued on her planned course to the east.

It was a near windless day, so the two ships remained in sight of each other for many hours, even though they were sailing in opposite directions. Aboard *Investigator*, Flinders had every sail set in a bid to catch even the slightest wisp of wind. But it was rare, and all the sails – from the jib set at the tip of the bowsprit through to the spanker on the mizzen mast – hung limply from their spars, roused only briefly into action with a thump as they turned inside out with the roll of the ship on an ocean swell. At one stage, the ship covered just two nautical miles in six hours, and that gain came only as a result of the slight current running along the coast. For the next eight days, the ship struggled to average the speed of a crawl – just one knot – covering a miserable 24 nautical miles a day.

These were testing times. Eventually, the weather went from one extreme to the other, and with land always in close proximity there was no room for errors of seamanship.

The long swell from the southward still prevailed, and the barometer was fast falling ... in a clear interval, land was seen bearing S. 51° E.; and a thick squall with rain coming on, in which the wind shifted suddenly from north-north-west to south-west, we were forced to haul close up and let out the third reefs in order to weather the coast. A constant succession of rainy squalls prevented us from knowing how the land lay for some time, nor could an observation for the latitude be obtained.

On entering the western part of Bass Strait, Flinders went in search of an island he had discussed with Baudin.

> I had received an account of its lying to the north-west of Hunter's Isles. It afterwards appeared that the northern part was seen in January 1801 by Mr John Black, commander of the brig *Harbinger*, who gave to it the name of King's Island. Of this I was ignorant at the time; but since it was so very dangerous to explore the main coast with the present south-west wind, I was desirous of ascertaining the position of this island before going to Port Jackson, more especially as it had escaped the observation of Captain Baudin.

On 23 April the call came from the lookout standing on the platform at the trestletrees, more than 40 feet up the mainmast, that there was land on the horizon – it proved to be the northern tip of the island Flinders was searching for. *Investigator* was soon anchored in the lee of the island, and over the following three days the captain and his scientists explored as much of the 423-square-mile island as possible. However, the approach of winter and the need for some particular provisions for the ship meant *Investigator* had to begin its journey to Port Jackson. They'd already been at sea for nearly ten months.

> I wished to finish as much of the South Coast as possible ... I determined to run over to the high land we had seen on the north side of Bass' Strait, and to trace as much of the coast from thence eastward as the state of the weather and our remaining provisions could possibly allow.

Conditions were perfect for a course to the north when *Investigator*'s anchor was weighed and her sails unfurled. In no time she was romping along in grand style on the face of a fresh southerly breeze, and sitting comfortably on six knots. It was only 50 nautical miles to Cape Otway, the reference point that Flinders wanted to sight before continuing his passage to the east through Bass Strait, and when the lookout shouted to those on deck that he could see their destination off the bow, the highest hills of King's Island were still in view astern.

Investigator came to within ten nautical miles of Cape Otway, and there Flinders called for the ship to be hauled up to starboard. Her sails were retrimmed so that her course would parallel the coastline – which ran to the north-east – and retain sufficient sea-room on what was, in the conditions, a lee shore.

On Monday, 26 April a deep bight was sighted off to leeward. Flinders immediately called for the ship to close on the coast so that better observations could be made.

> On the west side of the rocky point there was a small
> opening, with breaking water across it ... a large extent of
> water presently became visible within side; and although the
> entrance seemed to be very narrow, and there were in it
> strong ripplings like breakers, I was induced to steer in ...
> the ship being close upon a wind and every man ready for
> tacking at a moment's warning. The soundings were irregular
> between 6 and 12 fathoms until we got four miles within the
> entrance. In making the last stretch from the shoal the depth
> diminished from 10 fathoms quickly to 3, and before the ship
> could come round, the flood tide set her upon a mud bank
> and she stuck fast.

Fortunately, the tide was still flooding, so a boat was quickly lowered over the side and one of the ship's anchors put aboard so it could be set in deep water. With men hauling on the anchor cable, and with sails set to assist, *Investigator* was eased back into her element and anchored safely for the night.

Flinders later wrote of the day's 'discovery' in *A Voyage to Terra Australis*:

> The extensive harbour we had thus unexpectedly found I supposed must be Western Port, although the narrowness of the entrance did by no means correspond with the width given to it by Mr Bass. It was the information of captain Baudin, who had coasted along from thence with fine weather, and had found no inlet of any kind, which induced this supposition; and the very great extent of the place, agreeing with that of Western Port, was in confirmation of it. This, however, was not Western Port, as we found next morning [Tuesday, 27 April 1802]; and I congratulated myself on having made a new and useful discovery; but here again I was in error. This place, as I afterwards learned at Port Jackson, had been discovered ten weeks before by lieutenant John Murray ... He had given it the name of Port Phillip, and to the rocky point on the east side of the entrance that of Point Nepean.

While he never outwardly expressed the disappointment one might expect from an explorer who is beaten by just weeks from having his name put to a major discovery, Flinders no doubt cast his mind back to the excessive delay – literally months – that he had experienced at the hands of the Admiralty before sailing from England.

Being oblivious at the time to the fact that Murray had already discovered this bay and named it in honour of the colony's first governor, Arthur Phillip, Flinders took it upon himself to explore as much of it as possible before it became imperative for him to depart for Port Jackson. He was amazed that Baudin had not at least sighted the entrance from offshore.

The extent of this bay surprised Flinders. On the morning of 27 April he took one of the ship's boats and, accompanied by botanist Robert Brown and artist William Westall, set out to land at the foot of the mountain on the eastern shore (which Murray had named Arthur's Seat), and climb to its summit, which would prove to be 1000 feet above sea level. Much to Flinders' delight, he could see Western Port to the east, but most amazing for him was that, even from that height, he still could not clearly define the boundaries of the bay. Time would reveal that the surface area of Port Phillip Bay is around 745 square miles, and the length of its shoreline some 160 miles.

The following day Flinders attempted to sail *Investigator* deeper into the bay, but that plan was soon abandoned because of shallows and fickle winds. Instead, he had one of the ship's boats provisioned with supplies to last three days and, after directing Fowler to take the ship back to the entrance of the bay, he set off with a crew of chosen men to explore as much of the bay as possible. They sailed nine miles to the north of Arthur's Seat, then crossed to the western shore, before looping anticlockwise into the bay in which Geelong is sited today. There, the 1200-foot-high range of hills (the You Yangs) that stood ten miles to the north-west held his attention, so at dawn on 1 May he set out with three of his crew on a bid to reach the peak, which they achieved at ten a.m. 'I left the ship's name on a scroll of paper, deposited in a small pile of stones upon the top of the peak,' Flinders later wrote, 'and at three in the afternoon reached the tent, much fatigued, having walked more than twenty miles without finding a drop of water.'

It was an exhausting day across challenging and undulating terrain. The group boarded their boat almost immediately and sailed a few miles to the south to a headland (Indented Head) on the western side of the bay, where they camped for the night. The following morning, 2 May, they reboarded *Investigator*, and as soon as practicable after that Flinders recorded his impressions of the bay and its surrounds.

He referred to it as a 'useful but obscure port', then described the surrounding country as being 'pleasing and in many places a fertile appearance', and 'in great measure a grassy country, and capable of supporting much cattle, though much better calculated for sheep'.

Seaman Smith contributed his own interesting observations:

On the 28th we came to an anchor in a bay of very large size. Thinking there was a good channel in a passage through, we got aground; but by good management we got off without damadge. Here we caught a Shirk which measured 10 feet 9 inch in length; in girt very large ... May 2nd our boat and crew came on board. Brought with them 2 swanns and a number of native spears.

Twenty-four hours later, *Investigator* had cleared the entrance to the bay on the last of an ebb tide and was heading east through Bass Strait, along a coast already well documented. Five days later, in the early evening, the ship was closing on her ultimate destination, although a fading breeze and unfavourable tide stalled her progress. At dusk on Saturday, 8 May, the heads at the entrance to Port Jackson were in sight.

Flinders later reflected on the final stage of the voyage, and on the good condition of his crew as they arrived at Sydney Town:

I tried to beat up for the port in the night, being sufficiently well acquainted to have run up in the dark, had the wind permitted; but we were still to leeward in the morning. At one o'clock, we gained the heads, a pilot came on board, and soon after three the *Investigator* was anchored in Sydney Cove.

There was not a single individual on board who was not upon deck working the ship into harbour; and it may be averred that the officers and crew were, generally speaking, in better health than on the day we sailed from Spithead, and not in less good spirits. I have said nothing of the regulations observed after we made Cape Leeuwin; they were little different from those adopted in the commencement of the voyage, and of which a strict attention to cleanliness and a free circulation of air in the messing and sleeping-places formed the most essential parts. Several of the inhabitants of Port Jackson expressed themselves never to have been so strongly reminded of England as by the fresh colour of many amongst the *Investigator*'s ship's company.

CHAPTER ELEVEN

The Circumnavigation

It had been a two-year absence for Flinders and many of his men, so as soon as *Investigator*'s heavy iron bower splashed into the clear waters of Sydney Cove, he prepared to go ashore and report to the colony's new governor, Philip Gidley King. A boat was lowered over the side so the captain could be rowed to the southern shore of the bay before making the short walk up a gentle rise to the governor's home – a two-storey residence built using bricks brought from England. Inevitably, as Flinders made his way there, he would have been welcomed back as 'family' by many of the townspeople. The population at the time was around 3000.

King had taken up his posting in September 1800, six months after Flinders had returned home aboard *Reliance*, but he was no newcomer to Sydney Town. In 1788 he had served as a second lieutenant under Governor Phillip aboard *Sirius* as part of the First Fleet, and he had followed the development of the colony with great interest, including the success Flinders and Bass had enjoyed as explorers.

Following the formal introductions, Flinders presented Governor King with the orders from the Admiralty and the Secretary of State relating to his expedition. He then 'communicated a general account of our discoveries and examinations upon the South Coast', which he had made while sailing to Port Jackson.

Flinders then went to meet Captain Hamelin of *Le Naturaliste*, who had brought his ship into port two weeks earlier. He advised the Frenchman of Baudin's intentions to sail *Le Géographe* to Sydney once the weather in the south turned against him. Hamelin, in turn, informed Flinders that the boat and men lost from *Le Géographe* off Van Diemen's Land had been found by an English brig, *Harrington*, captained by William Campbell, and that the officers and crew were then safe aboard *Le Naturaliste* in Port Jackson.

There was no time for rest for Flinders and his men. The morning after their arrival in port, *Investigator* was warped to a position close to shore on the eastern side of Sydney Cove, and there the crew set about their assigned tasks. The ship's tents were set up close to the water's edge so the sailmakers could begin repairing sails and making new ones. The cooper was nearby, checking and mending the water casks, while Samuel Flinders was put in charge of checking the timepieces, navigation and surveying equipment. Other members of the crew, all seamen, were 'employed in stripping and re-rigging the masts, and preparing the hold to receive a fresh stock of provisions and water'.

Flinders wished to make modifications to the barricade that extended the full length of the quarterdeck on each side of the ship. As it was, it was too high for him to take effective sights while surveying the coast, especially when the wind was blowing offshore and the ship was heeling. Four convict carpenters and some dockyard workers made the changes to Flinders' requirements. A new cutter was built to replace the one lost so tragically off Cape Catastrophe. It was a near sister-ship to the whaleboat Bass had sailed on his Bass Strait expedition, a vessel Flinders knew was 'excellent in a sea, as well as for rowing and sailing in smooth water'. It was 28 feet ten inches overall, had the capacity to be rowed by eight oars, and was built using banksia for the frames and knees and cedar for the planking. It cost £30 to build.

If there was a disappointment for Flinders during this time, it was that he had not met up at any stage during the preceding two years with his good friend George Bass. They had not seen one another during the time they were in England, and now, while Flinders was preparing his ship for what promised to be his greatest expedition, Bass was sailing through the Pacific aboard his own trading vessel, which was to take on board a cargo of salted pork at Tahiti before returning to Port Jackson, thus fulfilling a contract he had signed with Governor King on behalf of the colony.

Bass's desire for a lifestyle built on commercial ventures on the high seas stemmed from the time he and Flinders had met Charles Bishop, the owner of the sealer *Nautilus*, while surveying the Furneaux Islands in what would soon be known as Bass's Strait. At this time in his life, Bass was questioning his future. His spirit of adventure was outweighing his desire to remain a navy surgeon, where the pay and commitments made life somewhat mundane. In Bishop's life he saw the best of both worlds, so that was the course Bass had decided to pursue, but it would have to start back in England.

Instead of waiting to sail home aboard *Reliance*, Bass had opted to join Bishop aboard *Nautilus* so he would get there sooner, even though she was first sailing to China. If Bass needed any convincing that there was good money to be made with a trading vessel, it certainly came when *Nautilus* reached Macao. There, Bishop sold the 9000 sealskins and sundry products he had on board at a handsome profit.

Nautilus next sailed to Bombay via the Straits of Singapore, and along the way Bass took the opportunity to chart coastlines and islands of interest. At some stage, possibly in Bombay, he parted company with Bishop and went aboard *Woodford* for the remainder of the voyage, arriving in England in July 1800.

There's no doubt that the seeds were sown during his time aboard *Nautilus* for a joint venture in which he and Bishop would buy a trading vessel suitable for carrying goods that they could sell back in Sydney Town. Bass's first step towards this project was to free himself of his obligations to the Royal Navy, and this came when the Medical Board granted him 12 months' leave.

Not long after Bass's marriage to Captain Waterhouse's sister, Elizabeth, he and his business partner had, with the help of Waterhouse, raised the near £11,000 they needed to buy their boat – *Venus*. She was an impressive little two-masted, 140-ton brig, with lines that left no doubt that she would be fast and seaworthy under sail. She was built from teak, the favourite timber of seafarers, and her hull was copper-sheathed. For protection – particularly because England was at war with the French – she carried 12 guns. Bass wrote that *Venus* was 'one of the most complete, handsome and strong-built ships in the River Thames, and will suit any trade ... very sound and tight, and bids fair to remain sound much longer than any of her owners'.

Bass stood proudly on *Venus*'s deck as she cruised downstream towards the mouth of the Thames. Her first destination was Portsmouth, where she would lie at anchor until final preparations were completed and the right conditions prevailed for an easy departure down the English Channel. As they sailed along the coast of southern England, the new owners were more than pleased with their vessel, and especially with her speed and manoeuvrability when fully loaded. When Bass wrote to his brother-in-law about the upcoming voyage, he reported that his ship was loaded 'as deep as she can swim and as full as an egg'.

Friday, 9 January 1801 emerged as the day they would sail out of the Solent and commence what would be an eight-month voyage to Port Jackson. It was a day of considerable sorrow for Bass and his wife, Elizabeth, who had been at his side for the three months since they had been married. As they embraced in farewell, Bass promised that he would be in her arms again as soon as humanly possible. Sadly, that would never occur.

When *Venus* reached Sydney Town, Bass and Bishop knew almost immediately that their business would not be as profitable as they had hoped. In fact, it would not be profitable at all because they had been beaten to the punch by other would-be entrepreneurs. The market had been 'glutted with goods beyond all comparison', Bass wrote within a month of arriving, adding, 'Our wings are clipped with a vengeance, but we shall endeavour to fall on our feet somehow or other.'

Fortunately, Bass's earlier exploits as an explorer placed him in good stead with Governor King, and this led to *Venus* being contracted to bring a cargo of much-needed salted pork from Tahiti. Instead of returning to England with cash in their pockets and a plan to purchase more merchandise for the colony, Bass and Bishop unloaded their cargo and stored it in Sydney Town, then set sail for Tahiti to procure the pork and, they hoped, repay their debts. It was a successful mission: they received some £3000 for their cargo on their return.

Bass was a much relieved man. He immediately sent money to Elizabeth back in England 'to stop a few holes in my debts'. Writing to his brother-in-law, Captain Waterhouse, he stated, 'That pork voyage has been our first successful speculation.' He also wrote very favourably of *Venus*: 'She is just the same vessel as when we left England, never complains or cries, though we loaded her with pork most unmercifully.'

It was evident that *Venus* would have to work out of Port Jackson and in the Pacific if the trading business was to become a profitable venture. Fishing and sealing concessions were secured for an expedition to New Zealand waters, and this prompted a jocular Bass to write to his wife that he intended to return to England and:

... seize upon my dear Bess, bring her out here, and make a
poissarde [fish wife] of her, where she cannot fail to find
plenty of ease for her tongue. We have, I assure you, great
plans in our heads, but, like the basket of eggs, all depends
upon the success of the voyage I am now upon.

Sadly, during the voyage he referred to, *Venus* and her entire crew would disappear in mysterious circumstances and never be seen or heard from again. It is possible that the ship sank and took all hands with her, yet that is unlikely, considering the secrecy surrounding the voyage and the few snippets of information that remain which relate to it.

Bass and Bishop still had creditors to appease, so they were eager to take up any voyage that would bring them the much-needed money. Bishop had taken ill when the opportunity arose to do a run to South America in search of provisions needed by the colony, and also take on board another load of salted pork from Tahiti, so Bass made the appropriate plans for the passage. It appears that Bass saw a secondary opportunity within this proposed voyage that made it very appealing to him. His and Bishop's unsold merchandise from London was still being stored in Sydney Town; Bass realised that this commission from the governor would allow him to take those goods to South America and sell them, even though it would be deemed smuggling by the Spanish, who controlled the coast of Chile.

Bass was very much aware of the risk, and so any such voyage would have to have a clandestine element. He alluded to this in a furtive manner when he wrote to Henry Waterhouse prior to departing Port Jackson on 5 February 1803: in order 'that they may not in that part of the world mistake me for a contrabandist, I go provided with a very diplomatic-looking certificate from the Governor here, stating the service upon which I am employed, requesting aid and protection in obtaining the food wanted'.

Was the 'diplomatic looking certificate' an effort by Governor King to provide some form of legitimacy to the voyage, and protection for his friend Bass, while knowing it could be deemed to be smuggling? Just days before *Venus* sailed, Bass left no doubt in another letter that the undertaking had a secretive nature and carried risks. 'In a few hours I sail again on another pork voyage, but it combines circumstances of a different nature also,' he penned, adding towards the end, 'Speak not of South America to anyone out of your family, for there is treason in the very name.'

When the outline of *Venus* fused into the horizon to the east of Port Jackson just a couple of hours after she had cleared the heads, it was the last anyone would see or hear of her and those on board. The only hint about what happened came later that year from the crew of *Harrington*, which had been involved in the smuggling trade along the west coast of South America. Their unconfirmed report was that *Venus* had been intercepted and captured by the Spanish in Peru, and that Bass and his crew had been arrested. As punishment, they had been consigned to the mountains, where they would work in the silver mines.

Rumours about the fate of Bass, his men and the ship abounded for years, but none could be substantiated. Elizabeth Bass lived in the desperate hope that the husband with whom she had spent just 12 weeks would one day return, but that was not to be. She lived alone until she passed away in June 1824.

Flinders would not learn of the unexplained disappearance of his friend Bass until after *Investigator* had completed her circumnavigation of New Holland.

On 20 June 1802, when *Investigator* was still being fitted out for that pioneering expedition, word reached Sydney Town that a large and unidentified ship was approaching Port Jackson. It appeared to be in some sort of distress: the ship was labouring, the sails were not trimmed properly and it was making very slow progress.

It soon became apparent that the ship was Baudin's *Le Géographe*, and the reason she was struggling to make headway was that there was virtually no crewman fit enough to stand a watch, let alone sheet home the sails or man the helm. Almost every one of them was afflicted by scurvy or some other debilitating ailment. Men were literally scattered across the deck, prone and moaning in pain, all desperate for medical care.

The moment word reached Flinders that it was *Le Géographe*, he sensed the problem and took immediate action.

A boat was sent from the *Investigator* to assist in towing the ship up to the cove. It was grievous to see the miserable condition to which both officers and crew were reduced by scurvy; there being not more out of one hundred and seventy, according to the commander's account, than twelve men capable of doing their duty. The sick were received into the colonial hospital; and both French ships furnished with everything in the power of the colony to supply. Before their arrival, the necessity of augmenting the number of cattle in

the country had prevented the governor from allowing us any
fresh meat; but some oxen belonging to government were
now killed for the distressed strangers ... The distress of the
French navigators had indeed been great; but every means
were used by the governor and the principal inhabitants of
the colony, to make them forget both their sufferings and the
war which existed between the two nations.

The depth of the caring and hospitality exhibited towards the
French by Governor King and the people of Sydney Town was
soon acknowledged by Baudin, who wrote:

Among all the French officers serving in the division which I
command, there is not one who is not, like myself,
convinced of the indebtedness in which we stand to
Governor King and the principal inhabitants of the colony
for the courteous, affectionate, and distinguished manner in
which they have received us.

While these gatherings were exceptionally polite and pleasant for
all concerned, no one knew that there were two 'rats' in their
midst – French spies. Their clandestine activities while in Sydney
Town are thought to have contributed to what would become the
worst period of Flinders' life, just 18 months later.

When the French ships finally sailed from Port Jackson in
November, Flinders was already well on his way around what he
and everyone else now knew was a relatively small continent – or a
very large island. But its actual outline was unknown.

By July 1802, almost everything was in readiness aboard
Investigator, and as a farewell gesture Flinders hosted some special
dinners aboard his ship.

His Excellency, Governor King, had done me the honour to visit the *Investigator*, and to accept of a dinner on board; on which occasion he had been received with the marks of respect due to his rank of captain-general; and shortly afterward, the Captains Baudin and Hamelin, with Monsieur Peron and some other French officers, did me the same favour; when they were received under a salute of eleven guns. The intelligence of peace [between the French and British in Europe], which had just been received, contributed to enliven the party, and rendered our meeting more particularly agreeable.

There was another special guest at this dinner enjoying the celebrations immensely. It was none other than Trim, the cat that continued to prove he had lost none of his prowess when it came to wheedling his way into a position where guests would slip him morsels of food.

Flinders decided that he would sail on 22 July, and while making final preparations, he was pleased to learn that a 60-ton brig, *Lady Nelson*, commanded by Acting Lieutenant John Murray, would be placed under his orders and act as a tender to *Investigator*. This vessel was quite radical in design. It had three sliding keels, and when all were raised 'she drew no more than six feet'. As Flinders noted, she 'was therefore peculiarly adapted for going up rivers, or other shallow places which it might be dangerous, or impossible for the ship to enter.'

The voyage that lay ahead of them was some 16,000 nautical miles – greater than the sailing distance from London to Port Jackson – and could take at least 12 months to complete. The coastline was dotted with more than 12,000 islands. Because of this, the victualling for the voyage was difficult for the cook, who could only speculate on what he might need to have aboard. The final inventory of provisions, however, gives an interesting insight into the diet of the seafarer of the day. Included were live sheep, pigs, geese and fowls, plus 30,000 pounds of biscuit, 8000 pounds of flour and 156 bushels of kiln-dried wheat. They also bore 1483 gallons of rum – almost a gallon for every ten nautical miles they would cover.

Before setting out, Flinders had to find 14 more crewmen to cover the eight men so dramatically lost at the entrance to Spencer's Gulf and others who were incapacitated; one crewmember had been bitten by a seal at Kangaroo Island. A new master was found – John Aken from the convict transport ship *Hercules* – and when Flinders advised the governor that he was struggling to find suitably qualified men, King agreed to allow nine convicts, most of whom were seamen, to join the crew. With these men King sent a document that no doubt pleased them immensely. It stated that 'on the return of that ship to this port, according to Captain Flinders' recommendation of them, severally and individually, they will receive conditional emancipations or absolute pardons, as that officer may request'.

The governor also agreed to two additional inclusions in the crew, as Flinders later recorded:

I had before experienced much advantage from the presence
of a native of Port Jackson, in bringing about a friendly
intercourse with the inhabitants of other parts of the coast;
and on representing this to the governor, he authorised me
to receive two on board. Bongaree, the worthy and brave
fellow who had sailed with me in the Norfolk, now
volunteered again; the other was Nanbaree, a good-natured
lad ...

There was one final official duty Flinders was obliged to execute prior to departure – all in the name of protecting the exceptionally valuable information he had gathered during his survey of the southern coast.

> I placed in the hands of governor King two copies of my chart of the south coast of Terra Australis, in six sheets; with three other sheets of particular parts, on a large scale. One copy I requested him to send with my letters to the secretary of the Admiralty, by the first good opportunity that offered; the other was to remain in his hands until my return, or until he should hear of the loss of the *Investigator*, when it was also to be sent to the Admiralty.

It was the perfect day to sail north when *Investigator* and *Lady Nelson* cleared the bold, rocky escarpments that stand like commanding custodians at the entrance to Port Jackson. The wind was 'fair and fresh' from the south-east, and the two vessels made good speed, running downwind under full sail.

Prior to going aboard their respective vessels, Flinders had Lieutenant John Murray receive his orders, which put him directly under Flinders' command for the duration of the voyage. Should the two ships become separated on the initial stage, *Lady Nelson* was to sail to Hervey's Bay so that contact could be re-established there. By 11 a.m. on the first day at sea, they had covered 17 nautical miles and Broken Bay was abeam; by midnight they were off Port Stephens, 90 nautical miles from Port Jackson.

Detailing and exploring the coastline on this first stage was not critical. Captain Cook had sailed the coast in *Endeavour* in 1770, and Flinders had added detail when he sailed *Norfolk* as far north as Hervey's Bay. Even so, eyes were forever alert, looking for noteworthy geographical features that might previously have been missed. Only after rounding Breaksea Spit would they need to be wholly diligent. Cook, whose schedule had been influenced by the weather at the time of year he sailed by, had recorded only limited detail of his passage through the Great Barrier Reef. Flinders' first major challenge would come when *Investigator* reached Torres Strait, off the tip of the cape. Governor King had directed him to further explore the waters of the strait before progressing south, down the western coast of the Cape York peninsula.

Overnight, the wind had moved into the westerly sector – an offshore breeze – and with it being midwinter there was crispness and chill in the air. As first light emerged subtly across the eastern sky and absorbed the night's stars into its expanding canopy, those on watch aboard *Investigator* began looking astern, in the hope they would see *Lady Nelson* in their wake – but she wasn't there. As a result, Flinders called for the ship to stop by laying-to until their tender caught up, which took an hour. A delay so soon in the expedition concerned the captain; the sailing conditions had been perfect overnight, yet *Lady Nelson*, which should have been fast downwind, was obviously not.

Investigator did not anchor at any stage between Port Jackson and the northern tip of Fraser Island, the point where Flinders would be entering territory that was new and largely uncharted. Smoke from fires in the area of Wide Bay confirmed for Flinders that the region was quite habitable: so many fires could only mean many people, and that meant fresh water was readily available. That night, the fires of the Aboriginal people along the shore of Fraser Island directed *Investigator*'s course, defining the limit of the land all the way through to Indian Head, 'so named by Captain Cook, from the great number of Indians assembled there in 1770'. Port Curtis, where Gladstone is sited today, was discovered on 7 August and named in honour of Sir Roger Curtis, the admiral at the Cape of Good Hope who had so ably assisted Flinders when he was there.

By now *Lady Nelson* was, through her slowness and the overly cautious approach to coastal navigation by Captain Murray, becoming more of a hindrance than an aid to the expedition, so much so that Flinders did not always wait for her to catch up. Two days later, after the discovery of Port Curtis, he was reminded how easily an expedition such as his could go to the edge of disaster.

On getting under way at daylight of the 9th, to prosecute the examination of the coast, the anchor came up with an arm broken off, in consequence of a flaw extending two-thirds through the iron. The negligence with which this anchor had been made, might in some cases have caused the loss of the ship.

Investigator then continued its coastal surveillance by proceeding north, rounding Cape Capricorn and entering Keppel Bay, which had been discovered and named by Cook in honour of Viscount Augustus Keppel, who 12 years later became the First Lord of the Admiralty. This bay was surveyed extensively by the crews of both ships for more than a week.

At one stage Flinders allowed some of his men to go ashore for recreation. Shortly after landing, this group was confronted by around 20 spear-wielding and obviously hostile 'Indians', who 'at first menaced our people with their spears; but finding them inclined to be friendly, laid aside their arms, and accompanied the sailors to the ship in a good-natured manner'. Before the friendly intention of these natives was realised, two of the crew took fright and ran off, only to find themselves trapped in a muddy mangrove swamp. They were forced to spend the night there, 'persecuted by clouds of mosquitoes', until they were found the following morning by another group of Aboriginals, who took the sailors to their camp, fed them broiled duck then returned them to their ship.

On 17 August *Investigator* and *Lady Nelson* weighed anchor in very light conditions and struggled for many hours to make headway against an adverse tide. Four days later, an impressive inlet, one which had not been sighted by Captain Cook, was discovered – but only just – by Flinders. A wind shift almost forced *Investigator* to sail wide of the coast, but Flinders called for a tack and subsequently sailed into a well-protected anchorage, 'where the hills rise abruptly and have a romantic appearance'.

> Instead of a bight in the coast, we found this to be a port of
> some extent; which had not only escaped the observation of
> captain Cook, but from the shift of wind, was very near
> being missed by us also. I named it Port Bowen, in
> compliment to Captain James Bowen of the navy.

This site, which in later years was renamed Port Clinton, provided the first opportunity for the ship's carpenters to go ashore and fell pine trees so that a replacement main sliding keel could be made for *Lady Nelson*, her original having been snapped off when she clipped a reef near Port Curtis. Since then, she had been unable to sail to windward – not that she sailed well upwind anyway – so she had been an even greater restraint on Flinders' progress. While the keel was being made, the scientists and surveyors went ashore and mapped the region. Meanwhile, Flinders continued with a study that he had consistently carried out since setting sail.

> At every port or bay we entered, more especially after
> passing Cape Capricorn, my first object on landing was to

examine the refuse thrown up by the sea. The French navigator, La Pérouse, whose unfortunate situation, if in existence, was always present to my mind, had been wrecked, as it was thought, somewhere in the neighbourhood of New Caledonia; and if so, the remnants of his ships were likely to be brought upon this coast by the trade winds, and might indicate the situation of the reef or island which had proved fatal to him. With such an indication, I was led to believe in the possibility of finding the place; and though the hope of restoring La Pérouse or any of his companions to their country and friends could not, after so many years, be rationally entertained, yet to gain some certain knowledge of their fate would do away the pain of suspense; and it might not be too late to retrieve some documents of their discoveries.

Islands large and small dotted the surface of the sea in every direction, and 50 miles on from Port Bowen, on 28 September, Flinders put another array of isles, the beautiful Percy Group, on the chart for the first time.

While the expedition was proving successful, as an explorer Flinders continued to feel frustration: there was so much that could be done, so many islands and coastal features to be documented, but he knew that the wet season and its accompanying monsoons would descend on that part of the world by year's end. This situation was compounded by the fact that he again had a leaky boat on his hands: *Investigator* was taking on five inches of water each hour, and the signs were that this situation would only deteriorate.

Accordingly, reaching Torres Strait and pressing on with the circumnavigation became his priority. Flinders decided to search for a gap in the long chain of coral reefs to the east, find the open sea then sail in relative safety to the strait, riding the south-easterly trade wind all the way. This, however, would prove to be an extremely difficult task – he needed to discover a passage through the wall of barely submerged reefs that was deep enough, wide enough and at the appropriate angle to the wind for his two vessels to sail through.

Every man on watch was put to the test, especially the lookouts aloft. The crew had to deal with the shadow of clouds and the often dazzling reflection of the sun, which danced on the surface of the sea like a million diamonds, effectively hiding the breaking water on the potentially lethal reefs. One wrong call on a sighting could easily bring disaster. Despite these dangers, Flinders also remained the surveyor, recording the height of the tides and the direction of the flow.

> We seemed at this time to be surrounded with reefs; but it was ascertained by the whale boat, that many of these appearances were caused by the shadows of clouds and the ripplings and eddies of tide, and that the true coral banks were those only which had either green water or negro heads upon them.

On 11 October both ships were confronted by considerable danger when their anchors were lost, the anchor cables being unable to cope with the razor-like coral and the loads placed on them by the tidal currents that were racing through a narrow channel in the reef. Flinders was chastened:

> The loss of anchors we had this day sustained, deterred me from any more attempting the small passages through the

Barrier Reef; in these, the tide runs with extraordinary
violence, and the bottom is coral rock; and whether with, or
without wind, no situation can be more dangerous. My
anxious desire to get out to sea, and reach the North Coast
before the unfavourable monsoon should set in, had led me
to persevere amongst these intricate passages beyond what
prudence could approve; for had the wind come to blow
strong, no anchors, in such deep water and upon loose sand,
could have held the ship; a rocky bottom cut the cables; and
to have been under sail in the night was certain destruction.

He changed his strategy to reach the open sea: the two ships would
run north, parallel to this extensive 'barrier' of reefs, 'until a good
and safe opening should present itself'. While trying to find a way
through the bastion of coral that was forever to the east of their
course, Flinders was becoming increasingly frustrated by the
contribution – or lack of it – by Captain Murray and *Lady Nelson*.
Finally he had had enough:

... hoping we should not meet with any more interruption
from the reefs, I resolved to send the brig back to Port
Jackson. The *Lady Nelson* sailed so ill, and had become so
leewardly since the loss of the main, and part of the after
keel, that she not only caused us delay, but ran great risk of
being lost; and instead of saving the crew of the *Investigator*,
in case of accident, which was one of the principal objects of
her attendance, it was too probable we might be called upon
to render her that assistance. A good vessel of the same size I
should have considered the greatest acquisition in Torres'
Strait and the Gulph of Carpentaria; but circumstanced as
was the *Lady Nelson*, and in want of anchors and cables

which could not be spared without endangering our own safety, she was become, and would be more so every day, a burthen rather than an assistant to me. Lieutenant Murray was not much acquainted with the kind of service in which we were engaged; but the zeal he had shown to make himself and his vessel of use to the voyage, made me sorry to deprive him of the advantage of continuing with us; and increased my regret at the necessity of parting from our little consort.

All excess provisions and equipment that would no longer be needed were transferred from *Lady Nelson* to *Investigator*, as was a launch that would replace *Investigator*'s cutter lost in Strong Tide Passage, 15 nautical miles north of Port Bowen. A request by Nanbaree, one of the two natives aboard *Investigator*, to return to Sydney with *Lady Nelson* was granted, and there was also a swap of three crew between the two vessels.

When the call of 'anchor aweigh' came from the master's mate at the bow, sails were again unfurled so *Investigator* could continue north in search of a way through the seemingly impenetrable system of reefs. Each time the man at the masthead called that a gap between the reefs had been sighted off the starboard bow, Flinders would order that the ship be hauled up to the east-north-east 'between them to look into the openings, and bearing away when repulsed'.

Finally, on 20 October, *Investigator* won some desperately needed respite. Flinders noted that they had sailed along the reefs 'which form so extraordinary a barrier to this part of New South Wales; and amongst which we sought fourteen days, and sailed more than five hundred miles, before a passage could be found through them, out to sea'. He explained the circumstances:

At four, the depth was 43 fathoms, and no reefs in sight; and
at six, a heavy swell from the eastward and a depth of
66 fathoms were strong assurances that we had at length
gained the open sea. The topsails were then treble reefed,
and we hauled to the wind, which blew strong at E. S. E.,
with squally weather. At eight, hove to and sounded: no
ground with 75 fathoms; and at twelve, none with 115.

Flinders Passage, as it is known today, is east-north-east of Townsville.

Investigator resumed her course towards Torres Strait, unimpeded
by the dangers of the reef or the sluggishness of *Lady Nelson*.
Looking back on the challenges the reef had posed for his ship over
such a great distance and time, Flinders wrote a warning for masters
of other vessels hoping to find a way through the reef. To achieve a
safe passage, a captain:

... must not be one who throws his ship's head round in a
hurry so soon as breakers are announced from aloft. If he
does not feel his nerves strong enough to thread the needle,
as it is called, amongst the reefs, while he directs the steerage
from the masthead, I would strongly recommend him not to
approach this part of the coast.

Once clear of the reef, *Investigator* averaged a leisurely three knots over
the next eight days before she was anchored in the lee of the largest of
the Murray Isles, the easternmost group in Torres Strait, about
100 nautical miles north-east of Cape York. It was 29 October 1802.

Remembering all too well the hostilities that had been
experienced with the Aboriginals of this region when he was there
aboard *Providence*, Flinders was apprehensive when the ship was
approached by canoes soon after arriving at the Murray Islands.

We had scarcely anchored when between forty and fifty Indians came off, in three canoes. They would not come along-side of the ship, but lay off at a little distance, holding up cocoa nuts, joints of bamboo filled with water, plantains, bows and arrows, and vociferating tooree! tooree! and mammoosee! A barter soon commenced, and was carried on in this manner: a hatchet, or other piece of iron (tooree) being held up, they offered a bunch of green plantains, a bow and quiver of arrows, or what they judged would be received in exchange.

Even so, as friendly as these people seemed, the captain remained wary of a surprise attack, especially overnight.

I did not forget that the inhabitants of these islands had made an attack upon the *Providence* and *Assistant* in 1792; nor that Mr Bampton had some people cut off at Darnley's Island in 1793. The marines were therefore kept under arms, the guns clear, and matches lighted; and officers were stationed to watch every motion, one to each canoe, so long as they remained near the ship. Bows and arrows were contained in all the canoes; but no intention of hostility was manifested by the Indians, unless those who steered for Darnley's Island might be supposed to go for assistance.

The following morning, Flinders seized on the opportunity to play the role of peacekeeper.

Soon after daylight, the natives were with us again, in seven canoes; some of them came under the stern, and fifteen or twenty of the people ascended on board ... Wishing to

secure the friendship and confidence of these islanders to
such vessels as might hereafter pass through Torres' Strait,
and not being able to distinguish any chief amongst them,
I selected the oldest man, and presented him with a hand-
saw, a hammer and nails, and some other trifles; of all which
we attempted to show him the use, but I believe without
success; for the poor old man became frightened, on finding
himself to be so particularly noticed.

The 'Indians' enjoyed the experience of being aboard the ship so
much that they simply ignored gestures from Flinders and the crew
indicating that they were about to sail – until crew started scurrying
aloft and unfurling the sails. In no time, the decks were cleared of
the visitors, who had rushed to their canoes. The anchor was
weighed and a course set that would see *Investigator* thread her way
through the natural hazards of the strait – islands, reefs and
sandbanks – while heading for the Gulf of Carpentaria.

To minimise the chance of running aground, Flinders had the
ship sail west-south-west, for much of the time through an area
where he knew there were fewer dangers. Wherever possible, he
went ashore with 'the botantical gentlemen' to research local flora
and fauna, and he was forever analysing tidal heights and current
flows. On 2 November, just 24 hours before entering the gulf,
Investigator was being guided through the waters around Thursday
Island when the captain decided to pay tribute to one of his
'gentlemen': 'Another island appeared ... to the south-west, which,
as it had no name, I called Good's Island, after Mr Good, the
botanical gardener.'

By now, *Investigator* was taking on water at an alarming rate,
particularly when sailing across the wind. This was when the gaps
between her planks began to open and the oakum caulking

between them came free. At best she was taking on ten inches of water an hour, and at worst, 14! Each ten inches of water equated to 46 tons in her bilge. Needless to say, the men manning the pumps were kept very busy.

After 20 days, Flinders and his assistants had surveyed the entire 500 nautical miles of the east coast of the gulf and reached Sweers Island, in the south-east corner. Here, the ship was positioned in sheltered water in the hope that the carpenters might rectify the leaks that were plaguing her, 'but as they advanced, report after report was brought to me of rotten places found in different parts of the ship – in the planks, bends, timbers, tree-nails, etc., until it became quite alarming'.

Flinders' only option was to order a complete inspection of the ship over the next two days. The report that came back from the master, John Aken, and the ship's carpenter, Russel Mart, delivered the information he dreaded most: *Investigator* was a rotting hulk.

The most concerning parts of the report declared that:

1st. .... in a strong gale, with much sea running, the ship would hardly escape foundering; so that we think she is totally unfit to encounter much bad weather.

2nd. We have no doubt but that, if the ship should get on shore under any unfavourable circumstances, she would immediately go to pieces.

3rd. It is our opinion that the ship could not bear heaving down on any account; and that laying her on shore might so far strain her as to ... make her unable to swim without vast repair.

4th. Mr Aken has known several ships of the same kind, and built at the same place as the *Investigator*, and has always found that when they began to rot they went on very fast.

From the state to which the ship seems now to be advanced, it is our joint opinion, that in twelve months there will scarcely be a sound timber in her; but that if she remain in fine weather and happen no accident, she may run six months longer without much risk.

As Flinders sat at the desk in his cabin and absorbed the report, he became increasingly exasperated. His expedition was facing defeat through no fault of his own.

I cannot express the surprise and sorrow which this statement gave me. According to it, a return to Port Jackson was almost immediately necessary; as well to secure the journals and charts of the examinations already made, as to preserve the lives of the ship's company; and my hopes of ascertaining completely the exterior form of this immense, and in many points interesting country, if not destroyed, would at least be deferred to an uncertain period. My leading object had hitherto been, to make so accurate an investigation of the shores of Terra Australis that no future voyage to this country should be necessary ... when circumstances were favourable, such was the plan I pursued; and with the blessing of God, nothing of importance should have been left for future discoverers, upon any part of these extensive coasts; but with a ship incapable of encountering bad weather — which could not be repaired if sustaining injury from any of the numerous shoals or rocks upon the coast — which, if constant fine weather could be ensured and all accidents avoided, could not run more than six months — with such a ship, I knew not how to accomplish the task.

This circumstance created a significant problem for the captain: how best should he attempt to sail back to Sydney Town in a vessel that 'would hardly escape foundering' in severe weather? While a return voyage sounded relatively straightforward, the time of the year made it otherwise. With the monsoon season about to descend on the region, a passage back through Torres Strait and down the east coast of Australia could see the ship succumb to the elements, if such a weather system developed. Also, there were considerably more hazards to navigation on that route.

The alternative was to continue on, circumnavigating the continent, but with relative haste instead of at a casual pace that suited exploration. It was likely that the wind strength and direction would be more favourable on this course, and therefore create the opportunity to at least complete a survey of the gulf. The major advantage associated with this option was that if the ship did not prove capable of continuing, then Flinders could run for the nearest port in the East Indies.

Comfortable with this choice, Flinders continued to carry out an exhaustive survey of the remainder of the gulf, and after sailing only 30 nautical miles he made his first discovery. Cape Van Diemen, which had been put on the chart as part of the mainland by the Dutch explorer Abel Janszoon Tasman in April 1644, was in fact the northern end of an island (now Mornington Island). As *Investigator* continued along the southern coast of the gulf, the same error was found with Capes Vanderlin and Maria: they too were, in fact, islands.

By 20 January *Investigator* was nearing the northernmost part of the gulf on the western side, and here Flinders found safe anchorage off Isle Woodah, just a few miles north-west of Groote Eylandt. As was almost always the case, the captain went ashore to take his bearings from various landmarks so he could plot the lie of the land as accurately as possible, while the botanists searched for unique flora and fauna. The ship lay at anchor there that night, and when the next morning a party went ashore to collect firewood, another tragedy occurred.

... a canoe, with six men in it, came over from Woodah ...
and when they appeared on the brow of the hill,
Mr Whitewood, the master's mate, and some of his wooders
went to meet them in a friendly manner ... This was at the
time that the appearance of my [own] party caused them to
run; but when we left the shore they had stopped, and our
people were walking gently up the hill. The natives had
spears, but from the smallness of their number, and our men
being armed, I did not apprehend any danger; we had,
however, scarcely reached the ship, when the report of
muskets was heard; and the people were making signals and
carrying someone down to the boat, as if wounded or killed.
I immediately despatched two armed boats to their assistance,
under the direction of the master; with orders, if he met with
the natives, to be friendly and give them presents, and by no
means to pursue them into the wood. I suspected, indeed,
that our people must have been the aggressors; but told the
master, if the Indians had made a wanton attack, to bring off
their canoe by way of punishment; intending myself to take
such steps on the following day, as might be found
expedient.

At five o'clock Mr Whitewood was brought on board,
with four spear wounds in his body. It appeared that the
natives, in waiting to receive our men, kept their spears
ready, as ours had their muskets. Mr Whitewood, who was
foremost, put out his hand to receive a spear which he

supposed was offered; but the Indian, thinking perhaps that an attempt was made to take his arms, ran the spear into the breast of his supposed enemy. The officer snapped his firelock, but it missed, and he retreated to his men; and the Indians, encouraged by this, threw several spears after him, three of which took effect. Our people attempted to fire, and after some time two muskets went off, and the Indians fled; Thomas Morgan, a marine, having been some time exposed bare-headed to the sun, was struck with a coup-de-soleil; he was brought on board with Mr. Whitewood, and died in a state of frenzy, the same night.

So soon as the master had learned what had happened, he went round in the whale boat to the east end of the island to secure the canoe ... in the dusk of the evening three Indians were seen by the wooders, and before they could be intercepted had pushed off in the canoe. A sharp fire was commenced after them; and before they got out of reach, one fell and the others leaped out and dived away. A seaman who gave himself the credit of having shot the native, swam off to the canoe, and found him lying dead at the bottom ...

The body of Thomas Morgan who died so unfortunately, was this day committed to the deep with the usual ceremony; and the island was named after him, Morgan's Island.

Fatalities were a readily accepted fact of life in this era, especially on an expedition such as this. In his very next sentence, Flinders returned to the cold, hard facts of the mission: 'The basis stone is partly argillaceous, and in part sand stone, with a mixture in some places of iron ore, but more frequently of quartz ...'

Nevertheless, the expedition leader formulated a theory on why the natives had shown such aggression towards his men: 'I can account for this unusual conduct only by supposing, that they might have had differences with, and entertained no respectful opinion of the Asiatic visitors, of whom we had found so many traces, some almost in sight of this place.'

Investigator was then closing on Cape Wilberforce, at the top of the western coast of the gulf, and as she rounded it the crew saw an unusual canoe full of men; nearby, there were six other large vessels of about 25 tons hauled up on the shore. Only days earlier, Aboriginals had made Flinders aware of the presence of Chinese sailors in the region, and that they had firearms, so every precaution was taken immediately to defend the ship. Flinders sent his brother Samuel in an armed boat to intercept the canoe, while he anchored *Investigator* within musket shot of it and had 'all hands at quarters'. These men turned out to be friendly Malays who had brought six prows south from Macassar in search of the highly prized *bêche-de-mer*, or sea cucumber.

By 6 March 1803 *Investigator* was sailing the coast of the Wessel Islands – a 70-mile-long, very narrow archipelago that gently arcs into the Arafura Sea from the north-west corner of the gulf. Here, with a stage of his planned circumnavigation complete, Flinders faced the brutal reality that his exploration, at least in the short term, had to be terminated. His decision was influenced by the approach of the end of the monsoon season, and the fact that, for the first time ever, he had an ailing crew.

> We had continued the survey of the coast for more than
> one-half of the six months which the master and carpenter
> had judged the ship might run without much risk, provided
> she remained in fine weather and no accident happened; and

the remainder of the time being not much more than
necessary for us to reach Port Jackson, I judged it imprudent
to continue the investigation longer. In addition to the
rottenness of the ship, the state of my own health and that of
the ship's company were urgent to terminate the
examination here; for nearly all had become debilitated from
the heat and moisture of the climate – from being a good
deal fatigued – and from the want of nourishing food. I was
myself disabled by scorbutic sores from going to the mast
head, or making any more expeditions in boats; and as the
whole of the surveying department rested upon me, our
further stay was without one of its principal objects. It was
not, however, without much regret that I quitted the
coast ...

Flinders had hoped to continue making observations by sailing
along the coast of New Holland, but a persistent south-westerly
breeze forced *Investigator* onto a course that took her towards
Timor, more than 700 miles to the west of the Wessel Islands, so
he opted to head for Kupang, a Dutch outpost at the western end
of the island:

I judged it advisable to obtain refreshments there for my
ship's company; under the apprehension that, as the winter
season was fast advancing on the south coast of Terra
Australis, the bad state of the ship might cause more labour at
the pumps than our present strength was capable of exerting.

Should there be a ship in Kupang that presented the opportunity
for a passage to Europe, Lieutenant Fowler would be put aboard
and returned to England, with two objectives: to convey to the

Admiralty the charts Flinders had completed to date, and to request from that noble body a new vessel, which Fowler could then sail back to New Holland as expeditiously as possible so that the exploration of the landmass could be completed. Unfortunately, there was no foreign vessel anchored off Kupang when *Investigator* reached the port, and no indication as to when one might arrive.

This meant that there was only one way home to Port Jackson, and that was aboard *Investigator*. While that was not the outcome Flinders had hoped for, there was one skerrick of good news regarding the deterioration of the ship:

> ... the carpenter being now directed to bore into some of
> the timbers then examined, did not find them to have
> become perceptibly worse; so that I was led to hope and
> believe that the ship might go through this service, without
> much more than common risk, provided we remained in
> fine-weather climates, as was intended.

When all work on board was completed and the ship was ready for sea, Flinders decided that some of the crew would be allowed to go ashore for recreation. One of the cooks and a young lad from Port Jackson saw this as an opportunity to start a new life and deserted. The entire town was searched the following day but the absconders were never seen again.

With her canvas barely stretched by a soft morning breeze, *Investigator* eased away from Kupang on 8 April at a slow rate of knots. It was the commencement of what would be a passage of some 4000 nautical miles to Port Jackson. Flinders set a course to the south-west, his destination being the coastline that the Dutch explorer Dirk Hartog had touched almost two centuries earlier. Before reaching there, however, and knowing that there was still some life in the rotting bones of his ship, Flinders decided to take the opportunity to look for Trial Rocks (today named Tryal Rocks).

In 1622, *Trial* (sometimes referred to as *Tryall*) was only the second ship out of England to attempt the passage to Batavia via the Cape of Good Hope. While doing so, she became the first English ship to be wrecked in Australian waters. The master, James Brookes, made a major navigational blunder by holding a course too far to the south of east, and on sighting the coast of what is now Western Australia, he was forced to change course dramatically to the north.

In pitch darkness, at around 11 p.m. on 24 May, *Trial* had ploughed into an unsighted reef and immediately started to break up. While her hull planks buckled and exploded into splinters, and as parts of the rig crashed to the deck, Brookes and nine crewmen managed to get aboard one of the ship's tenders and escape, as did another 36, who crammed aboard a longboat. Sadly, the 93 remaining crew had no way of escaping the rapidly submerging wreck and perished. Both the boats loaded with survivors managed to reach Java independently some weeks later.

Flinders' search for this reef, for which Brookes had given an approximate latitude and longitude, was one of many that failed to find anything; subsequently, in fact, the Admiralty declared Trial Rocks to be non-existent. However, in 1969 – 347 years after the tragedy – the wreck of the ship was finally discovered, and the location of the reef confirmed, near the Montebello Islands.

When Flinders abandoned his search for the reef on 27 April 1803, he was confronted by two predicaments: *Investigator* was beginning to take on an increasing amount of water through its expanding leaks, but more importantly there was a medical problem among his crew: 'the diarrhoea on board was gaining ground'. The probable reason for the men falling ill was their change of diet when they reached Kupang, a theory reinforced by the knowledge that Baudin had lost 12 of his crew to dysentery when *Le Géographe* was there. Flinders was in no doubt that he must not dawdle during the remaining voyage to Port Jackson, and, as a precaution against more of his men falling ill, he insisted that greater efforts be made to ensure that the ship remained dry and well aired below deck. He also divided the crew into three watches and the officers into four to reduce their fatigue.

Strong, squally and moist north-westerlies drove the heavily reefed *Investigator* for much of the time towards Cape Leeuwin, which she rounded on Friday, 13 May. From there her course was directly 'along the outer parts of the Archipelago of the Recherche ... and to stop a day or two in Goose-Island Bay, for the purposes of procuring geese for our sick people, seal oil for our lamps, and a few casks of salt from the lake on Middle Island'. The desired anchorage at Middle Island was reached on 17 May, but not before 'Mr Charles Douglas, the boatswain, breathed his last; and I affixed his name to the two lumps of land, which seemed to offer themselves as a monument to his memory'. He was buried on the island.

The ship lay at anchor for three days, and in that time one of Flinders' 'best men', William Hillier, also died from dysentery. At this time some 15 men were on the ship's surgeon's sick list.

At first light on 21 May, a fresh north-westerly wind brought whitecaps to the waters of the bay in which *Investigator* was anchored, meaning conditions were ideal for continuing the passage east. Recognising the favourable weather, Flinders ordered all necessary crew on deck to get the ship underway. However, the procedure went horribly wrong and *Investigator* went frighteningly close to being blown onto the rocky shore of the island. It started when a kedge dragged after the two main bowers had been raised clear of the bottom.

At this time we were not more than a cable's length from the
rocks of Middle Island; and the ship being exposed to great
danger with the least increase of wind, we ... began to heave
on the best bower. In the meantime the ship drove with
both anchors ahead, which obliged me, on the instant, to cut
both cables ... and run up the jib and stay-sails; and my
orders being obeyed with an alacrity not to be exceeded, we
happily cleared the rocks by a few fathoms, and at noon
made sail to the eastward.

Every man knew that *Investigator* had been incredibly lucky to
escape being wrecked on the island. With her frail hull being so
vulnerable, she would almost certainly have broken up on the rocks
in a very short time.

By now, any wish Flinders might have held to complete his
survey of Kangaroo Island on this return voyage had to be dismissed:
getting the ship and his crew home as soon as possible was the
priority. On 26 May, two days before *Investigator* entered Bass Strait,
James Greenhalgh, Flinders' sergeant of marines, succumbed to
dysentery. Others remained close to death.

... when I contemplated eighteen of my men below, several
of whom were stretched in their hammocks almost without
hope, and reflected that the lives of the rest depended upon
our speedy arrival in port, every other consideration
vanished; and I carried all possible sail, day and night, making
such observations only as could be done without causing
delay.

Two more crewmen died while *Investigator* tacked her way up the
coast towards Port Jackson into a 'foul' north-easterly wind.

Happily it veered to the southward at midnight, we passed
Botany Bay at three in the morning [Thursday, 9 June 1803],
and at daybreak tacked between the heads of Port Jackson, to
work up for Sydney Cove. I left the ship at noon, above
Garden Island, and waited upon His Excellency Governor
King, to inform him of our arrival, and concert arrangements
for the reception of the sick at the colonial hospital.

New Holland had thus been circumnavigated for the first time, and
the basic outline of this continent of near 3,270,000 square miles
could be revealed to the world.

CHAPTER TWELVE

A Fate Foretold

The return to Sydney Town was bittersweet for the 29-year-old Flinders after his voyage of nearly 11 months. He had achieved what he had set out to do by circumnavigating the continent and revealing its identity to the world, but this success was laden with disappointment. He had not been able to present as much fine detail of the coastline as he had hoped, and six of his crew (including one of the convicts) had died painful deaths as a result of the dysentery that came from their stopover in Kupang. Now he hoped to find a way to undertake another voyage in the near future so he could fill in the missing details on his charts.

Flinders' review of the expedition led to seven of the eight surviving convicts who had joined the ship being granted unfettered freedom by Governor King; the other returned to convict life, having failed to serve the captain well.

There was sad news awaiting Flinders in Sydney Town: his father had passed away while *Investigator* was at sea. Within 24 hours of his return he had penned a heartfelt letter to his stepmother, which expressed the respect he held for Flinders senior:

We arrived here yesterday from having circumnavigated
New Holland, and I received numerous and valuable marks
of the friendship of all those whose affection is so dear to me;
but the joy which some letters occasioned is dreadfully
embittered by what you, my good and kind mother, had
occasion to communicate. The death of so kind a father,
who was so excellent a man, is a heavy blow, and strikes
deep into my heart. The duty I owed him, and which I had
now a prospect of paying with the warmest affection and
gratitude, had made me look forward to the time of our
return with increased ardour ... Indeed, my mother,
I thought the time fast approaching for me to fulfil what I
once said in a letter, that my actions should some day show
how I valued my father. One of my fondest hopes is now
destroyed. O, my dearest, kindest father, how much I loved
and reverenced you, you cannot now know!

Numerous letters from his much adored wife were also awaiting
him, and he replied almost immediately in a manner that left no
doubt that his love for her was still strong. He also made reference
to his constant companion, Trim, saying that he, like his master,
had become grey during the voyage. He was very proud of the fact
that his well-travelled cat had now become the first feline to
circumnavigate New Holland as well as the first to sail around the
world.

Flinders wrote of the impact that the circumnavigation had on
Trim:

In the Gulf of Carpentaria, from the unhealthiness of the
climate, the want of his usual fresh food, and perhaps from
too much application to study, this worthy creature became

almost grey, lost much of weight, and seemed to be
threatened with a premature old age; but to the great joy of
his friends, he re-assumed his fine black robe and his
accustomed portliness, a short time after returning to
harbour.

Despite having been away for so long, and although he was suffering
from a number of ailments, Flinders initially took no time for rest.
He immediately began discussions with Governor King as to how
he might continue his exploration of New Holland, considering the
ships that were available in Port Jackson. The first priority,
however, was to make a thorough inspection of *Investigator*, and for
this the governor called on the commanders of *Porpoise* and
Bridgewater, which were both in port, and Thomas Moore, who was
'Master boat builder to the Territory of New South Wales'.

Just five days after *Investigator* had arrived back into harbour,
the men had completed their inspection. Little time was needed, in
fact, because *Investigator* was in a deplorable condition. The
inspectors concluded unanimously 'that she is not worth repairing
in any country, and that it is impossible in this country to put her
in a state fit for going to sea'. Flinders was present while the survey
was being done, and he reported:

I went round the ship with the officers in their examination,
and was excessively surprised to see the state of the rottenness
in which the timbers were found. In the starboard bow there
were thirteen close together, through any one of which a
cane might have been thrust.

Flinders realised just how fortunate he and his crew had been in
getting their ship back to Port Jackson, as he related in letters home

to England. In one he wrote that *Investigator* was 'worn out – she is decayed both in skin and bone'. In another, to his wife, he said, 'It was the unanimous opinion of the surveying officers that, had we met with a severe gale of wind in the passage from Timor, she must have crushed like an egg and gone down.'

Flinders described himself as 'distressed' at being unable to complete his task as planned; he wished to be under sail aboard another ship as soon as possible. However, he also realised that even if a ship was available, the mission could not proceed for some time simply because so many of his crew were still ailing. He used the enforced break as opportunity to accelerate his recovery from his own health problems. He made 'an excursion to the Hawkesbury settlement, near the foot of the back mountains; and the fresh air there with a vegetable diet and medical care soon made a great alteration in the scorbutic sores which had disabled me for four months'.

The well-rested and near fully recovered captain returned to his ship early in July. *Porpoise* arrived in port soon after, and so, as Flinders wrote, 'His Excellency, with that prompt zeal for His Majesty's service which characterised him, and was eminently shown in everything wherein my voyage was concerned, immediately ordered the survey to be made'. Unfortunately, *Porpoise* was found to be unsuitable – it would have taken 12 months to complete the required fit-out. Instead, she would return to England.

Flinders made further representations to the governor and received his responses in a matter of days. Of Governor King's suggestions, the one most suited to Flinders' desire to fulfil the orders for the mission as laid down by the Admiralty was to return to England and request another vessel. 'My election was therefore made to embark as a passenger in the *Porpoise*,' Flinders wrote, 'in order to lay my charts and journals before the Lords Commissioners of the Admiralty, and obtain, if such should be their pleasure, another ship to complete the examination of Terra Australis.' With that decision made, *Investigator* was decommissioned; she was moored in Sydney Cove so she could be used as a storehouse hulk. Her days as a history-making vessel of exploration were done.

At 11 a.m. on 10 August 1803, Flinders, accompanied by Trim and many of his crew from *Investigator*, farewelled Sydney Town from the deck of *Porpoise*, which then moved down harbour in the company of *Cato* and *Bridgewater*, bound for England via Torres Strait.

As previously recounted, one week later, on 17 August, a night of hell erupted for *Porpoise* and *Cato* when both ships blundered onto an unknown bastion of coral reef and were wrecked. The two crews managed to get to a nearby sand cay, while the captain of *Bridgewater*, it would appear, turned a blind eye to their predicament and sailed on.

No doubt, as the survivors stood on the sandbank and contemplated their fate while observing the remnants of the wrecked vessels in the distance, those who had been with Flinders aboard *Investigator* would have been reminded of the words of the fortune teller some of them visited before departing England. As Flinders noted with concern in *A Voyage to Terra Australis*, after predicting that *Investigator* was about to undertake a long voyage and that Thistle would lose his life, the 'cunning man' prophesied 'they would be shipwrecked, but not in the ship they were going out in [*Investigator*]: whether they would escape and return to England, he was not permitted to reveal'.

The only path to salvation for the stranded sailors was to orchestrate their own rescue. Thus, nine days after the catastrophe, Flinders and 13 men set out aboard the largest cutter available to them, which they named *Hope*. They were attempting to sail 700 nautical miles south to Port Jackson and raise the alarm.

Little more than 24 hours into this voyage, those aboard the cutter faced a frightening reminder of how life-threatening this undertaking would be. It came while they were mid-ocean with nowhere to hide.

> The wind freshened in the afternoon, and a cross sea rose
> which obliged us to reef the sails, and made the boat very
> wet. At four we close reefed and hauled to the wind, but this
> was not enough; the increased hollowness of the waves
> caused the boat to labour so much, that every plunge raised
> an apprehension that some of the planks would start from the
> timbers.

The treacherous sea state was being generated by wind against tide – the brunt of a current that was flowing rapidly to the south was being opposed by a strong south-easterly wind. Such was his concern for the safety of the boat that Flinders ordered the cutter to be lightened as quickly as possible so it would float higher and, he hoped, be safer in the conditions. The contents of a water cask were emptied over the side, while other crewmen threw overboard the fireplace stones they had on board, the firewood, a bag of food and whatever else they felt could be spared. It was a decision that probably saved them, Flinders later wrote, because 'the boat was then somewhat more easy'.

After two days of sailing, the cutter had covered 180 miles at an average of almost four knots. Considering the burden the vessel was still carrying – 14 men and their provisions and equipment – this was already a most admirable achievement.

The first sighting of land came late on 28 August. Flinders immediately called for the sails to be trimmed so that *Hope* could be hauled up onto a course that would see her parallel the coast while heading south. The captain was confident that this would minimise the risk of her being wrecked on unknown navigational hazards; it would also provide sufficient sea-room for a safe haven to be found, should a southerly gale sweep up the coast and endanger their progress.

The weather remained in their favour, and, much to everyone's delight, at sunset the following day Cape Moreton hove into view over the southern horizon.

> This was only the fourth day of our departure from Wreck
> Reef, and I considered the voyage to be half accomplished,
> since we had got firm hold of the main coast; for the
> probability of being lost is greater in making three
> hundred miles in an open boat at sea, than in running even
> six hundred along shore. It would have added much to our
> satisfaction, could we have conveyed the intelligence of this
> fortunate progress to our shipmates on the bank.

The need to replenish their water supply was becoming urgent, so Flinders altered course towards the coast and anchored the cutter just off the surf line at Point Lookout. As some of the crew prepared to swim ashore to collect water, Aboriginals were seen. Muskets were loaded to protect the men who were going to the beach, but the real threat came from a more sinister visitor.

> There were about twenty Indians upon the side of a hill near
> the shore, who seemed to be peaceably disposed, amusing us
> with dances in imitation of the kangaroo; we made signs of
> wanting water, which they understood, and pointed to a small
> rill falling into the sea. Two of the sailors leaped over-board,
> with some trifles for the natives and one end of the lead line;

with the other end we slung the empty cask, which they
hauled on shore and filled without molestation. A shark had
followed them to the beach; and fearing they might be attacked
in returning, we got up the anchor and went to a place where
the surf, though too much to allow of the boat landing,
permitted us to lie closer. The cask of water, a bundle of wood,
and the two men were received on board without accident.

Aided by the southerly current, *Hope* continued to make good time
on her voyage south. When the wind was too light for the sail to be
set the cutter had to be rowed. The crew, divided into two watches
of six, rotated day and night to keep the vessel moving. Flinders and
Captain Park, who had been the master of *Cato*, shared the helming.
By rowing when there was no wind, they were minimising their
time at sea, thus reducing their chances of encountering a southerly
gale, a weather front that could arrive almost unheralded off this
coast, with wind and waves of such ferocity that the boat and crew
would have no defence. Such a situation showed signs of arising on
Sunday, 4 September, when *Hope* still had 175 nautical miles to
cover before reaching Port Jackson.

On the 4th, we again attempted to beat to the southward;
but the wind being light as well as foul, and the sea running
high, not much was gained; at noon the weather threatened
so much, that it became necessary to look out for a place of
shelter, and we steered into a bight with rocks in it, which I
judge to have been on the north side of Tacking Point.

This would not be the last time they sought refuge from unfavourable
conditions, and it wasn't until 7 September that the men began to
believe that they would make it.

At eleven o'clock, the rain having cleared away, we stood
out to the offing with light baffling winds, and towards
evening were enabled to lie along the coast; but the breeze at
south-east not giving much assistance, we took to the oars
and laboured hard all the following night, being animated
with the prospect of a speedy termination to our voyage.
The north head of Broken Bay was in sight next morning,
and at noon the south head was abreast of the boat; a sea
breeze then setting in at E. N. E., we crowded all sail for
Port Jackson, and soon after two o'clock had the happiness to
enter between the heads.

The reader has perhaps never gone 250 leagues at sea in
an open boat, or along a strange coast inhabited by savages;
but if he recollect the eighty officers and men upon Wreck-
Reef Bank, and how important was our arrival to their
safety, and to the saving of the charts, journals, and papers of
the *Investigator*'s voyage, he may have some idea of the
pleasure we felt, but particularly myself, at entering our
destined port.

The weary shipwrecked sailors could not have wanted a more
favourable wind for the final five miles between the entrance to
Port Jackson and Sydney Cove. It was downwind all the way.
Relief poured through their bodies on sighting Sydney Town.

Flinders, sitting at the tiller in the sternsheets, guided the cutter
towards the southern shore until the bow gently nudged onto the
treeless bank. It was late afternoon, and the appearance of 14
unkempt and tired men from who knew where provided much
intrigue for the locals wandering along the shoreline.

No one was more surprised than Governor King, as Flinders
recorded:

I proceeded immediately to the town of Sydney, and went with Captain Park to wait upon His Excellency Governor King, whom we found at dinner with his family. A razor had not passed over our faces from the time of the shipwreck, and the surprise of the governor was not little at seeing two persons thus appear whom he supposed to be many hundred leagues on their way to England; but so soon as he was convinced of the truth of the vision before him, and learned the melancholy cause, an involuntary tear started from the eye of friendship and compassion, and we were received in the most affectionate manner.

The urgency of the moment led the governor to call immediately on the assistance of the captain of the merchant ship *Rolla*, which was in port and preparing to sail to China. *Rolla* was commissioned to sail to Wreck Reefs as soon as possible; it was to 'take every person on board and carry them to Canton'. Two colonial schooners were to sail in company: *Francis* would repatriate to Port Jackson those who wanted to do so, while *Cumberland* would become Flinders' new command for the purpose first of overseeing the rescue, then of sailing on to England as expeditiously as possible after completing another survey of Torres Strait.

While this gesture from Governor King might have sounded satisfying, it caused Flinders considerable concern. *Cumberland*, which had been built in Sydney Town, was tiny: just 29 tons burthen. Flinders described her, somewhat disparagingly, to be 'something less than a Gravesend Passage Boat'. Her actual dimensions are now unknown, but it is safe to say that she would have been no more than 50 feet length on deck, of 15 feet beam and five feet draft. She was so small that the crew would probably comprise only ten officers and men. Flinders wrote that, with the intended passage being 15,000 nautical miles, this offer 'required some consideration'.

> Her small size, when compared with the distance from Port Jackson to England, was not my greatest objection to the little *Cumberland*; it was the quickness of her motion and the want of convenience, which would prevent [me from working on] the charts and journal of my voyage … On the other hand, the advantage of again passing through, and collecting more information of Torres' Strait, and of arriving in England three or four months sooner [than by sailing aboard *Rolla*] to commence the outfit of another ship, were important considerations.

With *Cumberland* being so small, Flinders would be forced to stop at every convenient port over the long voyage so that the crew's food and water could be replenished. He envisaged these places to be Kupang, Île-de-France (Mauritius), the Cape of Good Hope, Saint Helena and some of the islands on the western side of the North Atlantic. On hearing this proposal, Governor King spoke strongly against going to Île-de-France because of the tenuous state of relations between France and Britain. He left the final decision on this matter to Flinders to make at the time he passed the island; as a precaution, he provided him with two letters for the governor of the island.

The captain's thoughts regarding *Cumberland* were influenced by two important factors. The idea of being the first person to successfully undertake such a long voyage in a vessel so small appealed to him, as did the opportunity 'to put an early stop to the account which Captain Palmer [the master of *Bridgewater*] would probably give of our total loss'. *Cumberland* it was!

Almost two weeks would pass before the vessels were ready to put to sea, however.

> This delay caused me much uneasiness, under the
> apprehension that we might not arrive before our friends at
> the reef, despairing of assistance, should have made some
> unsuccessful attempt to save themselves; and this idea
> pursued me so much, that every day seemed to be a week
> until I got out of the harbour with the three vessels.

It was still dark on the morning of Wednesday, 21 September 1803, when the decks of all three ships began to buzz with activity. Calls could be heard from the master and bosun as to what tasks needed to be undertaken; men made their way up the ratlines to unfurl the sails; and blocks carrying halyards, sheets, braces, buntlines and the like gave off high-pitched screeches in protest as loads came on them.

When all was ready, the capstan-bars were slotted into place, then, with the order coming to weigh anchor, the heavy wooden pawls clacked away as the crew worked the capstan. Within a few minutes, the bosun called 'anchor's aweigh' – it was clear of the bottom. Sails were trimmed, and before long, when first light was just a smear on the horizon, *Rolla*, *Francis* and *Cumberland* were sailing out of Port Jackson. The rescue mission was underway.

There were 13 crew sailing with Flinders: Captain Park plus his second mate from *Cato*, the bosun from *Investigator*, and ten seamen. All were busy learning how to handle their new charge, discovering the peculiarities she would display as she surged down the loping swells that had been generated by the very favourable south-easterly wind that was on hand. Their initial impressions were good, but as the day wore on and the wind strength increased, there was cause for concern: *Cumberland* was not as stable as they had hoped, and the more she began to heel the more water she took on. Flinders noted that 'instead of being tight, as had been represented, her upper works then admitted a great deal of water'. This certainly was not an encouraging sign at the start of a 15,000-nautical-mile voyage.

The dilemma for Flinders was immediate: on one hand he had the importance of the rescue effort, and on the other the safety of his own vessel and men. He was decisive: before dark, he signalled to *Rolla* and *Francis* that all three vessels should run for shelter in Port Stephens. Once there, the magnitude of the problem with *Cumberland* became apparent.

I anchored in a small bight under Point Stephens, in very bad plight; the pumps proving to be so nearly useless, that we could not prevent the water from half filling the hold; and two hours longer would have reduced us to baling [sic] with buckets, and perhaps have been fatal. This essay did not lead me to think favourably of the vessel, in which I had undertaken a voyage half round the globe.

An assessment of *Cumberland*'s problems brought only one conclusion: the saving of lives on Wreck Reefs was paramount, so there was no time to rectify the leaks. Instead, if the ship was to survive, sail would have to be greatly reduced every time the wind and waves issued a challenge.

Two days after leaving Sydney Town, the three vessels were back at sea and heading north once more.

Six weeks to the day after Flinders and 13 others had crammed aboard the small cutter *Hope* and set off from Wreck Reefs, desperate to save their owns lives and those of 66 other castaways, the lookout standing high in the rig aboard *Rolla* shouted with great excitement to those on deck that he had sighted in the distance ahead a flag flying from a pole. It could only be Wreck Reefs.

Simultaneously, close to the reef, a sailor – who was with Lieutenant Fowler testing the seaworthiness and sailing ability of one of the boats that had been built there – looked to the south and sighted what he thought was a large bird on the horizon. After focusing on it for a moment longer, he yelled, 'Damn my blood – what's that?' It was *Rolla*'s billowing white top-gallant. In an instant, Fowler had tacked the boat and was heading back to shore, and as they neared the edge of the cay, the two on board were hollering to their fellow castaways and pointing to the south: a ship was in sight.

By that afternoon, the three vessels were closing on their chosen anchorage in the lee of the bank. As they neared it, an eleven-gun salute boomed out from the carronades that had been salvaged from *Porpoise*. At the same time, Flinders noted with interest that *Porpoise* 'had not yet gone to pieces; but was still lying on her beam ends, high up on the reef, a frail, but impressive monument of our misfortune'.

An emotional reunion followed, as Flinders recorded: 'On landing, I was greeted with three hearty cheers, and the utmost joy by my officers and people; and the pleasure of rejoining my companions so amply provided with the means of relieving their distress, made this one of the happiest moments of my life.'

Flinders would learn that, after a month had passed at Wreck Reefs, his safe arrival at Port Jackson had been the subject of much conjecture but no one had given up hope. All had continued to work confidently towards the execution of the plan that Flinders had left with them before departing. Now it was time to return the survivors, including Trim, to safety: 'My plan of proceeding at the reef having been arranged on the passage, I immediately began to put it in execution.'

Everyone was assembled on the bank and told they had 24 hours to consider their options. Those sailors wanting to be discharged from service could return to Port Jackson aboard *Francis*; the rest would go aboard *Rolla* and sail to China – 'with the exception of ten officers and men,' Flinders noted, 'whom I named, to go to England with me in the *Cumberland*'. Knowing how unseaworthy his vessel was, however, Flinders confirmed that it was his intention to sail her at least as far as the first port, 'where a passage might be procured in a better vessel without losing time'. He also decided that some of those wanting to return to Port Jackson would do so aboard the new boat they had built during the previous six weeks: 'It was about the size of the *Cumberland*, had a deck, and was called the *Resource*.'

After three rousing and hearty cheers from those aboard, the four vessels went on their respective ways at midday on Tuesday, 11 October 1803. Unfortunately, because of the dire circumstances that lay ahead for Flinders, he would not learn for some years that the other three vessels reached their destinations successfully, and that, the following year, Lieutenant Fowler, Samuel Flinders, John Franklin and the remaining members of *Investigator*'s company were repatriated to England.

The passage to Torres Strait was uneventful for Flinders, his crew and Trim, although they still had to monitor the ingress of water into the ship's bilge constantly and man the pumps accordingly. They also had to reef the sails as soon as there was any sign of strong wind so that *Cumberland*'s frail hull was not overloaded. Both problems inhibited the ship's speed, leading Flinders to record his frustration: '... the indifferent sailing of the schooner was against making a quick passage, for with all the sail we could set, so much as six knots was not marked on the log board.'

Two days were spent in Torres Strait doing survey work. With that task complete, Flinders set a course to the west, first to the Wessel Islands and then to Kupang, where *Cumberland* arrived on 10 November – 30 days after departing Wreck Reefs.

As each day passed, the captain was becoming increasingly concerned about *Cumberland*'s vulnerability in rough weather and her ability to complete the voyage. He had hoped that while in Kupang he would be able to repair the ship's pumps and procure some pitch, which could be used to help stem the leaks in the topsides, but no opportunities were forthcoming.

With no reason to stay any longer, *Cumberland* was back at sea four days after reaching Kupang. Her next destination was the Cape of Good Hope, but the route would not be direct because of the ship's shortcomings. Instead, a course was plotted through regions where the wind was less likely to challenge the vessel's seaworthiness. Even so, the integrity of *Cumberland*'s structure continued to deteriorate, and Flinders' problems compounded.

> The schooner was leaky, more so than before, and the pumps were getting worse; but hoping to reach the Cape of Good Hope, I had wholly given up the idea of Batavia [as a potential destination] as lying too far out of the track; Île-de-France besides was in the way, should the vessel become incapable of doubling [sailing beyond] the Cape without repairs.

Within days, a decision on where to go next was being made for him. *Cumberland* was then trapped in a grotesque sea state, with the ground swell coming from the south-west while the large, wind-driven surface waves were coming from a different direction. The convergence of these systems created a situation where *Cumberland*'s hull was being twisted and contorted to a frightening degree, so much so that the one pump that was still operational had to be manned almost 24 hours a day. '... had the wind been on the starboard side, it is doubtful whether the schooner could have been kept above water,' wrote Flinders.

> After turning these circumstances over in my mind for a day
> or two, and considering what else might be urged both for
> and against the measure, I determined to put in at Île-de-
> France; and on the 6th ... altered the course half a point for
> that island, to the satisfaction of the people.

Île-de-France was a small dot on Flinders' chart – just 40 miles long and 30 miles wide – situated 550 miles east of Madagascar. He was mindful that Governor King had discouraged him from stopping there, but there was no alternative. Two options would be available to him once *Cumberland* was safely in port: he could pursue the long and arduous task of repairing it, or he could sell it and return home aboard another vessel. He was not overly concerned by the possibility that England and France might again be at war because he held a passport from the French government that would guarantee him, as an explorer, freedom of passage. This had been issued as a protection for the abandoned *Investigator* and not for *Cumberland*, but this caused Flinders no concern:

> ... I checked my suspicions by considering that the passport
> was certainly intended to protect the voyage and not the
> *Investigator* only. A description of the *Investigator* was indeed
> given in it, but the intention of it could be only to prevent
> imposition. The *Cumberland* was now prosecuting the
> voyage, and I had come in her for a lawful purpose, and
> upon such an occasion as the passport allowed me to put into

a French port. The great desire also that the French nation has long shown to promote geographical researches, and the friendly treatment that the *Géographe* and the *Naturaliste* had received at Port Jackson, rose up before me as guarantees that I should not be impeded, but should receive the kindest welcome and every assistance.

Unfortunately, as Flinders was about to find out, there were no guarantees. He was to be impeded – dramatically so – and he certainly wouldn't receive the kind welcome he was hoping for.

CHAPTER THIRTEEN

Passport to Imprisonment

It was the middle of the day on 15 December when *Cumberland*, having covered 3800 nautical miles from Kupang, was running along the eastern coast of Île-de-France. Her presence was there for all to see – sails billowing and a bold wave of white water bursting away from the bow each time she surged down an ocean swell. Still, Flinders was proceeding with caution; he had no charts on board relating to the size of the island and its anchorages, especially the location of the main harbour at Port Louis, so he was relying on scant information published in the *Encyclopaedia Britannica* to guide him. He was flying the French flag from the masthead as a signal to those on shore that a pilot was required.

Before long, a schooner was seen to sail out of a cove, which Flinders assumed to be a pilot vessel coming to guide him into port. His assumption appeared to be confirmed when the schooner turned in a manner that he interpreted as an indication that *Cumberland* should follow. But that wasn't the case.

In fact, England and France were once again at war. On sighting *Cumberland* flying the British jack from its stern, those on board the schooner believed that the English vessel was a ship of war and that the island was about to come under attack, so they ran for cover. Unaware of the political situation, Flinders followed the schooner into a bay, where he watched it anchor in a most unusual way.

If the schooner's actions were strange before, those of the people were now more so; for no sooner was their anchor dropped, than without furling the sails they went hastily on shore in a canoe, and made the best of their way up a steep hill, one of them with a trunk on his shoulder. They were met by a person who, from the plume in his hat, appeared to be an officer, and presently we saw several men with muskets on the top of the hill; this gave another view of the schooner's movements, and caused me to apprehend that England and France were either at war or very near it. To induce some person to come on board, I held up the letters for General Magallon, the governor; but this being to no purpose, Mr Aken went on shore in our little boat, taking with him the letters and French passport; in a short time he returned with the officer and two others, and I learned to my great regret that war was actually declared.

The arrival of *Cumberland* had caused great alarm not only among the crew of the schooner, but also among the local community. The belief that an attack was imminent resulted in the troops being called out, and women and children were ordered to escape towards the inland immediately. Orders were also given for cattle and sheep 'to be driven into the woods'.

When Aken returned to the ship, he had with him a military officer, Major Dunienville, to whom he had shown the passport. The welcome for Flinders was amicable, to the point that the major invited him to come ashore and join him for dinner that evening, but Flinders declined, preferring to concentrate on the problems his ship faced. Dunienville then advised that the pilot who was required to guide *Cumberland* to Port Louis would be available the following day.

On returning to shore, Dunienville wrote a report to the military governor of the island, General Decaen, who had replaced General Magallon. It was carried by messenger to Port Louis, some 20 miles to the north. The report detailed the circumstances around the arrival of *Cumberland*, the confusion over the possibility of an attack, and that Flinders had presented his passport. Dunienville ended by noting: 'Happily all these precautions, dictated by circumstances, proved to be unnecessary,' adding that Flinders 'did not know of the war, and consequently had no idea that he would spread alarm by following [the schooner]'.

Later the same day, Dunienville returned to *Cumberland* with an interpreter and a superior, the commandant of the region, Etienne Bolger, an abrupt and somewhat gruff man, who quickly pointed out that the passport was for *Investigator* and not *Cumberland*; because of this, the matter could only be dealt with by General Decaen. As a result, *Cumberland* sailed for Port Louis with the major on board as a guest.

During this passage to Port Louis, my mind was occupied in turning over all the circumstances of my situation, and the mode of proceeding likely to be adopted by the new governor. The breaking out of the war, the neglect of providing in the passport for any such case as that in which I stood, and the ungracious conduct of the commandant at the Baye du Cap, gave me some apprehensions; but on the other hand, the intention of the passport to protect the persons employed in the expedition, with their charts and journals, must be evident; and the conduct of a governor appointed by the first consul Bonaparte, who was a professed patron of science, would hardly be less liberal than that of two preceding French governments to captain Cook in the American, and captain Vancouver in the last war; for both of whom protection and assistance had been ordered, though neither carried passports or had suffered shipwreck. These circumstances, with the testimony which the commanders of the *Géographe* and *Naturaliste* had doubtless given of their treatment at Port Jackson, seemed to insure for me the kindest reception; and I determined to rest confident in this assurance, and to banish all apprehension as derogatory to the governor of Île-de-France and to the character of the French nation.

After a 40-nautical-mile overnight passage along the western side of the island, *Cumberland* sailed into Port Louis at four p.m. on 17 December 1803. The port was more an inlet than a harbour, and Flinders was directed to guide his vessel to an anchorage close to the settlement. The captain had hoped that he would see the French ships *Le Géographe* and *Le Naturaliste* in port, but he was soon to learn that the latter had already returned to France. Sadly, Captain Baudin had died aboard his ship on 16 September, little more than a month after *Le Géographe* arrived in Port Louis. The ship, with a new commander, had sailed for France just 24 hours earlier.

Anxious to get the issue of his passport resolved as quickly as possible, Flinders went ashore soon after *Cumberland* was anchored so he could present himself to General Decaen. Unfortunately, the governor was dining at the time, so Flinders had no option but to wait. He was taken by an aide:

> ... to a shady place which seemed to be the common lounge
> for the officers connected with the port. There were some
> who spoke English, and by way of passing the time, they
> asked if I had really come from Botany Bay in that little
> vessel ... Others asked questions of monsieur Baudin's
> conduct at Port Jackson, and of the English colony there; and
> also concerning the voyage of monsieur Flinedare.

Flinders struggled with the reference to 'Monsieur Flinedare' until he realised it was their way of pronouncing his name.

About two hours later, Flinders, wearing his frock uniform, was escorted back to Government House, where he was greeted by two men, one of whom immediately demanded his passport and papers. It was General Decaen, and assisting him was his aide-de-camp, Colonel Monistrol. After a cursory glance over the papers, the general asked in a terse manner why Flinders had arrived aboard *Cumberland* when his passport specified *Investigator*. Flinders explained the circumstances in detail, but this only prompted the general to become intolerant, as was evident in his response: 'You are imposing on me, sir! It is not probable that the governor of New South Wales should send away the commander of an expedition of discovery in so small a vessel!'

Little more was said, and the interpreter and a military officer were directed to take Flinders back to his ship so that his books and papers could be brought ashore for scrutiny.

By now, Flinders was feeling insulted by the treatment he had received from the general. He made sure that the interpreter knew it, telling him that 'the captain-general's conduct must alter very much before I should pay him a second visit, or even set my foot on shore again'.

But Flinders had no choice in the matter; he was to be taken ashore once the documents had been assembled because the general had ordered that he be confined at a lodging in the town. 'What! I exclaimed in the first transports of surprise and indignation – I am then a prisoner!' He was then told that his detention in Île-de-France was likely to last only a few days, and that in the meantime he would be treated in the most cordial manner possible.

This meant little to the incensed Flinders.

Aken was ordered to join the captain on shore that night, but it wasn't until one a.m. that all the documents had been gathered and placed in a trunk, along with some clothes that would be needed. As they were rowed ashore, the remainder of the crew – and Trim – were left aboard *Cumberland*, under the watch of guards on deck.

Despite being told that they would want for nothing, Flinders and Aken were accommodated that night in a dark, dingy and dirty tavern, Café Marengo, in the middle of the town, with a sentry posted outside their room. After just a few hours of fitful sleep, which was constantly punctuated by squadrons of mosquitos and bedbugs, the pair were rudely awoken by the sound of two armed grenadiers striding into their room at six a.m.

That afternoon Flinders was taken to an office for a lengthy interrogation. When that was complete, and much to Flinders' surprise, the governor, who had not been present, invited him to dinner on behalf of his wife, Madame Decaen. Flinders rejected the invitation; in hindsight, this would be the gravest mistake he could have made.

This invitation was so contrary to all that had hitherto passed, and being unaccompanied with any explanation, that I at first thought it could not be serious, and answered that I had already dined; but on being pressed to go at least to the table, my reply was, that 'under my present situation and treatment it was impossible; when they should be changed, when I should be set at liberty, if His Excellency thought proper to invite me, I should be flattered by it, and accept his invitation with pleasure'.

Flinders scored a direct hit on the Frenchman's supercilious ego. Decaen considered the response a personal affront and fired back a menacing retort: he would renew the invitation to Flinders as he requested – when he gained his liberty.

In his memoirs, Decaen later wrote that:

... he had given me cause to withhold the invitation on account of his impertinence; but from boorishness, or rather from arrogance, he refused that courteous invitation, which, if accepted, would indubitably have brought about a change favourable to his position through the conversation which would have taken place.

Unbeknown to Flinders, the man he was dealing with was one of Napoleon's rising stars. Decaen was born in 1769 in Caen, the capital of Normandy, and orphaned at age 12. A family friend guided him through his school days, after which he studied law. A staunchly patriotic man, he responded to a call to arms when aged 22. His rapid rise through the ranks of the French military was due primarily to his courage, intelligence, aggression and fervent determination to impress his superiors.

By 1795 Decaen was serving in the army in the Rhine, under the command of Jean Victor Moreau, the general who stood just one step down from their great leader, Napoleon Bonaparte. It was because of Decaen's leadership and success while holding this post that he came to the attention of Napoleon, and this led to the two men developing a strong bond of friendship. In time, through their conversations, Napoleon became aware that Decaen held a desire to carry the French flag in India, and he arranged for him to be posted there.

Decaen sailed from Brest in February 1803 bound for Pondicherry, on the east coast on India, where he would become captain-general of all French-held territories to the east of the Cape of Good Hope. It is probable that part of his commission was to expand the French influence in the region, but when the declaration of war by England against the French came earlier than expected, those plans were quickly brought to a halt. Decaen's opportunity for greatness in the east had suddenly been stymied, causing him to detest the British even more. His only apparent option was to become governor of Île-de-France, and he arrived in Port Louis on 15 August 1803, just four months before Flinders sailed in aboard *Cumberland*.

Decaen was a blunt and plain-spoken man, who could also be 'the very pineapple of politeness' when he was angered by others. His temper had a very low flashpoint, so quarrels were common. Flinders would later describe him as a man with 'the character of having a good heart, though too hasty and violent'.

Flinders' refusal to dine with Decaen and his wife, and his subsequent communiqués, ignited the governor's ire: he became determined to ensure that the Englishman knew who was calling the shots. Decaen realised that he could paint Flinders as being involved in espionage, particularly after finding a reference in one of his journals that could be interpreted to say as much. It would be an excellent opportunity to impress the government and his military superiors back in France.

A report from the commandant at La Savanne, where *Cumberland* had first come to anchor, did Flinders no favours, bringing into question Flinders' real identity and accusing him of 'imposture'. Decaen also held meetings with François Péron and Lieutenant Louis de Freycinet, both crewmembers of *Le Géographe*, who told the governor that they had conducted espionage activities while in Port Jackson, even though they'd had no authority from the French government to do so.

The pair had decided that their circumstances in Sydney Town provided the perfect opportunity for the surreptitious gathering of information that might aid any future French attack on the colony. The men hoped that they would be well recognised for taking the initiative in this way, and that consequently they would be looked upon favourably when it came to promotion.

One of the reasons for the British government's authorisation and support of Flinders' circumnavigation of New Holland was its fear that the French might establish an outpost somewhere on the coast, but while Baudin was holed up in Sydney, receiving unfettered hospitality and medical treatment from Governor King, he had declared that the French held no interest in such a move.

Within days of the two French vessels departing Sydney in November 1803, however, word filtered through to King that the French, while in port, had let it slip that they hoped to establish a settlement in the D'Entrecasteaux Channel in southern Van Diemen's Land. King struggled to believe what he was hearing, especially after the way in which he had hosted and cared for the French, despite the food shortages that were confronting the colony. Yet the thought that he had been duped by his guests angered him so much that he immediately put Acting Lieutenant

Charles Robbins and a crew aboard *Cumberland* and sent them south to intercept Baudin's ship and demand an explanation.

Le Géographe had eventually been sighted near King Island, and from the moment Robbins advised Baudin of the reasons for the pursuit the Frenchman was shocked and highly embarrassed. He was adamant that no such plan existed, and in his defence he reminded Robbins that he had clearly conveyed his appreciation for the considerable support he and his men had received in Port Jackson in a personal letter he had presented to King. The contents of this letter expressed deep gratitude and paid great tribute to the leadership of Governor King. It was a letter that could well have helped Flinders' cause in Port Louis, but unfortunately he did not carry a copy.

In his meeting with Decaen, Peron convinced the governor that Baudin's voyage of discovery was indeed a guise for an espionage mission to New Holland and surrounding regions, and that it had been authorised by Napoleon. No papers supporting this claim have ever been found. With Baudin having passed away, it was not possible for Decaen to confirm Peron's assertion, so he listened intently and read a written report. Peron's lengthy dissertation stated that:

> ... my opinion, and that of all those among us who have
> been particularly occupied with the organization of that
> colony, would be that we should destroy it as soon as
> possible. To-day we can do that easily; we shall not be able
> to do it in a few years to come.

In another report, Peron, who said Port Jackson was 'perhaps the most beautiful port in the world', outlined how an invasion could best be accomplished: 'The conquest of Port Jackson would be very easy to accomplish, since the English have neglected every species of means of defence. It would be possible to make a descent through Broken Bay, or even through the port of Sydney itself.'

There is no evidence that implicates Baudin in any of this espionage activity; however, when Peron returned to France aboard *Le Géographe* in late March 1804, he furnished the French Minister of Marine with the same information, all in the ardent hope that it would put Freycinet and him in good favour with the military hierarchy. Unfortunately for both men, that wasn't to be.

In truth, it would have been almost impossible for the French to mount an attack on Port Jackson. At this time, the Royal Navy was the undisputed master of the high seas, so it would have been incredibly difficult for a French fleet to reach New Holland without being intercepted and coming under attack. In fact, seven years later, in 1810, Napoleon did issue an edict calling on a squadron to 'take the English colony of Port Jackson, where considerable resources will be found', but it was wishful thinking. After 1805, when the Battle of Trafalgar was fought and won by the English, the French navy was an ineffectual force.

Right now, though, Flinders was cornered. Decaen held the upper hand, and he soon devised a manoeuvre that would keep Flinders detained for some considerable time. Instead of personally adjudicating on the matter of the 'imposter' Flinders, who could well be a spy, he would refer the matter to the government in France for consideration. As Decaen well knew, the obstinate Englishman would have to be detained until a response reached Port Louis.

Realising he had been outmanoeuvred, the fuming Flinders did his best to retain his composure. More than two-and-a-half years later, when writing of the situation, he recalled that:

My refusal of the intended honour [to dine] until set at
liberty, so much exasperated the captain-general that he

determined to make me repent it; and a wish to be acquainted with the present state of Île-de-France being found in my journal, it was fixed upon as a pretext for detaining me until orders should arrive from France, by which an imprisonment of at least twelve months was insured.

The reference in Flinders' journal actually related to his wish to investigate what benefits the island might hold in the way of the procurement of food and livestock for New South Wales. Despite this, with England and France back on a war footing, it was easy for Decaen to see Flinders as a spy on a military mission. He was a Royal Navy man aboard a vessel that was ridiculously small for a passage between Port Jackson and England, he was holding the wrong passport, and he was pretending to have been forced into port under the guise of having a sinking boat. Along with Decaen's inherent dislike for the British – which was commonplace across the French military forces – the governor had all the ammunition he needed to fire off his report to Paris.

What could well have been just a few days of detention in Port Louis had just become at least a year. The situation would soon spiral out of control, becoming an emotionally tormenting and extremely frustrating six-and-a-half years of internment.

Further compounding Flinders' predicament was that when Decaen's officers searched *Cumberland* they found despatches the ship was carrying from Governor King to the Secretary of State in London. Flinders did not know the contents of these documents, but when they were translated in Port Louis they were found to contain information regarding military matters. This led to a declaration that 'this officer is not engaged on purely scientific work; he is the bearer of despatches which might if delivered have an influence upon the present war'.

Fortunately, Flinders had some underground support from people who were convinced of the veracity of his presentation to Decaen, and this enabled him to write to Sir Joseph Banks, alerting him to his detainment in Île-de-France and his worsening situation due to the translation of the despatches. It seemed that everything that could go wrong for him was going wrong, and Decaen was building a stronger case against him. Flinders wrote:

> I have learnt privately that in the despatches with which I
> was charged by Governor King, and which were taken from
> me by the French General, a demand was made for troops to
> be sent out to Port Jackson for the purpose of annoying
> Spanish America in the event of another war, and that this is
> considered to be a breach of my passport. 'Tis pity that
> Governor King should have mentioned anything that could
> involve me in the event of a war ... or that, having
> mentioned anything that related to war, he did not make me
> acquainted in a general way with the circumstances, in which
> case I should have thrown them overboard on learning that
> war was declared ... To be the bearer of any despatches in
> time of peace cannot be incorrect for a ship on discovery
> more than for any other; BUT WITH A PASSPORT, AND
> IN TIME OF WAR, IT CERTAINLY IS IMPROPER.

Decaen was soon drafting his report concerning Flinders' arrival in Île-de-France, knowing he would be believed when he referred to the Englishman as being impertinent and arrogant. While listing his reasons for detaining Flinders, Decaen's mind must have returned to the discussion he had had with Peron regarding his espionage in Sydney Town, and to his own theories on the intentions of the English. This led him to write: 'There is no doubt that the English

Government have the intention to seize the whole trade of the Indian Ocean, the China Seas and the Pacific, and that they especially covet what remains of the Dutch possessions in these waters.'

The war of written words between Decaen and Flinders was regular and did nothing to appease the situation. In one letter, Flinders declared that 'I cannot think that an officer of your rank and judgment to act either so ungentlemanlike or so unguardedly as to make such a declaration without proof; unless his reason had been blinded by passion ... I AM NOT and WAS NOT an imposter.' Decaen returned the fire, saying that his detainee's 'unreserved tone' was due to 'the ill humour produced by your present situation'. He then drew a line in the sand, stating: 'This letter, overstepping all the bounds of civility, obliges me to tell you, until the general opinion judges of your faults or of mine, to cease all correspondence tending to demonstrate the justice of your cause, since you know so little how to preserve the rules of decorum.'

On 28 December 1803, Flinders wrote in a seemingly sarcastic tone to Decaen:

> From my confinement ...
> Sir,
> Since you forbid me to write to you upon the subject of my detainer I shall not rouse the anger or contempt with which you have been pleased to treat me by disobeying your order. The purpose for which I now write is to express a few humble requests, and most sincerely do I wish that they may be the last I shall have occasion to trouble your Excellency with.

Flinders requested that the books, private letters, charts and papers that had been aboard *Cumberland* be returned to him so he could continue his work. He also asked that his crew be better accommodated and fed on shore, adding that 'the people with whom they are placed are much affected with that disagreeable and contagious disorder the itch; and that the provisions with which they are fed are too scanty'. In closing the letter, he restated the importance of having access to his charts and documents:

> A compliance with the above requests will not only furnish me with a better amusement in this solitude than writing letters to your Excellency, but will be attended with advantages in which the French nation may some time share ...
>
> Your prisoner,
> Matthew Flinders

Within hours, Colonel Monistrol advised the 'prisoner' that the requested documents and charts would soon be delivered to him at the inn in which he remained confined. At the same time, Monistrol furnished Flinders with a word of warning, saying that the tone of his letters to the general 'might tend to protract rather than terminate' his internment.

Over the next few weeks, Flinders tried in vain to have an audience with the general. In February 1804 he wrote to him suggesting that one of the most expedient and easiest ways to resolve this matter was to send him to France for trial. Other options were to simply let him and his crew depart aboard *Cumberland* with the promise that no information regarding Île-de-France would be divulged within an agreed period of time, or that his crew alone be allowed to depart the island aboard *Cumberland*. In making these suggestions, he sought some compassion from Decaen towards his crew, reminding him that they had been shipwrecked on a small sand cay for six weeks prior to being aboard *Cumberland*.

Receiving no response from Decaen, Flinders accepted that his hope for liberation in the near future had disappeared, so he wrote to the Lords Commissioners in England explaining his internment in Île-de-France, in the hope that they might pursue a release for his crew and himself. The letter reached its destination six months later.

On 16 March 1804, Flinders spent his 30th birthday in the stifling atmosphere of Café Marengo. By then, the claustrophobic and clammy environment of the inn was having a debilitating impact on his health, so he requested that he be transferred to Maison Despeaux, otherwise known as the Garden Prison. It was a large home about a mile out of town, which was 'surrounded with a wall inclosing about two acres of ground, within which the prisoners were allowed to take exercise'. The inmates he referred to were mainly British prisoners of war, primarily officers.

This request was approved, so Monistrol took Flinders, Trim and Aken there to choose their rooms, which, Flinders noted, 'in comparison with our place of confinement, made me think it a paradise'. At the end of the month the pair 'took possession of our new prison with a considerable degree of pleasure; this change of situation and surrounding objects producing an exhilaration of spirits to which we had long been strangers'.

Within two weeks of arriving at Maison Despeaux, Flinders' emotions were torn asunder: Trim, who had been ashore with him for much of the time, had disappeared. Flinders did everything he could to locate his loyal companion of the previous seven years, but not even the offer of a reward led to his return. '... poor Trim was effectually lost,' Flinders lamented, 'and it is but too probable that this excellent, unsuspecting animal was stewed and eaten by some hungry black slave.'

It was not until August 1804 that Decaen's despatch reached its addressees in France; not surprisingly, its contents were not seen as a high priority. Napoleon had become emperor only three months earlier, and the war with England was demanding the attention of almost every one of his officers. A seemingly minor matter at a French outpost in the Indian Ocean was trivial for the Departments of Marine and War.

Decaen did not deliver all the charts, papers and logbooks that had been requested, and Flinders was becoming increasingly frustrated at being unable to continue his writing and the marking up of his charts. Yet he could not show his chagrin in any way, as this would only give Decaen more personal gratification. Flinders recognised the general's 'desire that nothing should take off my attention from feeling the weight of his power'.

Flinders and Aken befriended a number of the British sailors and merchant mariners also being held behind the stone walls of the prison. This would become an experience 'by which our society was enlivened'. Flinders noted that 'between the employments of copying my bearing book and defaced journals, making some astronomical observations, reading, and the amusements of music, walking in the inclosure, and an old billiard table left in the house, the days passed along rather lightly than otherwise'.

Had everything progressed as planned for *Cumberland*'s passage to England, Flinders would have been treading English soil by this time and in the embrace of his wife, whom he had not seen for four years. His ardour for Ann remained abundantly strong throughout this ordeal, and he often reread the letters she had sent him in Port Jackson. He bared his feelings in a letter to her in August 1804:

> I yesterday enjoyed a delicious piece of misery in reading
> over thy dear letters, my beloved Ann. Shall I tell thee that I
> have never before done it since I have been shut up in this

prison? ... I cannot connect the idea of happiness with
anything without thee. Without thee, the world would be a
blank. I might indeed receive some gratification from
distinction and the applause of society; but where could be
the faithful friend who would enjoy and share this with me,
into whose bosom my full heart could unburthen itself of
excess of joy? ... I am not without friends even among the
French. On the contrary, I have several, and but one enemy,
who unfortunately, alas, is all-powerful here; nor will he on
any persuasion permit me to pass the walls of the prison,
although some others who are thought less dangerous have
had that indulgence occasionally.

His personal opinion of Decaen also appeared in his writings at this
time:

The truth I believe is that the violence of his passion outstrips
his judgment and reason, and does not allow them to
operate; for he is instantaneous in his directions, and should
he do an injustice he must persist in it because it would
lower his dignity to retract. His antipathy, moreover, is so
great to Englishmen, who are the only nation that could
prevent the ambitious designs of France from being put into
execution, that immediately the name of one is mentioned
he is directly in a rage, and his pretence and wish to be polite
scarcely prevent him from breaking out in the presence even
of strangers. With all this he has the credit of having a good
heart at the bottom.

The same month as Decaen's letter arrived in France, Flinders
managed to find the means to send a letter to Governor King. The

true explorer that he was, he informed the governor of what he had learned on his second passage through Torres Strait before detailing his imprisonment in Île-de-France. Details from this letter were subsequently published in the *Sydney Gazette*, and, more than a year later, in *The Times* in London.

On 27 August 1804, four ships of the Royal Navy presented a threatening show of force by appearing from beyond the horizon and cruising along the coast of the island. This presented an opportunity for *Cumberland*'s bosun and six merchant officers, who had been held in another prison in Port Louis, to escape and be secreted to the squadron offshore by small boat, but Flinders and Aken had no such luck. Between 19 and 21 September, HMS *Phaeton*, a 38-gun fifth-rate frigate, stood off Port Louis flying a flag of truce while the master, Captain Cockburn, went ashore, hoping to meet Decaen and arrange an exchange of prisoners. Instead, he was blindfolded the moment he stepped ashore and held captive on a guard ship. He eventually returned to his ship in total disgust, not having met the general. As Flinders noted, 'His mission, we were told, was to negotiate an exchange of prisoners, particularly mine; but in the answer given by General de Caen it was said, that not being a prisoner of war, no exchange for me could be accepted; nor did any one obtain his liberty in consequence.'

The months ticked by, and in December 1804 Flinders wrote a letter to Decaen with an aide-mémoire: 'Permit me to remind you that I am yet a prisoner in this place, and that it is now one year since my arrestation. This is the anniversary of that day on which you transferred me from liberty and my peaceful occupations to the misery of a close confinement'. He also drew the general's attention to the possibility that the existence of war between France and England could well make the arrival of any despatches from France uncertain. This letter, and another that detailed how well Baudin and his crew had been treated in Port Jackson, were ignored.

The fact was that Decaen was caught in the crosshairs. Even if he wished to release Flinders, he could not now do so: he was obliged to await formal directions from France. He had forwarded his despatch to Paris in the hands of one of his aides-de-camp, insisting that he bring the issue to the attention of Napoleon in person. This was eventually achieved; however, the emperor's response was non-committal. He simply said he had full faith in Decaen – and with that, Flinders' life went into limbo. No response from the military regarding 'l'affaire Flinders' could be drafted and sent to Île-de-France until someone actually made a decision.

The arrival of summer in 1804–05 brought a recurrence of an intestinal complaint for Flinders, and this led to the jail's principal physician recommending that he be moved to the highlands in the island's interior, where a more acceptable climate might bring him relief, if not a cure. At the same time, Aken became so ill that it was thought he might die, so an application was made for him to be released and sent to New York aboard a ship that was currently in port. Surprisingly, Decaen agreed, so on 20 May Aken departed, carrying with him for the Admiralty all the papers from the voyage of *Investigator*, as well as a number of charts that Flinders had completed in prison, and another large general chart of New Holland, which detailed Flinders' discoveries.

By August, with an exchange of political prisoners complete, only three Englishmen remained in detention: Flinders, his dedicated servant and a 'lame seaman'. The remainder of the crew of *Cumberland* had, by this time, been repatriated.

With no despatch from Paris having arrived by August 1805, Decaen showed some sympathy towards his detainee: he would be transferred to Plaines Wilhems in the interior of the island, where he would be accommodated in a large and comfortable country residence owned by one Madame d'Arifat. While he was still considered to be in confinement, he would be granted greater personal liberties. This probably saved Flinders' life, as by the time he stepped outside Maison Despeaux on 19 August he appeared a feeble and emaciated old man who could barely walk. The 20 months in Port Louis had taken such a toll on his health that he was hardly recognisable to those who knew him previously.

If there was a saviour for Flinders while he was in Maison Despeaux, it was Thomas Pitot, a young, intelligent and well-educated French merchant who wrote and spoke English. For Flinders, he was 'the most agreeable, most useful, and at the same time durable' friend he had found during his entire incarceration. Pitot arranged Flinders' new accommodation and assisted him in every way he could.

Flinders rested for a few days in Port Louis, and while there visited the office of one of Decaen's city administrators, where he wrote out the conditions for his own parole:

> ... I do hereby promise, upon my parole of honour, not to go more than the distance of two leagues from the said habitation, without His Excellency's permission; and to conduct myself with that proper degree of reserve, becoming an officer residing in a country with which his nation is at war. I will also answer for the proper conduct of my two servants.

Flinders also drafted a letter to the Admiralty in London that was a signal for salvation, but he did not know if or when it would reach its destination. '... my hopes were expressed that their Lordships would not suffer an imprisonment, contrary to every principle of justice and humanity, to continue without notice,' he wrote, 'without such steps being taken to obtain my release and the restitution of my remaining charts and papers, as in their wisdom should seem meet.'

Plaines Wilhems was a paradise for Flinders after his experiences in Port Louis. The climate was refreshingly cooler, and his surrounds comprised lush gardens, waterfalls and an abundance of greenery. Intrigue was encountered wherever he ventured, and he explored and detailed as much of the region as possible. Most importantly, his accommodation was a comfortable free-standing pavilion in the grounds of Madame d'Arifat's residence; much to Flinders' delight, he was accepted as a member of the family, to the point that he had the pleasure of dining with them daily.

I cannot enough be grateful to them for such kindness to a stranger, to a foreigner, to an enemy of their country, for such they have a right to consider me if they will, though I am an enemy to no country in fact, but as it opposes the honour, interest, and happiness of my own. My employment and inclinations lead to the extension of happiness and of science, and not to the destruction of mankind.

This new environment was the panacea Flinders needed to reinstate his health. Long and relaxing walks through the gardens, forests and fields, and mentally stimulating human contact brought him back to being the energetic man he once was. His days were filled with many and varied activities, including studying and becoming fluent in French, and reading Latin.

Flinders' mind had also developed another, completely different, mission: he now hoped to explore the inland of New Holland from north to south – from the southernmost point of the Gulf of Carpentaria to the northern waters of Spencer's Gulf, a distance of around 1000 miles. It would be a venture into the unknown – a trek across some of the harshest, hottest and driest land imaginable, which included the Lake Eyre basin, at 463,000 square miles one of the largest endorheic basins in the world. Although Flinders did not realise it at the time, this venture, had he undertaken it, could easily have been fatal.

In October 1805 he received, for the first time in three years, a packet of letters from family and friends at home. One, from Sir Joseph Banks, explained that while no direct line of communication existed between the British and French governments due to the war, he had made a personal appeal for Flinders' release to the National Institute in Paris, and a 'favourable answer' had been received. Thus, there were strong hopes that, as soon as Napoleon returned from Italy, an order for Flinders' liberation would be obtained.

Flinders knew better than to rely on what could be a false hope. He knew, too, that he should never let the burden of boredom enter his life: he needed to keep his mind active. During this period, then, he put every available moment to good use. His pen was forever busy, preparing his charts, logs and memoirs for publication. All the time, the challenge of completing his mission of charting the coast of New Holland in the most accurate possible manner was foremost in his mind.

Should an opportunity present itself, Flinders would choose duty over a homecoming, as he made clear in a letter to Sir Joseph Banks in March 1806. Interestingly, in this same letter he refers to New Holland as 'Australia'.

Should a peace speedily arrive and their Lordships of the
Admiralty wish to have the north-west coast of Australia
examined immediately, I will be ready to embark in any ship

provided for the service that they may choose to send out.
My misfortunes have not abated my ardour in the service of
science. In the event of sending out another *Investigator*
immediately after the peace, probably Lieutenant Fowler or
my brother might be chosen as first lieutenant to bring her
out to me.

Despite Flinders' obvious dedication to his duty, and although he
was continuing to work diligently on his charts and documents, the
Admiralty decided that he was not actually on active service and
put him on half pay. Understandably, his steadfast and faithful wife
was not impressed: 'The Navy Board have thought proper to
curtail my husband's pay,' she wrote, 'so it behoves me to be as
careful as I can; and I mean to be very economical, being
determined to do with as little as possible, that he may not deem
me an extravagant wife.'

Newspapers in England were by now carrying stories detailing
Flinders' plight, and an ever-increasing number of representations,
many from French citizens, were being put to the French government
on the English captain's behalf. The famous French explorer and
hydrographer Charles Pierre Claret, the Comte de Fleurieu, went
public, declaring 'the indignities imposed upon Captain Flinders were
without example in the nautical history of civilised nations'.

On 1 March 1806, Flinders' case finally went before the Council
of State in Paris. Sir Joseph wrote to Ann Flinders with the news:
'After many refusals on the part of Bonaparte to applications made to
him from different quarters, he at last consented to order Captain
Flinders' case to be laid before the Council of State.'

In the council's verdict, Decaen, while not being criticised for
his actions, was informed via the despatch sent to him that 'by a
sentiment of generosity, the Government accord to Captain

Flinders his liberty and the restoration of his ship'. He was also sent a copy of the minute relating to the matter:

> The Council of State, which, after the return of His Majesty the Emperor and King, has considered the report of its Marine section on that of the Minister of Marine and the Colonies concerning the detention of the English schooner *Cumberland* and of Captain Flinders at Île-de-France ... is of opinion that the Captain-General of Île-de-France had sufficient reason for detaining there Captain Flinders and his schooner; but by reason of the interest that the misfortunes of Captain Flinders has inspired, he seems to deserve that His Majesty should authorise the Minister of Marine and the Colonies to restore to him his liberty and his ship.

Today, such an edict would be cause for instant celebration, but it would not be until July 1807 – 16 months after the pronouncement in Paris – that the despatch finally reached Île-de-France. Most remarkably, it was not a French ship that delivered the verdict to Decaen, but the Royal Navy frigate HMS *Greyhound*, which was sailing under a flag of truce. At this time, Royal Navy ships were the enforcers on the high seas, especially after the crushing victory over the French at Trafalgar, and the taking of the Cape of Good Hope in January 1806. The original document had been sent from France aboard a French vessel, but it was captured by the British almost immediately after departure. The contents of the document were passed on to the Admiralty in England, and Rear-Admiral Sir Edward Pellew directed that the despatch, addressed to Decaen, should be taken to Île-de-France.

Pellew also wrote to Flinders and informed him of the news. Flinders immediately sent a note to Decaen requesting that he receive his liberty after three and a half years of internment on the island. Decaen's response was direct: '... so soon as circumstances will permit, you will fully enjoy the favour which has been granted you by His Majesty the Emperor and King.'

Flinders had hoped that he might depart aboard *Greyhound*, but, unfortunately for him, she set sail on a battle mission towards Java within two days of arriving in Port Louis. Consequently, he was back in the hands of Decaen, who was about to emotionally crush Flinders once more.

Incredibly, Decaen did not follow Napoleon's orders but instead wrote back to Paris:

I did not consider that the present moment was favourable for putting into operation that act of indulgence on the part of His Majesty. I have since received the second copy of the same despatch; but, the circumstances having become still more difficult, and that officer appearing to me to be always dangerous, I await a more propitious time for putting into execution the intentions of His Majesty.

Île-de-France was a remote outpost holding little, if any, strategic value for France and the war. Decaen was certainly feeling the isolation, however, and he did everything possible to create the impression that it must be boldly defended. The fact was that he was desperately in need of reinforcements, but there was no way he was ever going to see them while the Royal Navy remained so dominant. He knew that, should he release Flinders, the British would immediately become aware of the real state of the island's defences. Flinders had always hoped the British would attack Île-de-France and rescue him; he noted that 'if attacked with judgment, it appeared to me that a moderate force would carry it'.

So, after holding Flinders on the island for nearly four years, Decaen now had a prisoner whom his emperor had signalled should be released. Yet Flinders was now of greater value to Decaen in detention than being free. Flinders knew too much, leading Decaen to deem him to be 'dangerous'.

Over the years a number of opportunities had presented themselves for Flinders to escape the island, but he had always refused them – for two very honourable reasons. Firstly, he would stand by the document he had signed detailing his parole. Secondly, should he make good an escape, it would be without his most prized possessions – the charts and documents detailing his exploration of the coast of New Holland aboard *Investigator* – and he saw those as being more valuable than his liberty.

In May 1806 (just a few weeks after the hearing in Paris) Flinders was visited at Plaines Wilhems by Captain Gamaliel Matthew Ward of the American ship *Recovery*, which was visiting Port Louis. Ward had heard that the famous English explorer and naval man Matthew Flinders was being detained in the highlands, so he decided to visit him and arrange to secret him aboard *Recovery*, but Flinders declined the chance.

However, just one month later, on Sunday, 22 June 1806, the pressure of waiting for news from France was getting to him, and for the first time he seriously contemplated 'dishonouring' his parole.

Disappointed in finding no orders arrived from France, and having nearly lost all my confidence in the French government (the great events in Europe which they had to occupy their attention prevented me from losing it wholly) I had formed a plan of getting back my parole and making my escape. I had even everything arranged, but not being able to get back the parole, the design could not be accomplished.

After the time of my premeditated escape, I remained some time in a state of sullen tranquillity. Revolving circumstances in my mind, two plans presented themselves. The one to escape from my parole, leaving a letter for Gen. D.C. explaining my motives, and to give myself up to the French government in Europe, with a demand for examination and justice: the dread of dishonouring my parole made me however contemplate this plan with a fearful eye. Another was to tell Gen. D.C. directly that I would no longer remain upon my parole, and after giving him a week to take his measures, to make my escape if I could.

In December the same year, his frustration again showed through in a letter to John Aken: 'Since I find so much time elapse, and no attention paid to my situation by the French Government, I have been very heartily sorry for having given my parole, as I could otherwise have made my escape long ago.'

For three more exasperating years, Decaen held onto his man. Only the improved health that Madame d'Arifat's residence brought Flinders kept him going.

In June 1809, the powerful Royal Navy squadron that was based in the Indian Ocean loomed over the horizon and commenced a blockade of Île-de-France, but no attack was launched because of a lack of intelligence on the state of the island's defences. After some six months of continuing his bluff, Decaen had to face the inevitable: his time would soon be up.

In December 1809, Hugh Hope was sent to Île-de-France by the governor-general of India, Lord Minto, to negotiate an exchange of prisoners with General Decaen. Naturally, Flinders hoped that his internment would be considered during these negotiations, but after so many years of bitter disappointment, he was far from optimistic. He maintained his work ethic, continuing his experiments and observations, and his writing. However, in case a quick departure should be necessary, he requested his good friend Pitot 'to order for me some shirts, jackets, and pantaloons, of which I should have need in case of departing in the cartel'.

Flinders' anxious wait continued over the following days.

> In the time of waiting for this event, I revised some notes upon the magnetism of the earth and of ships, and considered the experiments necessary to elucidate the opinions formed from observations made in the *Investigator*; and I was thus occupied when, on March 13th, a letter came from Mr Hope ... to inform me that he had obtained the captain-general's promise for my liberty, and departure from the island with him in the *Harriet*. This unhoped for intelligence would have produced excessive joy, had not experience taught me to distrust even the promises of the general; and especially when, as in the present case, there was no cause assigned for this change in his conduct.
>
> I dared not therefore allow my imagination to contemplate a meeting with my family and friends as likely to soon take place, nor to dwell upon any subject altogether English.

Flinders' 'state of suspense between hope and apprehension' remained with him until 28 March, when the information he had always longed for, but never expected, came from Colonel Monistrol: 'His Excellency the captain-general charges me to have the honour of informing you, that he authorises you to return to your country in the cartel Harriet, on condition of not serving in a hostile manner against France or its allies during the course of the present war.'

On 6 May 1810 the ship *Harriet*, which had been commissioned as a cartel for the safe conduct of exchanged prisoners during the war, was anchored in Port Louis. During the course of that day, Matthew Flinders was welcomed aboard and directed to his accommodation. He was one of only five men on board to have a cabin to himself, so he immediately set about arranging it to his liking, a project that involved bringing aboard two chairs from the port. He and everyone else on board hoped that they would be sailing within a matter of days under the sanction of the general, but that was not the case: Decaen had far more important things to do, such as visit all the forts on the island to make sure they were prepared for the anticipated attack by the British squadron, which was continuing to blockade the island.

It would not be until 13 June that Decaen agreed that *Harriet* could depart the port, so in the meantime Flinders continued working on his charts and documents. He also began learning Malay, reasoning that 'this language may be useful to me in exploring the islands between Timor and New Guinea which I propose to do in my future voyage'.

There was no time to be lost once the authorisation to sail came through. Late that day, the call came from the captain of *Harriet* to make sail and head out of the port. Flinders enjoyed this familiar but long-missed situation, and as he strolled along the deck a wave of adrenaline surged through his body: his liberty was finally there to be savoured.

Before long, there came the near forgotten sound of the anchors being weighed, then, after observing the hive of activity aloft and on deck, he watched as the sails were unfurled and trimmed to capture the evening breeze. *Harriet* was under sail, and he was on his way home.

An hour or so later, as the setting sun cast a soft shade of light on the island, Flinders looked back at its profile and treasured one thought: '... after a captivity of six years, five months and twenty-seven days, I at length had the inexpressible pleasure of being out of the reach of General de Caen.'

CHAPTER FOURTEEN

'Let Us Dismiss ...'

As *Harriet* eased away from the coast, the ships of the Royal Navy's blockading squadron – three frigates and a sloop of war – were seen in the distance to the south. This caused Flinders to request of the master, Captain Ramsden, that he change *Harriet*'s course so they could close on those ships and communicate with the fleet's commander, Commodore Rowley. The captain agreed and, a few hours later, communications regarding the blockade were exchanged between the vessels.

Flinders also took the opportunity to inquire if, per chance, any of the ships under Rowley's command might be bound for the Cape of Good Hope in the near future. He was advised that the 106-foot, 16-gun sloop HMS *Otter* was about to quit the squadron and do just that. Flinders could not have received a better response. Should he be able to transfer to *Otter*, he could take a more direct route home, instead of having to sail the considerably more circuitous passage via India, which was where *Harriet* was headed. He made the request to transfer and the commodore agreed; the following day, he and his trunks and documents were transported by cutter to *Otter*.

MUNDLE

At nine p.m. that evening, when everything was stowed and secure, *Otter* – which was then at the southern end of the island's west coast – was eased away on to a course to the south-west and headed towards the Cape of Good Hope. There was a fresh and squally trade wind blowing and the ship made good time, so much so that within 24 hours those on deck, peering through the murk, could make out the white water breaking on the reefs off the coast of the cloud-capped Reunion Island.

It was a 2300-nautical-mile run to Cape Town, and after averaging 3.6 knots *Otter* arrived there on 11 July. Unfortunately, Flinders had to wait there for six weeks before a ship en route to England came into port. This was the cutter *Olympia*, and on 28 August 1810 she departed Simon's Bay at the start of the 6500-nautical-mile voyage up the Atlantic to home waters.

One final life-threatening experience awaited Flinders. *Olympia*, while closing on the approaches to the English Channel on 21 October, was confronted by a violent maelstrom that swept in unannounced from the west. The conditions were so extreme that the 'very leaky, and excessively ill-found' *Olympia* was almost overwhelmed. For more than a day the crew battled the ferociously wild winds and huge breaking seas in an effort to weather the Casquets Rocks, which lay directly to leeward. There was little doubt that all on board would perish if the ship came to grief in the massive waves that were pounding the rugged and rocky shore, but good fortune was with them. The wind began to abate, then it turned in their favour and *Olympia* made good her escape. Within 48 hours the ship had passed the Needles, entered the Solent and was at anchor at Spithead.

On 23 October 1810, after an absence of nine years and three months, the 36-year-old Matthew Flinders stepped onto English soil once again. In true naval fashion, he immediately went about formal procedures with his superiors, and while doing so he was excited to learn that news of his return had preceded him; his wife, Ann, had travelled from Lincolnshire to London to greet him.

Understandably, he wasted no time, climbing aboard a carriage and heading 'to town' to meet his beloved.

> I had the extreme good fortune to find Mrs Flinders in London, which I owe to the intelligence of my liberty having preceded my arrival. I need not describe to you our meeting after an absence of nearly ten years. Suffice to say I have been gaining flesh ever since.

John Franklin, who had sailed under Flinders' command as a young midshipman, also made a special trip to London to welcome the captain, only to realise that he had, quite embarrassingly, intruded on the reunion. He later wrote to Flinders:

> Some apology would be necessary for the abrupt manner in which I left you, except in the particular circumstances wherein my departure was undertaken. I felt so sensibly the affecting scene of your meeting Mrs Flinders that I would not have remained any longer in the room under any consideration.

Being home brought new responsibilities for Flinders. Most importantly, he had to calculate where he stood in life, both financially and in rank within the Royal Navy. Both matters would be resolved during his discussions with the Admiralty, but sadly he was treated very poorly on both fronts.

Charles Philip Yorke, the man whose name Flinders gave to Yorke's Peninsula while exploring the southern coast of New

Holland, was the First Lord of the Admiralty when Flinders returned from Île-de-France. Unsurprisingly, he was one of countless military and public officials who feted the explorer, but regulations were regulations when it came to rank. Although he returned a hero, Flinders soon realised that he was again the victim of circumstance: there would be no post-dating of promotions.

A regulation adopted at the Admiralty forbids any officer to be promoted whilst a prisoner, upon the principle apparently, that officers in that situation have almost always to undergo a court martial, which cannot be done until they are set at liberty. My case was made subject to this regulation, although it required no court martial; and was moreover so different to that of prisoners in general, that nothing similar perhaps ever occurred ... On my representations to the Right Hon Charles Yorke, first lord commissioner of the Admiralty, by whom I had the honour to be received with the condescension and feeling natural to his character, he was pleased to direct that it [a commission for post rank] should take date as near to that of general De Caen's permission to quit Mauritius, as the patent which constituted the existing Board of Admiralty would allow. A more retrospective date could be given to it only by an order of the King in council; unhappily His Majesty was then incapable of exercising his royal functions ... It was candidly acknowledged, that my services in the *Investigator* would have been deemed a sufficient title to advancement in 1804, had I then arrived in England and the Admiralty been composed of the same members; but no representation could overcome the reluctance to admitting an exception to the established rule; thus the injustice of the French governor of Mauritius,

besides all its other consequences, was attended with the loss
of six years post rank in His Majesty's naval service.

The situation was no different when it came to his remuneration
from the Admiralty. Flinders made the point that he and his wife
were required to reside in the considerably more costly city
environment of London, rather than the less expensive countryside,
while he completed his extensive works on his charts and writings
which were to be published, but again the Admiralty said they
could not break with precedent. Flinders' submission to the Lords
stated that by remaining ashore to complete this work, he would
be between £500 and £600 out of pocket, as against being back at
sea – yet the Admiralty granted him only £200.

A seafaring colleague, Captain Kent of HMS *Agincourt*, strongly
suggested that Flinders consider abandoning the work: 'I conjure
you to give the subject your serious attention, and do not suffer
yourself to be involved in debt to gratify persons who seem to have
no feeling.'

As always, however, Flinders' dedication to duty went way
beyond the reality of the moment. His attitude to reward for effort
was apparent in a letter he wrote to Sir Joseph Banks, in which he
recognised the difference between being a sailor and being an
explorer within the Royal Navy: 'I chose a branch which though
less rewarded by rank and fortune is yet little less in celebrity. If
adverse fortune does not oppose me, I will succeed.'

Committed as he always was to his men, Flinders also took
time to inquire as to the whereabouts and condition of those who
were with him aboard *Investigator*. Some had passed away, while
others had gone on to greater things within the navy or simply
joined new ships as seamen. There was, however, one surprise: the
rotting *Investigator* had, somehow, been patched up, re-rigged and

nursed back to England to deliver despatches. The captain, William Kent, reported after the voyage that a '... more deplorable crazy vessel than the *Investigator* is perhaps not to be seen'. But her life didn't end there. After being condemned by the Navy Board in 1810 she was rebuilt once more and sailed back as a cargo vessel to Geelong where she joined the fleet owned by the Melbourne Steamship Company. Incredibly, she continued to sail until 1872 when she was finally broken up at Williamstown, at the entrance to Melbourne's Yarra River.

Flinders' exceptional efforts as an explorer saw him received 'with flattering attention' by the Admiralty, across society and by the public. Lord Spencer, who had authorised the *Investigator* expedition, conversed with him at length about his discoveries and experiences; Sir Joseph Banks hosted a Royal Society dinner in his honour; the seafaring Duke of Clarence met with him so he could peruse and appreciate his charts; and the soon to be Rear Admiral of the Blue, William Bligh, introduced him to the then Prince Regent who, in 1820, would be crowned King George IV.

As soon as practicable after his homecoming, Flinders turned his attention to his immediate priority: preparing his written works and charts for publication and presentation. He became so engrossed in the project that he referred to the time as his equivalent of 'being at sea'. Part of this commitment required the completion of what would become his legendary publication, *A Voyage to Terra Australis*. During his forced confinement at Île-de-France, he had written some 151,000 words for this tome, but there was still much to be done. That project alone would become a 350,000-word masterpiece.

The reality is that Flinders, during his all too brief life, demonstrated a personal genius that went well beyond that of a great explorer. His attention to detail and clarity of observation during every expedition were beyond compare, as was his seamanship and care for his men, but of equal significance was his contribution to the science of navigation. Following Flinders' death, his talents were lauded by no less than Conrad Malte-Brun, the acclaimed Danish-French geographer and journalist who became the first general secretary of the Société de Géographie in France. When Flinders died Malte-Brun wrote that 'the geographical and nautical sciences have lost in the person of Flinders one of their most brilliant ornaments'.

That brilliance was obvious in his research into the cause and effect of variations in a ship's compass, and the relationship between the rise and fall of the barometer and the direction and strength of the wind.

In 1805, while confined at Île-de-France, Flinders wrote an impressive document on 'the Differences in the Magnetic Needle, on Board *Investigator*, arising from an Alteration in the Direction of the Ship's Head[ing]'. Navigators had long been aware that a compass needle would show deviations when moved from one part of a ship to another, but it was Flinders who deduced the reason for this and invented a method that would correct the problem. It was because of compass deviation that 'ships running three or four days without an observation [a sun or star sight] should be found in situations very different from what was expected, and some of them lost'.

The thoroughness of his experiments led to the realisation that, in the Northern Hemisphere, the magnetic influence on the compass needle was the opposite of what it was at a similar latitude in the Southern Hemisphere, and that there was virtually no deviation when the ship was at the equator. Also, he proved that varying deviations came with a change in the ship's heading, and that the iron on board the ship – from cannons to fastenings and equipment – also caused differences in readings.

These variations influenced Flinders' work both as a navigator and an explorer – activities that demanded the finest accuracy. He was aware that when Captain Cook was conducting surveys ashore near Cape Townshend, the needle of his compass could differ up to 30 degrees in some locations. This led Cook to theorise that there was iron ore in the surrounding hills – which, in time, would prove correct. Flinders had a similar experience in the same region:

> It has been more than once observed, that granite is amongst
> the substances which exert an influence upon the magnetic
> needle; and it is to the attraction of the ridge of mountains to
> the south and westward, that I attribute the great variation
> found in the bearings at this station.

Flinders modestly regarded his findings as being 'most probably vague and unscientific', but after a presentation on the subject to the Admiralty following his return to England, the Royal Navy was directed to assist him with further experiments. This led to his declaration that 'the magnetism of the Earth and the attraction forward in the ship must act upon the needle in the nature of a compound force, and that errors produced by the attraction should be proportionate to the sines of the angles between the ship's head and the magnetic meridian'.

A solution was needed, and Flinders joined forces in London with James Inman, a highly regarded mathematician who some years earlier had been sent to Port Jackson as the replacement astronomer for *Investigator*. With Inman's assistance, Flinders devised what became known as the 'Flinders bar'. Made from soft iron, the bar counteracts the vertical magnetism within a ship and, therefore, corrects deviation. To achieve this, the Flinders bar is attached to the forward side of a ship's binnacle, where the compass is mounted.

As part of this finding, Flinders strongly recommended to the Admiralty that, in future, a ship's compass – which, until then, had been considered to be just another piece of navigational equipment – be treated as a delicate item of high priority. When not in use, he wrote, it should be stored with considerable care in an officer's cabin.

Flinders' works extended to essays regarding his theories on tides and the magnetism of the Earth. Later, in an essay on his theories on the magnetic compass, he detailed his observations of the marine barometer and how it indicated a change in weather conditions. In doing so, he had discovered the correlation between a rising and falling barometer and the velocity of the wind. Once again, Flinders' careful and concise observations led him to present clearly defined and irrefutable explanations. His experiments were conducted on passages along the east coast of New Holland and through the tropics, and he declared that a rise or fall in the barometer would precede a change in wind strength and/or direction. In March 1806, while he was still captive in Île-de-France, his paper was presented to the Royal Society, whose president was still Sir Joseph Banks. A report on this presentation that appeared in the *Edinburgh Review* soon after read:

It is very easy for us, speculating in our closet upon the theory of winds and their connection with the temperature, to talk of drawing a general inference on this subject with confidence. But when the philosopher chances to be a seaman on a very dangerous coast, it will be admitted that the strength of this confidence is put to a test somewhat more severe; and we find nevertheless that Captain Flinders staked the safety of his ship and the existence of himself and his crew on the truth of the above proposition.

Flinders' life in London revolved around his seemingly tireless dedication to his experiments, writings, wife and family. It appears that he put off all thoughts regarding a return to Australia until after all his other work for the Admiralty was completed, even though 'authorship sits awkwardly upon me'. He always longed for the sea and adventure, but he accepted, probably reluctantly, that 'Seamanship and authorship make too great an angle with each other; the further a man advances upon one line the further distant he becomes from any point on the other'. A similar thought was expressed in one of the many letters he wrote to family and friends: 'I am at my voyage, but it does by no means advance according to my wishes. Morning, noon and night I sit close at writing, and at my charts, and can hardly find time for anything else.'

For relaxation, he and Ann attended church regularly and enjoyed evening walks through the streets around Soho, where they were renting accommodation. At home, they spent many hours playing chess, and Flinders' brother Samuel was a regular visitor. They also visited friends and reciprocated that hospitality as often as possible. The vast majority of these experiences were laden with pleasure, but, as Flinders revealed at times in his journal, there were moments which he wished he could have avoided: 'We dined today, stupidly, with Mrs Major and a small party of Goths.'

In 1811 Ann Flinders became pregnant, but apart from mentioning occasionally that she was unwell with headache and pains, Flinders made only one direct reference to this in his journal, in January 1812: 'Sunday 17. Foggy and moist. Writing at rough voyage in the day, and fair copy in the evening. Mrs F taken very unwell this evening; being threatened with a miscarriage.'

After 11 years of marriage, their first child arrived, yet even then Flinders remained the master of understatement. His journal entry for the day retained the formality and familiar form of every preceding day: 'April Wednesday 1. Foggy, calm morning, after a boisterous night. Went to my brother upon the subject of the observations. Occupied in correcting the bearing book, by a just proportionate variation. This afternoon Mrs Flinders was happily delivered of a daughter; to her great joy and to mine.' The daughter was named Anne.

———

Considering the magnitude of Flinders' exploration, which included the first circumnavigation of Terra Australis – an event that proved it was the world's largest island and smallest continent – it is only appropriate that history has credited Flinders with giving Australia its name.

The word 'Australia' was not new at the time, but Flinders' dedication of it to a single entity – the continent – was. Two centuries earlier, in 1606, the Spanish had referred to 'Austrialia del Espiritu Santo', but this referred to the part of the world that extended from the New Hebrides to the South Pole. There were several other references to the region using the word 'Australia', or another form of it, through to 1770, when a work published by the Scottish geographer Alexander Dalrymple, who later became the first hydrographer of the Admiralty, applied the term to what he surmised to be a landmass of significant size that was yet to be discovered in the South Pacific Ocean. In fact, this was the year that Captain Cook discovered the east coast of that continent.

It is apparent that Flinders was well aware of the term 'Australia', which appears on a number of occasions in *A Voyage to Terra Australis*. As early as 1804, when he was ensconced at Plaines Wilhems, he wrote in a letter to his brother: 'I call the whole island Australia, or Terra Australis. New Holland is properly that portion of it from 135 degrees of longitude westward; and eastward is New

South Wales ...' In an essay that was published in France three years later, Flinders wrote:

> The examination of the eastern part was commenced in 1770
> by Captain Cook and has since been completed by English
> navigators. The first [the west] is New Holland properly so
> called, and the second bears the name of New South Wales.
> I have considered it convenient to unite the two parts under
> a common designation which will do justice to the discovery
> rights of Holland and England, and I have with that object in
> view had recourse to the name Austral-land or Australia. But
> it remains to be seen whether the name will be adopted by
> European geographers.

When it came time to publish *A Voyage to Terra Australis*, there was great debate over whether the title of the publication should refer to 'Australia' or 'Terra Australis'. After Flinders had returned to England in 1810, he advised Sir Joseph Banks that he desired to use the word 'Australia' when referring to the entire continent; however, Banks was swayed by the publisher of Flinders' charts, who did not approve of the change: his company had always referred to 'New Holland'. Regardless, Flinders continued to pursue his case with Banks, who came around to that way of thinking. But Banks was again persuaded to change his mind, this time by an associate from the era of Captain Cook, Captain James Burney, who said that 'Terra Australis' was a name 'more familiar to the public'.

Flinders accepted the defeat, but he still took the opportunity to present his case via a footnote in his publication: 'Had I permitted myself any innovation upon the original term, it would have been to convert it into Australia; as being more agreeable to the car, and an assimilation to the names of the other great portions of the earth.'

Just three years after the publication of *A Voyage to Terra Australis*, the name 'Australia' was used in an official format. This was in a despatch dated 4 April 1817 from Governor Lachlan Macquarie at Port Jackson to Lord Bathurst, which acknowledged the receipt of 'Captain Flinders' charts of Australia'. Macquarie later confirmed his desire to see that name officially recognised. The first step towards this came in 1824, when the Admiralty declared that the continent should be known officially as 'Australia'. Seventy-seven years later, on 1 January 1901, the grand moment arrived when the 'Commonwealth of Australia' was proclaimed.

Pain was never far from Flinders during the latter part of his life, a consequence of ailments that he had developed during his incarceration at Île-de-France. The first real cause for concern had emerged soon after he arrived at Plaines Wilhems. On 10 September 1805 his journal revealed: 'All this day I have found myself unwell, either from a cold or from an approaching fit of the gravel' – or kidney stones, a complaint often caused by dehydration.

His health deteriorated after he returned to England, due in part to his intense dedication to the publication deadline for the completion of his writings and charts. On the weekend following the birth of his daughter, he wrote in his journal:

Saturday 4. Find myself very unwell today, with an attack of the gravel. Employed at times, nevertheless, with the bearing book.

Sunday 5. Foggy, still morning. Occupied in putting the directions of the ship's head, and the true variations, into the bearing book; though very far from being well.

Twelve months later, the ailment was ravaging his 39-year-old body, so much so that Ann wrote to a friend that her husband looked 70 and was 'worn to a skeleton'.

In February 1814 the family of three moved to a new residence at 14 London Street, Fitzroy Square, just one and a half miles north of Buckingham House. That Flinders' medical condition was deteriorating at this time is apparent in his journal entry for the day prior to the move:

> Sunday 27: Frosty. Examining quire for the printers and correcting proof. Communicated to Mr Hayes our surgeon all the symptoms of the complaint which alone ever troubles me, and which appears to be either stone or gravel in the bladder. It is troubled me more within some months and become painful.

Flinders' surgeon advised that walking was one way of helping his condition, but within weeks of moving to the new address he was struggling even to do that. His increasing pain and associated problems led to him noting one day that he had been 'obliged to rise 12 times in nine hours in the night'. The treatments prescribed by the surgeon represented the medications of the day: citric acid, distilled water, barley water, gum arabic, muriatic acid and tea.

Still Flinders continued to work, spending hours editing and proofreading his manuscripts, and checking his charts for accuracy. He applied the same dedication to this project that he had as an explorer – all was in the quest for perfection.

The last entry in his journal came on Sunday, 10 July 1814: 'Did not rise before two being I think, weaker than before.'

Eight days later, Flinders' publisher, G. & W. Nicol of Pall Mall, delivered the first copy of the two volumes of *A Voyage to Terra*

Australis to his residence; sadly, by then Flinders was unconscious. Ann, the loving wife who had supported her remarkable husband for so many years – the majority alone – is said to have positioned the leather-bound book on the bed, then taken his hand and placed it gently on top.

The following day the end was nigh, and as he drew his final breaths, Flinders' mind must have drifted back to the close of a memorable evening with his shipmates aboard *Investigator*. At that moment he was heard to whisper, ever so faintly, 'But it grows late, boys – let us dismiss ...'

List of Illustrations

Glossary

abaft Towards the stern of a ship. 'Abaft the beam' means aft of abeam

abeam A point 90 degrees out from anywhere along the centre-line of a ship

anchor Bower, the biggest anchor; stream, the next largest anchor; kedge, a smaller anchor for special purposes, usually stored below decks

athwartships Directly across the ship, from side to side

baffling winds An erratic wind that frequently changes direction

ballast Any heavy material (like gravel, iron, lead, sand, stones) placed in the hold of a ship to provide stability

beam-ends The sides of a ship. 'On her beam ends' is used to describe the rolling effect of very rough seas on the ship; the ship is almost on her side and possibly about to capsize

beat, to Sailing upwind

belay To secure a rope

belaying pin Wooden pins found around the mast at deck level, or at the side of a ship which are used to secure a rope

best bower anchor The starboard of the two anchors carried at the bow of the ship. That on the port side is known as the smaller bower, even though the two are identical in weight

bight Loop of rope

bilge The curved portion of a ship's hull immediately above the keel

block A single or multiple sheaved pulley

boatswain/bosun Warrant or non-commissioned officer responsible for the maintenance of the ship's rigging, anchors and cables

bower Bow anchor or cable

bowsprit A pole extending forward from a vessel's bow

brace A rope or line attached to the end of a yard which is either eased or hauled in so that the sail is trimmed to suit the wind direction

breadfruit A large, round fruit from the Pacific Islands

brig A two-masted square-rigger

buntlines Ropes tied to the foot of a square sail that keep it from opening or bellying when it is being hauled up for furling to the yard

burthen Displacement

cable 1. A long, thick and heavy rope attached to the ship's anchor

2. A naval unit of distance – ten cables is one nautical mile

canton A usually rectangular division of a flag, occupying the upper corner next to the staff, or any quarter of a flag, commonly the upper hoist (left) quarter

capstan A large waist-high vertical winch turned by crew manning the capstan bars which lock into the head of the winch. The crew then walk in a circle to work the winch. Used to raise the anchor and other heavy objects

carronade A short-barrelled limited-range gun, used for close-quarter action, which was enormously destructive to a ship's timbers

cartel A commissioned ship sailing under a flag of truce in time of war to exchange prisoners or to carry a proposal from one enemy to another

cat-head A sturdy timber projection near the bow to hold the anchor

cat-tackle A tackle for hoisting an anchor into place so that it is secured to the side of the ship

caulking The material which makes the ship watertight (such as cotton fibres or oakum), forced between the planks to stop leaks

cay A low bank or reef of coral, rock or sand

chains The area outside the ship where the deadeyes, rigging and other hardware come together to support the mast

chain shot Two solid cannon balls linked by chain and fired from a cannon to inflict major damage to a ship's rigging or masts

chain-wale A broad, thick plank that projects horizontally from the side of a ship immediately abreast of the mast. Its purpose is to provide a wider base for the shrouds which support the mast. This is where the leadsman is said to be 'in the chains' when he stands on the chain-wale to heave the lead and measure the depth of the water

clew The bottom corners of the square sail, or the lower back corner of a triangular sail

clew up To draw up a square sail to the yard by hauling on the clew lines

clinker A construction method for ships and boats where the external planks overlap each other and are fastened together with clenched copper nails

close-hauled Sailing with the sails trimmed in as close as possible to the centre-line. This allows the ship to sail as close to the direction of the wind as possible

collier A cargo ship that hauls coal

commander The next rank above lieutenant in the Royal Navy prior to the introduction of the rank of lieutenant-commander in the early twentieth century

counter Stern

cutter A fast sailboat with one mast that carries several headsails

dead reckoning The method for estimating a vessel's current position based on its previously determined position then advanced by estimating speed and course over an elapsed time

deck beams Timbers running from side to side of a ship to support the deck

draught The measurement from the waterline to the deepest point of the vessel in the water

fathom A unit of measurement for depth – one fathom is 1.83 metres or six feet

flush deck Any continuous, unbroken deck from stem to stern

forecastle [foc'sle, fo'c's'le] The living quarters in the bow of the ship where the crew is accommodated

foremast The first mast, or the mast fore of the main-mast

fothering To seal a leak by lowering a sail over the side of the ship and positioning it to be sucked into the hole by the rushing sea

foul wind An adverse wind, usually blowing from the ship's desired direction of travel

freeboard The distance from the water to the ship's gunwale

full and by Sailing a few points below close-hauled

gig A light and narrow ship's boat of clinker construction capable of being rowed or sailed; generally used by the commander

grog A mixture of rum and water served to a ship's crew

gunwale/gunnel The top edge of the planking at the sides of the ship, named for the place where you rest your gun to take aim

halyard A rope used for raising or lowering a sail, yard, spar or flag

hauled onto the wind, or haul up To change a ship's course so that it is sailing closer to the direction from which the wind is blowing. At the same time the ship's sails are trimmed to suit the new course

hawse-holes Cylindrical holes in the bow of a vessel for the anchor cable to run through

headed When the wind changes direction so that it is coming from a point closer to the ship's bow, causing the ship to change course to leeward so that it can continue sailing effectively

heel To tilt to one side

helm The apparatus used to steer the vessel by moving the angle of the rudder

HMS His/Her Majesty's Ship. The prefix given to Royal Navy ships since 1789

hove to Slowing a vessel's forward progress by fixing the helm and foresail so that the vessel does not need to be steered; a procedure usually applied in very rough weather

hull The main body of the ship

irons, to go into When a ship fails to complete a tack and therefore lies head to wind with fore-and-aft sails flapping and square sails aback

jib A triangular headsail set from the foremast which is the foremost sail

kedge A small anchor used to keep a ship steady and clear from her bower anchor

keelson A piece of timber fixed to the keel to provide additional strength

knees A piece of timber usually shaped at a right angle that secures parts of the ship together, especially the beams and timbers. For example, a hanging knee is used to support the ends of the deck beams

knot A unit of speed equal to one nautical mile (1.852km) per hour or approximately 1.151 miles per hour

larboard The old name for port, the left-hand side of the ship

lay-line When a vessel can sail to a desired destination at the optimum upwind or downwind angle

league A unit of distance in the eighteenth century equal to three nautical miles

lee The sheltered side

leeward The direction away from the wind; opposite of 'windward'

lieutenant Lowest rank of commissioned officer in the Royal Navy, prior to the introduction of the rank of sub-lieutenant in the twentieth century

log *1.* A device for measuring a ship's speed
2. A record of a ship's movements, the weather for navigational purposes, and general and pertinent information regarding incidents, observations and shipboard routine. Usually kept by the captain, masters and lieutenants

luff The leading edge of a fore-and-aft sail; or to change course into the wind so that the sails flap

lying to / lying a-hull Waiting out a storm by lowering all sails and letting the vessel drift

marines Seaborne contingent of soldiers

master The most senior non-commissioned officer or warrant officer in the Royal Navy at the time responsible for the navigation of the ship, subject to the command of its officers

masthead The very top part of the mast

mate Assistant warrant officer to a senior warrant officer, hence bosun's mate and master's mate

messed Dined

mizzenmast The mast nearest the stern of a three-masted vessel

nautical mile A mathematical calculation based on the circumference of the Earth at the equator

negro head A vertical outcrop of coral that sits upon a reef

oakum Old pieces of rope picked to shreds and tarred for use as caulking. Known as rope junk

offing Distance from shore/land or other navigational hazards

packet (ship) A vessel that sailed a regular service between two ports, usually carrying mail.

pawl A hinged or pivoted catch on a ratchet wheel which prevents it from slipping back

pinnace A small vessel which can be rowed or sailed that usually carries men between shore and ship

plantain A banana-like fruit

point A compass aboard ships of this era was divided into 32 'points', so to change course two points meant that the vessel changed direction by just over 22 degrees on a modern-day compass

poop deck The short deck towards the stern above the quarterdeck of a ship

pooped To have a wave break over the stern of the ship and onto the deck

port The left-hand side of a vessel

prow An alternative term for the bow – the front end of the vessel

quadrant A very simple instrument used to determine the altitude of a heavenly body

quarterdeck The exposed upper deck at the stern of the ship from the main-mast to the back, usually the territory of the ship's officers

quitted the chains The crewman heaving the lead (to check the water depth) leaves his post in the chains and returns to the deck

ratlines Bands of ropes lashed across the shrouds like steps that allow crew to easily climb aloft

reef/reefed To take in or reduce the area of a sail without furling it

reeved Threaded or re-led

rhumb line The path taken by a vessel that maintains a constant compass direction, i.e. the shortest possible route

rigging All ropes, wires and chains used to support the masts and yards

schooner A fore-and-aft rigged vessel, originally with two masts, but later with three or more. Designed for blockade running and as a fast naval vessel

scorbutic sores Ulcers related to scurvy that can appear anywhere on the body

sextant A navigational instrument used to measure the angle of elevation of an object above the horizon

Sheerness Docks An important naval dockyard at Sheerness, on the Isle of Sheppey in the Thames estuary

sheet anchor Traditionally, the largest of a ship's anchors carried so it can be quickly dropped in the event of an emergency

ship-of-the-line A warship built to fight in the line of battle – the traditional form of battle in the late eighteenth and early nineteenth centuries where the ships formed a line so that they could fire broadsides at the enemy

shoot the sun Taking the altitude of the sun with a sextant

shroud The standing rigging on the ship that provides lateral support to the mast

sloop A single-masted sailing ship usually carrying a mainsail and a single jib or headsail

slops Ready-made clothing from the ship's stores which is sold to the seamen

spanker A large fore-and-aft sail set from the mizzenmast (aft-most) using a gaff – a wooden spar which supports the top of the sail

spars A general term relating to all the poles in a vessel's rig, such as masts, yards, booms and gaffs

Spithead A stretch of water at the eastern end of the Solent located between Portsmouth and the Isle of Wight

FLINDERS

starboard The right-hand side of a vessel

stay A large, long rope which acts as a piece of standing rigging to support the mast either athwartships or fore-and-aft

sternsheets The stern area of an open boat

strake A line of planking on the side of a vessel

supercargo A merchant ship officer who is in charge of the cargo and the commercial concerns of the voyage

taffrail A railing around the stern of a ship

tender A small vessel that attends a man-of-war, primarily in harbour. Usually used to carry munitions, provisions, mail and despatches to and from the ship

thole pins Wooden rowlocks

timoneer Helmsman

topgallant In a square-rigged ship, these are the spars and rigging at the very top of the masts above the topsails

trestletrees Framing comprising two short, strong parallel timbers fixed fore-and-aft on the opposite side of the lower masthead to support the topmast, or at the top of the topmast to support the topgallant mast

warp A rope attached to a ship which is used to move it from one place to another by men pulling on it when the ship is in harbour; to move or reposition a ship by hauling on a line or anchor line

warped To manoeuvre a ship along by pulling on a warp

wear ship, to A manoeuvre that comes when a square-rigged ship changes course by turning the ship's stern through the wind so that the direction of the wind comes onto the opposite side of the ship. Today it is referred to as a gybe

windage The exposed part of the hull and rig of a vessel causing wind resistance

windlass A horizontal and cylindrical barrel used as a lifting device for a rope or anchor cable. It is turned by rods called handspikes

yard A slender wooden spar slung at its centre on the forward side of a mast on a square-rigged ship

yardarm The outer end of each yard where, on square-rigged ships, signal flags were flown or from where men sentenced to death following a court martial were hung

A Note on Sources

In detailing the research sources I used when writing *Flinders,* it comes as a delight to be able to actually thank the subject, Matthew Flinders, for supplying such a vast and detailed amount of information for the story. His own publications, the two volumes of *A Voyage to Terra Australis,* delivered invaluable material for this book. It was information straight from the captain on the most significant elements of his numerous adventures, his life in general, and the periods dominated by total exasperation – especially during his enforced detainment on Île-de-France courtesy of General Decaen. In these volumes, Flinders recounts his expeditions and experiences – structured from information contained in his logs and journals, and from indelible memories, which makes for enthralling reading for any student or historian. On many occasions, when I sourced interesting snippets of material from elsewhere, it was a pleasure to so often be able to revert to Flinders' tomes for confirmation on them being fact or fiction.

As unfortunate as his extended stay at Île-de-France was, Flinders put the time to good use: this incarceration gave him ample time to work on his publications and his superbly detailed charts, all of which were published in conjunction with the release of *A Voyage to Terra Australis.* Interestingly, Flinders also took the time to make a seafaring feline the lead character in another book – a short story written as a tribute to his constant and much-loved companion on sea and land, Trim.

There was one other book, a biography, I used as a primary source for research material – *The Life of Matthew Flinders* by Ernest Scott, first published in 1914 and to this day considered by many to be the most authoritative work on Flinders. Scott migrated from England to Melbourne in 1892 and continued his career as a journalist with the *Herald* newspaper. He was fascinated by early Australian history, so much so that, despite a lack of academic qualifications, he became chair of history at the University of Melbourne the year prior to the publication of his extremely well researched writings on the great explorer.

Besides these foundation stones of my research, there was a considerable amount of information located in other publications, and online, which were subsequently authenticated and applied to the work. One important find that carried an interesting enlightenment on Flinders' life and career was *The Indomitable Captain Matthew Flinders, Royal Navy*, written by Lt Cdr Peter Ashley, RN, of the Society for Nautical Research in England. Published in 2005 after considerable research on Ashley's part in the UK and Australia, this stimulating little book provided fascinating material and prompted additional investigation on my part in other areas.

It was through the guidance of Paul Brunton, the Manuscripts Curator at the State Library of NSW, that I was able to secure much of the material that really mattered for this book. The National Maritime Museum in Greenwich, London, was also supportive with the supply of information.

As was the case when writing *Bligh: Master Mariner*, Google Earth and Google Images gave me considerable insight when it came to researching – and 'visiting' – places Flinders explored. From his birthplace in Donington to any point of importance on his voyages, Google Earth took me there so I could appreciate the location and its surrounds. Similarly, Google Images provided quick access to a myriad of photographs and illustrations of destinations, ships or individuals that needed to be seen to be appreciated and described.

Other sources of information for this book included:

- George Tobin's narrative from the voyage of HMS *Providence:* Twenty-three-year-old Tobin, a third lieutenant aboard HMS *Providence,* provided a colourful perspective of life on board and ashore from a completely different aspect to the primary characters, Bligh and Flinders.
- National Maritime Museum, London – *The Flinders Papers:* Comprising 150 documents that include papers, charts, journals, letterbooks and books relating to Matthew Flinders. They have been on long-term loan to the National Maritime Museum and, having been transcribed, are available for public scrutiny.
- National Archives, UK: The National Archives in the UK provided the journal from *Investigator* which Flinders kept with him while in Île de France, subsequent to his completion of the circumnavigation of Australia in 1802/03.
- 'Notes on the Sealing Industry of Early Australia' [J.C.H. Gill, B.A. LL.B., published in the *Journal of the Royal Society of Queensland,* volume 8, issue 2, Brisbane, 1967]: This document, found on the website of the University of Queensland, provided information on Captain William Reed, who was the master of *Francis* – sent to Preservation Island in Bass Strait to rescue crew and recover cargo from the wreck of *Sydney Cove.* The paper was presented to a meeting of the Royal Historical Society of Queensland on 23 February 1967.
- *The Navigators: Flinders vs Baudin* [Klaus Toft, published by Duffy and Snellgrove, Sydney, 2002]: This book was the original source of online information that provided brief descriptions of Ann Flinders and numerous highlights of Matthew Flinders' life. The site from which it came, Villanova College, Queensland, was part of the Royal Geographic Society of Queensland's *Flinders 2002* Project.
- Dr Mathew Flinders' Diaries: A webpage detailing the family tree of descendants of Matthew Flinders – the Genealogy Report of

Chambers/Snodgrass Family History – provided details of the diaries kept by Dr Mathew Flinders, father of explorer Matthew Flinders.

- 'The Uses of Adversity: Matthew Flinders' Mauritius Writings' [Gillian Dooley, published in *Alas, for the Pelicans!*, Wakefield Press, Adelaide, 2002]: Gillian Dooley of Flinders University, South Australia, was the author of this impressive document which primarily related to Flinders' time in Île de France. It carries many interesting descriptions of the lifestyle and environment Flinders endured while incarcerated on the island.

- *Investigation of a survivor camp from the Sydney Cove shipwreck* [Michael Nash]: The Tasmanian Parks and Wildlife Service website was the source of a very interesting report by Michael Nash. It was based on a 2002 investigation into the remnants of the camp established by survivors of the *Sydney Cove* wreck on Preservation Island, off the north-east corner of Tasmania. The same document detailed the history of the wreck, including events leading up to the ship being deliberately run aground, the establishment of a survivors' camp on the island, and the rescue effort that came later from Port Jackson.

- 'Matthew Flinders put "Australia" on the map' [Paul Brunton]: Paul Brunton, the Manuscripts Curator at the State Library of New South Wales, is arguably the leading authority on early Australian maritime history. This article by him appeared on the Australia's Maritime World website. As well as providing solid reference material, the site also led to the State Library of New South Wales' site titled 'Matthew Flinders' Journeys'.

Acknowledgements

With just one name on the cover of this book recognising the author, it would be easy to assume that it was a solo effort – but it was far from that. To get a book such as this all the way from concept to consumer requires a team effort, and fortunately I have had an exceptionally good team assisting me.

The genesis of *Flinders: The Man who Mapped Australia* came from Helen Littleton, a very talented publisher who worked with me on my previous book, *Bligh: Master Mariner*. She saw the story of Matthew Flinders as the next logical step following on from the success of *Bligh*. For *Flinders*, I was fortunate to have Matthew Kelly, the non-fiction publisher at Hachette, become the guiding light in the project, and his constant encouragement went hand-in-hand with broad-based assistance from that organisation. Here I must recognise the support of the team at Hachette, in particular Malcolm Edwards, Fiona Hazard, Matt Richell, Kate Stevens and Jess Luca, for committing to this journey 'under full sail'.

As was the case with *Bligh: Master Mariner*, it was Paul Brunton, the Manuscripts Curator of the State Library of New South Wales, who once again kept me on course with what material should form the foundation of my research for the Flinders story. Later, with my writing complete, he took time to read the manuscript and tender additional guidance. For this I am most appreciative.

As an author I am very much hands-on when it comes to the writing and research for the story, but even so, I could not have achieved this without my first-class office support team ... comprising just one person: my assistant, Liz Christmas. Her commitment and contribution to every aspect of the task was exceptional, and I am exceedingly grateful to her for this. I couldn't have asked for anyone better to work with.

On a personal note, I must recognise the encouragement and understanding of my partner, Prue Stirling. I'm sure there were times when she believed my mind was perennially locked into Matthew Flinders' era, and there was no turning back.

News that I was writing this tribute to Matthew Flinders was well received in many quarters and as a result I received numerous offers of assistance. In particular, I must thank 'Flinders fanatic' Peter Bourne who, while on a trip to England, sought out some interesting information for my project. I must also recognise from the Society of Nautical Research in England, Lt Cdr Peter Ashley, RN, author of *The Indomitable Captain Matthew Flinders, Royal Navy*, for the valuable information he supplied in communications with me.

Finally, I want to acknowledge the support that the all-important booksellers showed for this book prior to its release, and thank them for what they have achieved with my previous publications.

Rob Mundle
2012

Index